THE QUANTUM TRAVERSE

THE QUANTUM TRAVERSE

Unlocking the Mysteries of Life's Origin, Consciousness,
Extraterrestrial Life and Physics through the Quran

Nadeem Haque

Foreword by Bradley Steffens

BEACON Signature PRESS

First published by Beacon Signature Press

Copyright © Nadeem Haque, 2025

First edition published in 2025

Paperback ISBN 978-1-916955-42-4

Ebook ISBN 978-1-916955-43-1

Cataloging-in-Publication record for this book is available from the British Library

In the real-world, illusions become (seemingly) real
If you know the secret of the Universe
Space-time is merely a quantum traverse
From a poem by Nadeem Haque

The greatest unsolved mysteries are the mysteries of our
existence as conscious beings in a small corner of the
Universe.
Physicist, Freeman Dyson

About the Author

Nadeem Haque is a researcher and author of numerous interrelated areas that connect with Islam.His work has thus far focused on the following areas: animal rights and environment/ecology; the origins and nature of consciousness; the unification of physics; origin of life and history/history of science, and extra terrestrial life and the Qur'an.

Contents

Preface

The Backstory to this Book

I have been studying Islam since the age of nine years old; that is around 54 years now. It seems hard to believe that over half a century has gone by, just like that—at warp speed. Yet, such is the psychological nature of time. When I was a child in Kampala, Uganda, the 'Pearl of Africa's Crown', as they called it in their National Anthem, I used to ponder whimsically what it would be like when I would be *really* old—that is when I would be 17 years old. Now even that 'old age' to a child seems a distant past!

I wondered about God at an early age, and remember that when I was just over 3 years old I asked my mother (Tahera Haque) where God was, and she pointed up to the sky. As a child, I started to think of God as some type of majestic gaseous form—a voluminous cloud! Subsequently, as I grew older, my father, Zeya Haque (1932-2005), instilled pride in me of this belief system of Islam and the fact that its truth was being covered up by various groups interested in greed and power. At the age of nine years old, in 1969, I used to have discussions with my best friend on evolution—which is the subject discussed in Part 1 of this book; that may seem odd—back in 1969? There were no cell phones, computers, databases, internet/websites, even fax machines, and USBs—only books, typewriters, landlines, radio and one black and white TV set. These days kids that age are not exactly discussing such abstruse subjects; but how come I was doing it back then, and what is more, in the eyes of many in the West, in the very heart of the 'Dark Continent'? It so happens that 'back in the day', East Africa was hypothesized as being the place where 'early man' arose, especially due to the Leakey family. My father, a lawyer—coincidentally —had to, once, cross-examine Louis Leakey in a case—Leakey was in the opposing party. My father told me that he completely decimated Leakey in the cross-examination (it was a civil case). Due to this reason of me being exposed to 'evolution' at an early age, and the fact that the Ugandan Government presented evolution as fact, by having a permanent exhibition at a Museum in Kampala, I became very intrigued and took a particular stance on the subject at a very early age.

My father, even though he did not say too much about Islam, was truly a Muslim in behaviour, and what he said on the subject was quality, rather than quantity, which is what counts the most. He had arranged a teacher for me—a 'Mwalimu' (a native Ugandan Imam from Kibuli mosque in Kampala) to teach me basic Arabic reading from the Quran, and a biography of Prophet Muhammad. My Mwalimu was brilliant in his recitation of the Quran and to this day I have not come across anyone as good as him (and I am including the most renowned Quranic reciters in the world!). I specifically checked the internet many times for different Qari just to see if I could find a better reciter, but have not been able to do so, so far—he truly had a gift from God for this! This highlights a fact that there may be someone better at something than anyone else but is not well known at all or is very obscure. We often forget that limelight is not always directly proportional to ability, talent or truth. May God exalt the Mwalimu wherever he is. My father, Zeya Haque, or Bwana Haqqa as the native Ugandans called him, became a famous lawyer and former judge (magistrate) in Uganda and indeed the whole of East Africa in the early 1970s, after the international case concerning the kidnapping of the British Diplomat (Brian Lea) which turned out to be fake kidnapping done for political/monetary gain—my father corroborated this through investigation in which he sailed to a remote island in Lake Victoria. He, in fact, 'won the enquiry/hearing' for his client (Rao) who was a co-defendant with the Ugandan Government against the British Government; this simultaneously collapsed the British government's serious accusations against the Ugandan Government. Early on in my life, events such as this showed me that truth is often hidden or distorted by parties with vested interests; one therefore needs to explore things to discover the truth: *always question the narrative*! The authority is not the truth—truth is the authority. The path may not be easy, but it is a duty incumbent upon each and every one of us to seek the truth about important and relevant issues.

Chronologically speaking, a further great influence on me was my group at the University of Toronto which had the name ANALYS (Associates for Knowledge **Analys**is and Synthesis). Except for a few intervals, we met for 15 years almost every week (starting in 1978). In the interlude, (1981 to 1985) I went to England to study Civil Engineering at King's College London where I co-founded a group called King's College Islamic Society, in 1985, that has grown and is still extant today. Back at University of Toronto ANALYS assisted and MSA in holding the Embryology and Quran symposium (in 1989) with the top embryologists Keith Moore, T.V. N. Persaud and Marshall Johnson. It was in my private discussion with the most brilliant Marshall Johnson where I was given extremely motivational words. Dr. Johnson told me that the Muslims were not doing enough to tell the non-Muslims about the amazing scientific things in the Quran. He also said he was also looking into the whole business of the human being, being created from clay, stated in the Quran, and that it really puzzled and intrigued him. This made me ponder more on clay in the Quran, until many years later, I published the book; its expanded, re-titled and updated version forms Part 1 of this book.

The last lecture we organized as ANALYS was by the late Imam Heshaam Jaaber (in 1993), who was the closest companion to Malcolm X and the one who led his Janaza (Funeral) prayers despite death threats (he had written the book "I buried Malcolm X"). Imam Jaaber became a close friend from whom I learned about the machinations against Malcolm X, and his (Malcolm's) steadfastness in the face of danger. Jaaber loved my article on Malcolm X and also was given my co-authored book, *From Facts to Values*, to distribute in the USA, that he also saw as being *the* book for the methodology of truth. This is aside from the Mathematician Gary Miller (Abdul Ahad Omar) lectures which we held over the years in the 1980s with MSA—Gary was, in a way part of our group at ANALYS. We even ended up inviting the late Hans Kung to the apartment of one of us, and Gary Miller dropped by as well; Hans Kung—we came to realize firsthand—was no friend of Islam but was more like a strategic advisor about it, for the Christian world, through his studies. Gary Miller's best lectures were: *The Amazing Quran*; *The Quran, the Final Revelation* and his brilliant booklet on Christianity, logic and Islam[1]. However, the greatest impact on me was my grandfather, Al-Hafiz B.A. Masri who was the once (Sunni) Imam of Shah Jehan Mosque in Woking, England and later became a pioneer in research on Animals and Islam and then concerning the environment. I ended up publishing two books: *Ecolibrium - The Sacred Balance in Islam* (I was a co-author) and

---

1 *A Concise Reply to Christianity: A Muslim View*, published in 1983 by Gary Miller (Abdulahad Omar) can be found here: https://www.islamicboard.com/comparative-religion/134282066-concise-reply-christianity.html

See also: https://noranazmy.com/gary-miller where a number of his lectures are posted. *A Concise Reply to Christianity* is a transcript of his lecture. As of April 24, 2021, I lost touch with Gary Miller, as he was retired by the Petroleum Institute, Abu Dhabi, UAE. He moved to British Columbia, Canada. Part of his last message to me was: "I was retired by management last year and I have returned to Canada, now living in B.C." (Email to Nadeem Haque).

the re-publication of Masri's *Animals in Islam*, with essays from other scholars incorporated as a preamble, where I was the main Editor. *Ecolibrium* was 34 years in the making!

All of this begs a pertinent or crucial question: many other people who met these extremely knowledgeable and amazing people I mention above did not embark on such an extensive and deep writing career, so to speak—what was *my* underlying motivation? What has led me to put together "The Quantum Traverse"? One of the main driving forces was yearning to discover if God really existed and whether there actually was a life after death. This made me investigate the Quran more deeply, especially after 1977 (I was 17 years old), when I read about the Big Bang and discovered that it was clearly mentioned in the Quran itself. After this point, I was hooked onto the Quran. I then thought of writing a series of books but it seemed like a daunting prospect and appeared almost impossible at the time. I did make a start, eventually—in 1990! The first major non-fiction book I wrote was *From Facts to Values*, with my ANALYS colleague and friend Mehran Banaei, and it was completed in 1995. That book is way more relevant today than it was back then, and efforts are being made to get it re-published, including an online version. In the 2000's, I co-wrote two books with my close colleague and unique friend, M. Muslim. Aspects of these have been incorporated in this book in Parts 2 and 4. Part 2 is largely the foundational work by Muslim, with my extensive elaboration of it, and Part 4 is based on our earlier joint work on physics.

In tackling the issue of God's existence and life after death, I had to delved into the Quran extremely deeply, as well as into nature, and I came to starkly realize that the Quranic information corroborates logic and facts found in nature and history, and that knowledge is truly one, there being no separation into 'religious' and 'secular'. It was indeed beyond uniting science and religion, as there was no disunity in the first place. I had also realized that not only had the Quran given birth to the inductive method, but that the West had learned from this and they had therefore learned the use of nature, but tragically not the converse—*the nature of use*. In addition, although the West had started surpassing the nominal and declining Islamic world after the 16th and 17th centuries in terms of scientific creations, and later on, 'industrial development', they had done so by utilizing the knowledge sprouted from, but also in critical aspects, divorced from the Quran's ethical components, chief of which was *al-mizan* (the balance); hence, my two co-authored books on that vital subject: *From Facts to Values: Certainty, Order, Balance and their Universal Implications* and *Ecolibrium: The Sacred balance in Islam*. Since the West had taken only half the parachute, to quote Gary Miller, their fall from a very high precipice had become exceedingly dangerous. They needed and still badly need the other half, that is, a radical shift in ethics and morality (as described in *Ecolibrium*) so that Earth and its inhabitants can flourish and live interesting lives in full tranquility, peace and justice, where *every* man *and* woman is enabled and encouraged to fulfill their diverse potential. Furthermore, since a unificatory outlook was missing, closure on several Big Questions has become literally impossible for current views/theories being espoused. The Quran *has to* 'kick in' again just as it had about 1,400 years ago; it has to raise humankind from the New Dark Ages, just as it had from the 'classical' Dark Ages. A valid human civilization worthy of being called "civilization" needs to evolve; we cannot forevermore be encaged, enraged and upstaged in the proclivities of semi-barbarism that we seem to be mired in.

I believe that human knowledge has matured through the following phases, to uplift humankind, 'The 5 Stages in the Intellectual Evolution of Humanity':

Stage 1: Pre-History

- Simple observations of nature by *very early* humans.
- Refined observations in early human history.

Stage 2: Ancient history

- Ancient History—mainly deduction but not much induction (scientific method of testing). Evolution of deductive reasoning. High point: Greatest scientist of the ancient times: Archimedes.

Stage 3: Pre-Middle Ages

- Quran: Deduction + Induction (exemplars Ibn Al-Haytham, Al Biruni, Ibn Rushd, Ibn Sina and others) and early harmony with scripture. Greatest scientist of the 'middle period': Ibn Al- Haytham—the prime developer of the scientific method.

Stage 4: Post-Middle Ages

- *Refinement* of Induction in the West (with Newton etc.). Greatest scientist of the 'Pre-modern' period: Isaac Newton.

Stage 5: 20ᵗʰ Century & Beyond

- Relativism, Indeterminism, Positivism and the harming of the Scientific Method with further confusion due to introducing the counter-reaction of mysticism into scientific thought.

- The Quran re-establishing the scientific method with deduction and induction + the Quran being part of the process of investigation. I argue that this is the final and complete methodological phase. In this book I hope to show you this methodology and its results in action.

No scientist/thinker since Archimedes, Al-Haytham and Newton (the top three in history—in my opinion—based on their discoveries and impact) has arisen in the modern or postmodern period, so far, with respect to their stature and influence. But I am hopeful that someone or a group will arise in the not too distant future, and that this book and my other works and those of my erstwhile colleagues will be somewhat influential in consolidating the answers to the Big Questions, or resolving in more detail the deeply mysterious questions, at the interface of science and philosophy!

This area of studies involving the interrelationship between the knowledge in the Quran (the verses in the Quran) and knowledge in the Universe, is a logical outcome of the signs in the Universe and the signs mentioned in the Book (the Quran), because they have the same Structurer known by the dreaded (for atheists) three letter word—G O D. *Therefore, by investigating the Universe and the Quran in an intervolved way, more of their secrets can be discovered.* The epistemology of a Muslim (that is, one who submits to One God) is far more extensive and incorporates both scientific knowledge and the linguistic evidence in the Quran *as an inseparable unity.* I have attempted to convey this methodology and discoveries in this book, which is a work that amalgamates what I have written about before, but is re-organized into this single volume, with totally new material to boot, to cover four critical areas: life's evolution and development, consciousness, extraterrestrial life and physics. I hope that the reader will join me in critically and passionately assessing this book, and will seriously engage in a fruitful and constructive dialogue, so that we may all come closer to truth.

Nadeem Haque
nhaque@mail.com
August 12, 2023

Foreword

Bradley Steffens

Ibn al-Haytham and the Origins of Modern Science

The Quantum Traverse tackles major scientific questions in the same vein as the prime founder of the scientific method. That there is an actual founder of the scientific method might be surprising and new to many. Sometime around 1028, the Islamic mathematician Alhasan ibn al-Haytham was putting the finishing touches on his magnum opus, *Kitāb al-Manāzir*, or *The Book of Optics*—a compendium of all he had learned about light, vision, reflection, refraction, and the perception of visible phenomena—when he made a simple but astonishing statement, words all the more remarkable for their humility. Ibn al-Haytham said he had written an earlier treatise on optics, but that readers should disregard it. The problem was not that it contained errors, although it undoubtedly did. Rather, he had come to realize that the methodology he had employed in his earlier work was fatally flawed. He had developed a new paradigm for research, and it had changed everything. He wrote:

> I formerly composed a treatise on light and vision in which I employed persuasive methods of reasoning, but when true demonstrations relating to all objects of vision occurred to me, I started afresh. Whoever, therefore, comes upon the said treatise must know that it should be discarded.[1]

For those who wonder when and where modern science got its start, Ibn al-Haytham's statement offers a valuable clue. Before *Kitāb al-Manāzir*, natural philosophers, from the ancient Greeks forward, including Ibn al-Haytham himself, had used reason to formulate conclusions about the workings of nature. But as Ibn al-Haytham worked on various problems presented by the propagation of light, he devised simple, physical tests to see if his hypotheses were correct. He called these tests "true demonstrations." We call them experiments. What may have started as a one-off test of his most radical idea—namely, that vision is caused by light rays entering the eye, an idea that contradicted everything known about vision up to that point—soon became a systematic practice.

As Ibn al-Haytham realized the power and immutability of experimental research, he resolved that he would not put anything into *Kitāb al-Manāzir* unless he had established its truth through a mathematical proof or a physical demonstration. This would be his approach to research for the rest of his career. Accordingly, one can reasonably say that the advent of modern science occurred not just somewhere in the eleventh century, but at a precise moment in the life of Ibn al-Haytham—the moment he realized that logic and reason were no longer sufficient for explaining natural phenomena, and that they must be abandoned in favor of experiment.

Ibn al-Haytham's pioneering of the scientific method was a natural outgrowth of his religious faith. Islam teaches that only God is perfect, and human beings are deeply flawed. To learn the truth about natural phenomena, one must remove human opinions and even human logic from one's investigation and enter into a dialogue with the Universe itself. In a later treatise, *Doubts on Ptolemy*, Ibn al-Haytham describes the importance of relying on experiment rather than on human opinions:

> The seeker after truth is not one who studies the writings of the ancients and, following his natural disposition, puts his trust in them, but rather the one who suspects his faith in them and questions what he gathers from them, the one who submits to argument and demonstration, and not to the sayings of a human being whose nature is fraught with all kinds of imperfection and deficiency.[2]

Ibn al-Haytham recognized that the abnegation of opinion must apply to one's own thoughts, goals, and pet theories as well. To the sentence above, he added: "He should also suspect himself as he performs his critical examination of it, so that he may avoid falling into either prejudice or leniency.[3] Ibn al-Haytham realized that one's own opinions worked like a lodestone, bending the evidence toward a favored result. Hoped-for outcomes had a way of making themselves manifest. One must purge oneself of one's hopes if one wishes to discover the truth. Better to submit to the Creator, he reasoned, and allow Him to reveal what He wishes you to know. In *Doubts on Ptolemy*, the Islamic scholar concluded:

> We are not free from that human turbidity which is in the nature of man;
> but we must do our best with what we possess of human power. From
> God we derive support in all things.[4]

Had Ibn al-Haytham's methodology been lost in the sands of time, it could not be seen as the progenitor of the modern scientific method. This was not the case, however. *Kitāb al-Manāzir* made its way to the Iberian Peninsula, where it was translated into Latin by Roman Catholic monks. Unfortunately, Ibn al-Haytham's introduction, in which he described the importance of "true demonstrations," was not included in *De Aspectibus*, the Latin translation *Kitāb al-Manāzir*. Nevertheless, his methodology was clearly revealed in the dozens of experiments he described throughout the book.

De Aspectibus was quoted by the Franciscan friar Roger Bacon, in Book Five of his *Opus Majus*, or *Greater Work*. Another Franciscan friar, John Pecham, summarized *De Aspectibus* in his circa 1279 work *Perspectiva communis*, referring to Ibn al-Haytham as "the Author" or "the Physicist." Art historian Francesca Fiorani has established that Leonardo da Vinci—identified by Michael White as the earliest practitioner of modern science in his 2001 book *Leonardo: The First Scientist*—was influenced by Ibn al-Haytham's work as well. "There was an eleventh-century manuscript titled *Book of Optics* by the Arab philosopher known in the Renaissance as Alhacen—his real name was Abu Ali al-Hasan Ibn al-Haytham—that Renaissance artists knew about, because it had been translated into the vernacular. A copy of this Italian translation was in the hands of an artist Leonardo knew… . Not surprisingly, written on scraps of paper and in his notebooks are thoughts that are so deeply aligned with Alhacen's book that they seem, at times, nearly direct quotes from it—such as Alhacen's belief in the truthfulness of sensory experience."[5]

Ibn al-Haytham's methodology gained even wider circulation when the Swiss publisher Frederick Risner published *De Aspectibus* and Erazmus Ciolek Witelo's *Perspectiva* together in one book entitled *Opticae thesaurus* in 1572. Galileo Galilei, who is credited by Frederick Aiken as the pioneer of experimental science in his 1971 book *Galileo: the First Modern Scientist*, was undoubtedly aware of Ibn al-Haytham's work, considering his interest in optics and the development of the telescope. So great was Ibn al-Haytham's fame that when the Polish astronomer Johannes Hevelius published an atlas of the moon in 1647, the frontispiece bore the likenesses of the two pillars of experimental science up to that time: Galileo, shown holding a telescope, and Ibn al-Haytham, depicted with a geometric drawing in his hand.

Assiduously applying Ibn al-Haytham's methodology to all manner of research, Western scientists outpaced their counterparts in the rest of the world for the next several centuries, and interest in Ibn al-Haytham waned until his rediscovery in the early 2000s. As awareness about Ibn al-Haytham spread, the United Nations General Assembly designated 2015 as the International Year of Light and Light-based Technologies. As part of the celebration, the United Nations Educational, Scientific and Cultural Organization (UNESCO) teamed up with the cultural heritage organization 1001 Inventions to launch a series of interactive exhibits, workshops and live shows depicting the life and work of Ibn al-Haytham. Announcing the program, International Year of Light and Light-based Technologies (IYL2015) Chairman John Dudley stated: "Ibn Al-Haytham was a remarkable pioneer known for his insistence on understanding our world through experimental verification, and it will be a pleasure to work throughout 2015 to make his story known worldwide."[6] Today, Ibn al-Haytham is widely recognized as the world's first experimental scientist and it is in the same spirit of rationalism, evidence and inspiration from the Quran, that Nadeem Haque has written *The Quantum Traverse*, one thousand years later.

Bradley Steffens is a novelist, a poet, and an award-winning author of more than seventy nonfiction books for young adults. He is the author of *Ibn al-Haytham: First Scientist* (Morgan Reynolds, 2007), the first full biography of Ibn al-Haytham to appear in the West. An updated an expanded version of the book, *First Scientist: Ibn al-Haytham*, was published by Blue Dome Press in 2021. He is also the author of *The Prisoner of Al-Hakim*, a novel based on the life of Ibn al-Haytham (Blue Dome Press, 2017).

i. Ibn al-Haytham, *The Optics of Ibn al-Haytham*, tr. A.I. Sabra. London: The Warburg Institute, 1989, vol. I, p. 6.

ii. Quoted in Abdelhamid I. Sabra, "Ibn al-Haytham, Brief life of an Arab mathematician: died circa 1040," *Harvard Magazine*, September-October 2003. https://harvardmagazine.com/2003/09/ibn-al-haytham-html

iii. Quoted in Abdelhamid I. Sabra, "Ibn al-Haytham, Brief life of an Arab mathematician: died circa 1040," *Harvard Magazine*, September-October 2003. https://harvardmagazine.com/2003/09/ibn-al-haytham-html

iv.   Ibn al-Haytham, *The Optics of Ibn al-Haytham*, tr. A.I. Sabra. London: The Warburg Institute, 1989, vol. I, p. 5.

v.   Francesca Fiorani, *The Shadow Drawing*. New York: Farrar, Straus and Giroux, 2020, p. 3.

vi.   Quoted in "Ibn Al-Haytham to be a focus of the International Year of Light through partnering with 1001 Inventions," International Year of Light and Light-based Technologies.
https://web.archive.org/web/20211222071447/https://www.light2015.org/Home/About/Latest-News/November2014/Ibn-Al-Haytham-to-be-the-focus-of-the-International-Year-of-Light-through-partnering-with-1001-Inventions-.html.

PART 1

Cosmobiosys:
Beyond Darwinism and Creationism

In Part 1, it is clearly and conclusively proven that the Quranic view of life describes the origin of life of all species, including Man. Part 1 is a major revision of Volume 3 of the Microbits Series, entitled: *From Microbits to Everything: Beyond Darwinism and Creationism: The Evolutionary Implications*[2]. Here, a radically new model for the development of all life, that has absolutely no connection with natural selection, but is based on the unity of physics and biology, is presented. These realizations are a natural outcome of understanding the *fundamental* structure of space and time discussed in discussed in Volumes 1 and 2 of the *From Microbits to Everything* series[3], by myself and M. Muslim and the intra-relationships between the verses in the remarkable Quran that bear on this crucial subject. The readers will get an opportunity to get a basic understanding of Microbits in Part 4 of this book.

2 Haque, Nadeem. (2009). *From Microbits to Everything: Beyond Darwinism and Creationism: Volume 3: The Evolutionary Implications.* Optagon Publications Ltd., Toronto.
https://www.academia.edu/38349135/From_Microbits_to_Everything_Beyond_Darwinism_and_Creationism_Vol_3_The_Evolutionary_Implications
3 Haque, Nadeem. (2007). *From Microbits to Everything: Universe of the Imaginator: Volume 2: The Philosophical Implications.* Optagon Publications Ltd., Toronto.
https://www.academia.edu/38368823/From_Microbits_to_Everything_Universe_of_the_Imaginator_VOLUME_2_The_Philosophical_Implications

Chapter 1

Clay-based Evolution in the Quran

Introduction

It has become somewhat common knowledge that the Quran contains many verses that pre-empt scientific discovery, such as those pertaining to cosmology, embryology, etc. But what does the Quran say about evolution, if anything? Indeed, the origin and development of life and human beings is one of the greatest unresolved mysteries. In this book, we shall examine some intriguing verses in the Quran which depict the origin of life forms and their development.

All species were created from clay, including humans. The Quran depicts the creation of human beings that is generalizableto all species.

The Quran on Clay

If we are to understand the verses in the Quran on the subject of origins, we need a systems view, where the Quran best explains the Quran itself. In particular, in this connection, the system of Quranic verses is indeed akin to algebraic mathematical equations that need solving. For example, if we have an equation: y=2x +z and want to solve for y, then if we know what x and z are, we can indeed solve for y. We simply plug the values for x and z into the equation y=2x+z and get the answer for y. Analogously, the Quranic verses discussed in the next section, that are designated as 1 , 2 and 3, are at the core of the above-referenced thesis, and are akin to equations that need to be solved by plugging into the *general equation*, which is taken to be verse 1, it being the most general and basic one.

Primary Passages on Clay and Man

Let us use the following Quranic verses as equations, where we have three primary verses and hence 'equations':

1. I am about to create man from (*min*) clay (*tiin*). (38:71)
2. We *began* the creation of man from clay. (32:7)
3. We created man from (*min*) an extract (*sulaalatin*) from/in (*min*) clay. (23:12)

Now when it says in verse 1 that God is going to create man from clay, all that the Quran is referring to, is the *initiation* of life, or its origin. However, we need to factor in verses 2 and 3 to clearly realize this, for if we keep staring at Equation 1, we will not get any further in our understanding. What happens when we do this? Plugging in verses 2 and 3 into 1, we get:

We began the creation of man from an extract from clay.

Or:

We originated the human being from an extract *in* clay.

Or, yet again, in present scientific parlance:

We originated [the species] *homo sapiens* from an extract [present] in clay. *Equation 4*

It must be noted that when it says that God is going to create man from clay, it does not mean from the clay itself, but *from* something *in* the clay. This is how the Arabic word *min* is used here. An example of this type of usage of the word *min* is as follows:

We created man *min* [from] *nutfatin amshaajin* [the mingled fluid from both male and female partners]. (76:2)

It is an obvious fact now (post-mid 20th Century C.E.) that we are not created from such fluid but *from* the germ cells *in* those mingled fluids. The important clue to the realization that we are not made from clay, but from some components *in* clay, is the fact that we are carbon-based entities, yet clay is silicon based! How did the transformation occur, if we are made from clay itself? This precludes the theory that some espouse, that although life *began* in clay, it was also *completed* in clay for the verse pertains only to primal origination[4].

---

4   The late Dr. Maurice Bucaille, in his book "What is the origin of Man?", on page 173- 174, discusses the word *sulaalatin*, which he says means "one thing extracted from another thing". Bucaille, beleives in the general concept of the advancement of hominin species in terms of physical attributes and that evolution has proceeded because of the emergence of 'new' information in the genes; however, Bucaille also ascribes verses 76:28 and 6:133 as proofs of successive hominin species replacing or evolving into one another. These verses, to the contrary, as can be easily evinced by the context in which they occur, refer to a decadent civilization or people being replaced by another *after* the advent of neolithic societies by social upheavals/wars, cataclysms etc, not one hominin group replacing an older version. See Maurice Bucaille's: *What is the Origin of Man? The Answers of Science and the Holy Scriptures*,1983, Seghers, Paris.

There is another intriguing verse, call it equation 5, which is the key to solving the issue of how evolution has occurred, and what organisms were evolved:

> He it is who has created you from clay, and then has decreed a term—a term known to Him. And yet you still continue to remain doubtful... (6:2) *Equation 5*

Now recall that Equation 5 includes Equation 1. But Equation 1 turned into Equation 4: so now we can substitute Equation 4 into Equation 5 and we get the following:

> He it is who has originated *homo sapiens* from an extract in clay, and then has decreed a term—a term known to Him. And yet you still continue to remain doubtful... (6:2) *Equation 6*

Simplifying this verse into its essentials, we have: God originated man from specific components(s) extant in clay and after a long duration, decreed a fixed term. Now at this juncture one may rightly enquire: What is the meaning of 'term'? To know this, one requires an even deeper analysis of the verse:

The first part of this passage (Equation 5) can be divided into three sections:

1.1 He it is who has created you out of clay.

1.2 THEN has decreed a term.

1.3 a term known to Him...

Let us analyse 1.1 and 1.2 further:

The first part of this passage (*Equation 5*) can be divided into three sections:

Let us analyse 1.1 and 1.2 further:

1.1.1 We have seen that the first part of this verse is a short form for:
He it is who has originated *homo sapiens* from an extract in clay.

1.2.1 The word "THEN": *thumma*. This is a very significant word. When it is used in embryology (in the Quran) it means a long duration or slow process relative to the other components of the whole process being elucidated, and is a 'time-gauge' for a transformation process. In the Quran, when *thumma* is used it has three properties: Firstly, it denotes a change from one state to another, in time, from A to B. Secondly, there is a long duration relative to the processes being discussed; in other words, the transformation process from A to B is long. Thirdly, *then* separates A and B, although they are contiguous processes.

This is how the verse is to be understood: The transformative process from A to B is very long. What this verse is saying is that clay is like an ideal cooking pot that re-organizes matter (chemicals, so as to form enzymes etc.). The origination process is the development of the machinery of life: the enzymes, RNA and DNA that got produced. *These processes take time and do not happen suddenly.* The clay structures the initial process and then the process itself develops into a fully formed human being.

The Quran then talks about duration with other words. The words used here are *qadha ajalan* (decreed a term) and *waajalun musamman* (there is a term fixed with/known to Him). The word *ajala* is used many times in the Quran and with respect to durations of processes/movements in nature. For example, refer to chapter 13, verse 2.

What is this duration? If man's developmental process was *not* complete in the creation of man from clay, since the verse states that God *began* the creation of man from clay, the Quran could not have been talking about man's life on Earth, resurrection etc., that most older and contemporary scholars opine when they address this verse in their comments on the meaning of 'duration'. For example, Muhammad Asad, in a footnote to his English translation of the Quran on this verse, states that:

> ...Some of the authorities are of the opinion that the "term" refers to the
> end of the world and the subsequent resurrection, while others relate it
> to individual human lives. Other commentators, again, see in the first
> mention of this word a reference to individual lives, and in the *second*, to
> the Day of Resurrection; "and there is [another] term...", etc. However,
> in view of several other occurrences of the expression *ajal musamma* in
> the Quran, it is best rendered here as "a term set [by Him]" or "known [to
> Him]" i.e. relating both to individual lives and to the world as a whole.[5]

This erroneous view espoused by many commentators arises because of the position taken by such writers on the Quran in terms of most of them assuming that man was wholly completed in clay (fully formed) without a process of development. They then go on to further interpret, based on this flawed inter-

---

5 Asad, Muhammad, Translator. (1980). *The Message of The Quran*, pp. 171-172.

pretation, that when it says that God decreed a time/period, God is referring to the individual duration on earth, whereas others take it to mean the duration until Resurrection.

Let us examine the meaning of "...decreed a term" and also "...a term known to Him", even further. Firstly, let us construct a parallel sentence so that we can understand this verse better. Verse 6:2 is equivalent to the following statement, *in terms of pattern*: The process for creating a car (any group of objects known as a car and not any specific car with a unique license plate) is initiated by melting iron ore. Then there is decreed period which is fixed for the development of the car. It is fixed because it is known. Now we may ask: fixed for what? Following the car production analogy, obviously for the evolution of the car, that is, through the production of metal and then car parts and then assembly etc., rather than the following, incorrect conclusion: that the car is taken to the scrap heap (analogous to resurrection/day of judgment) which is an *end* process, once the car is fully formed. Indeed, why would it be taken to the scrap heap? What about all the intermediate processes, especially when the first part of the sentence in the Quran in the final *Equation 6*, on page 29, does not, using the analogy of cars, even speak about the completion of the car, by iron ore, and in fact talks of the *beginnings* of the car explicitly and literally!

The duration referred to in 6:2 then, refers to the development of the full human that emerged after the creation of DNA etc. through clay, in turn, leading to the human line. For the individual 'advanced' organism, the completion process does not occur in clay but through DNA etc., in an embryological-like process (more about this in Chapter 3). This view then, discounts an evolutionary view of 'a first man' being completely formed within a cocoon of clay, and by the clay material itself, rather than by the other components found *in* clay.

It must be pointed out, that in the Quran there is no concept of the Universe having been created in seven, twenty-four hour days as per Christian Fundamentalist Creationism. Far from it, in the Quran, in numerous passages, it is pointed out that the Universe was created in six *periods*. It is well known that the word in the Quran normally translated as day (*yaum*) means an unspecified division of time. It could be a picosecond or one billion years. These six periods, however, appear to coincide with the six divisions for the development of earth and life on earth. In the Quran, it states that the first two periods were spent in the creation/evolution of the Earth itself:

> Say: What! Do you indeed disbelieve in Him Who created the Earth in two periods, and do you set up equals with Him? That is the Lord/ Sustainer of the worlds. (41:9)

The total timeline is six periods[6]:

> Surely your Lord/Sustainer is God, who created the galactical systems and the Earth in six periods of time; then He ascended on the throne (of power); He throws the veil of night over the day, which it pursues incessantly; and [He created] the sun and the moon and the stars, made subservient by His command; surely His is the creation and the command; blessed is God, the Lord/Sustainer of the worlds.(7:54)

The possibility that God created man from clay in a sudden fashion is ruled out by two factors: It is not the clay from which man is created, but *other* elements that are 'entrapped' in the clay. The amazing fact is that there is an even more complex process hinted in Quran 23:12, "...*from an* extract *from* clay" implies that not only is biological life derived from the constituents *within* clay, that is, the extract *in* clay, but that life also develops *from* something within the extract itself, the Arabic word "from", *min*, being used twice in that verse. This is a linguistic 'double derivative'. Keep in mind that the chemical transitions of the elements to form nucleotides, RNA and eventually DNA *cannot* occur overnight.

Sequence of Creation

Since clay-based evolution has occurred, and clay was not isolated on one spot on the Earth, according to the previous analysis of the Quran, life did not develop on one spot on Earth, but throughout the Earth. There was not just one 'primeval pond' but many on the Earth. In 24:45 it is stated that all carbon-based life began from water after the big bang:

> Do those who cover the truth not see that the rest of the Universe and the Earth were one piece and We [God] suddenly (rapidly) ripped them apart

---

6 If we assume that the Earth is 4.5 billion years old and the periods are time periods and not stages, then the total age of the Universe (according to the Quranic statements) would be three times that of the Earth (because the Earth alone is two periods and the Universe is six periods in age) which would be (4.54 x 6/2) =13.62 billion years old. The current estimate is 13.77 billion years, as of 2021, with data from the Hubble Space telescope, plus or minus 40 million years.

> and made every living thing (*shayin hayin*) from water (*min al-mai*); will
> they even then not—through confirmation— believe? (Quran: 21:30)

> God has created from water every solid bodied creature (*dabbatin*). (Quran: 24:45)

Note that the Quran literally states that every *dabbah* is created from water. This verse is taken to mean both that water is the prime ingredient for carbon-based life and also that life needed water as a necessary ingredient for development. Since, like clay, water was not only on one spot on Earth but universal, it means that life originated throughout the various parts of Earth where clay and water existed.

To continue with an analysis of Quran 24:45, the sequence in which the major current groups of animals: mammals, birds, reptiles and amphibians is described is as follows:

> .... so of them is that which walks upon its belly, and of them is that which walks upon two feet, and of them is that which walks upon four; God creates what He pleases; surely God has power over all things. (24:45)

Here, four groups of animals are mentioned. The order of appearance, according to these verses is: *1. reptiles and amphibians, 2. birds* and then *3. mammals.*

Chapter 2

Clay as Catalyst

Recent research is pointing to the Quranic solution that we have been created from clay and indeed in the manner presented in this book. The general problem regarding the origin of life has been how DNA, the source of organisms, has been formed. Since you need RNA for DNA, then how did *that* begin in the first place? In Graham Cairns-Smith's theory[7], it was suggested that since clay has a crystalline structure, perhaps it formed a template through which life emerged. Eventually this formed life, and the initial template or scaffolding that assisted its formation, has vanished, much like when a building is being constructed. In other words, at a certain point, the organic molecules took over and started replication. However, more recently, the relation of clay and the origin of life is converging on the view being presented in this book through the work of the late James P. Ferris and his colleagues. Ferris has discovered, as stated in the Quranic verses cited in the previous chapter, that clay served as a cooking pot which contained, protected, molded and synthesized enzymes to produce RNA and thence DNA, that is, the road to life. In their technical paper, Ferris and Shin Miyakawa state the statistically phenomenal improbability for the minimal requirements for the origin of life based on the RNA world model. They state that:

> The random formation of two RNAs containing 40 nucleotides would require the formation of 10^{48} isomers weighing 10^{28} g, an amount comparable to the mass of the earth.[8]

Clay and the Origin of Life

In the 1990's, James Ferris, of the Rensselaer Polytechnic Institute discovered that montmorillonite clay can serve as a catalyst in forming RNA. When nu-

---

7 Cairns-Smith, A.G. (1985). *Seven Clues to the Origin of Life.*

8 Miyakawa, Shin, and Ferris, James P. (2003). *Journal of the American Chemical Society* "Sequence- and Regioselectivity in the Montmorillonite-Catalyzed Synthesis of RNA" citing Joyce G.F., Orgel, L.E. from the book *In the RNA World: The Nature of Modern RNA suggests a Prebiotic RNA*, pp. 49-77.

cleotides were poured onto its surface, this type of clay caused the fusion of the nucleotides. Up to 50 nucleotides at a time accreted together to produce a sole RNA molecule. Currently, many chemists, biologists, physicists, astronomers, and geologists who are researching the origins of life believe that RNA molecules were capable of performing both enzymatic activity and self-replication, defining what is known as the "RNA world" scenario. Today, proteins are built through the use of both transfer and messenger RNAs; these proteins then can act as enzymes to catalyze a variety of chemical reactions, including the formation of nucleotides. According to the supporters of the RNA world concept, there would be no protein enzymes in existence to form the first nucleotides or catalyze the first formation of RNA strands because these proteins are only formed by RNA (the chicken and the egg problem). Therefore, the phosphate, sugar, and base groups must have bonded through abiotic (non-biological) means.

Thus far, scientists have been unable to bind the phosphate to the sugar and base group using conditions that were thought to have been present on the early Earth; this is a very active, current field of research. However, once a full nucleotide unit has been formed, scientists have been able to make extended chains of RNA, of up to 50 units (mers) in length, which could then fold to perform catalytic activity, accelerating the ease of synthesis for future molecules and initiating the RNA world. If free nucleotides are combined in solution, they do not react at all. Therefore, many scientists have been searching for what types of activating groups and inorganic catalysts must have been involved in the polymer bonding process. Dr. Ferris, discovered one inorganic material which facilitates this reaction: montmorillonite clay. The particular structure of this clay serves to provide a medium in which the individual activated RNA units combine to form larger chains. Montmorillonite clay is currently the only mineral discovered which catalyzes the synthesis of RNA polymers (containing a minimum of 10 nucleotides) from their single units.

The Role of Water

In verses 21:30 and 24:45 it states that God created every carbon-based/visible living creature (not jinn or angels) from water. What role would water have played in conjunction with clay? We know the following facts about the involvement of water: It has been realized that four ingredients are required for the origination of life: nucleotides, fatty acids and water and that montmorillonite clay facilitates the two crucial processes that form a rudimentary vesicle analogous to a cell from these components. Firstly, as has been described earlier, montmorillonite clay can combine nucleotides to form RNA; secondly, it is simultaneously able to insert the concomitant RNA into a vesicle that forms as a result of mixing all these components. The next step is to produce more complex reactions from within the RNA housed in the membraned vesicle, in other words, watch a basic level of RNA based development occur before one's eyes![9] Note the amazing verse 37:11 that links the creation of man with sticky clay, implying wetness.

The Evolution of Clay itself

The creation of man from *turaab* (which means "dust" in Arabic) is the creation of man from the pre-clay situation, because even clay had an evolution! Remember: the Earth was formed from the accretion of gas and dust which gradually produced a planet replete with rock and mud. But how did clay form? Most of what we call "dirt" is a mixture of decomposed organic material and inorganic material; leaves, bark, and insects with rocks interspersed, for example. Clay forms in a dramatically different manner, however. When rocks, specifically feldspar, weather by chemical and physical means, they dissolve into their various elements and compounds. These molecules often form into mainly organized layers as they settle, based on charge, weight and other considerations. This is basically how the clays form their layering and crystal structure, which is based on the charges of the individual molecules. The following verses speak about the creation of man from dust or clay: 7:12; 17:61; 18:37; 22:5; 30:20; 35:11; 40:67. Other verses elucidate the evolution of clay from mud:

> He [Iblis] said: I am not such that I should prostrate to a human being, whom you have created from sounding clay (*salsaal*) of altered black smooth mud (*hamaa masnun*). (15:33)

> And when your Lord said to the angels: Surely, I am going to create a mortal out of sounding clay of altered, black, smooth mud. (15:28)

The other similar verses are: 15:26; 23:12 and 55:14.

---

9   Zimmer, Carl, (2004), *Discover*, "How did life on earth begin?", pp. 40-41.

Researcher Hideo Hashizume[10], in the open access book *Clay Minerals and Nature,* states:

> Most experiments related to the origins of life on Earth use specific clay minerals, such as montmorillonite and kaolinite. Volcanic rocks from the magma ocean would be enriched in Mg^{2+} ions. On this basis, we have investigated the interactions of Mg-rich clay minerals...with organic molecules, including bio-organic compounds. It is further suggested that the atmosphere of the early Earth contained little oxygen. This condition would be conducive to the formation of Fe^{2+}-rich clay minerals which, therefore, might have played an important part in the synthesis of simple bio-organic molecules.

> ...clay minerals can also control the surface arrangement of adsorbed nucleic acid bases or amino acids. By using a mixture of different clay mineral species, it may be possible to select a given bio-molecule over another for adsorption and polymerization. Although there is an element of trial and error in investigating the role of clay minerals in chemical evolution and the origins of life, we may yet be surprised by the outcome.

Yes, indeed! The surprise is going to be that without clay there would have been no life; that this is the way it is on all planets with life, and the fact that this is what the Quran had been saying all along! In addition, some more research has been reported by Jacob Teunis Theo Kloprogge, and Hyman Hartmann in the paper "Clays and the Origin of Life: Experiments".[11]

> The clay data coming from Mars and carbonaceous chondrites have necessitated a review of the role that clays played in the origin of life on Earth. The data from Mars have suggested that Fe-clays such as nontronite, ferrous saponites, and several other clays were formed on early Mars when it had sufficient water. This raised the question of the possible role that these clays may have played in the origin of life on Mars. This

---

10 Hashizume, Hideo. (September 12, 2012). "The Role of Clay Minerals in Chemical Evolution and the Origins of Life", *Clay Minerals and Nature,* Ed. Marta Valaskova and Grazyna Simha Martynkova, IntechOpen.
https://www.intechopen.com/chapters/38858
11 Kloprogge , Jacob Teunis (Theo) and Hartmann, Hymann, *Life (Basel),* 2022 Feb, "Clays and the Origin of Life: Experiments", 12(2): 259, Published online 2022, Feb. 9. https://pubmed.ncbi.nlm.nih.gov/35207546/

has put clays front and center in the studies on the origin of life not only on Mars but also here on Earth.

It is interesting to see that even though no life may ever be found on Mars, it is yielding clues to the origin of life on Earth and corroborating the Quran.

Chapter 3

Outlines of a New Mechanism for Life's Origin

The true nature of information

To see how life and all species have originated and developed, we need a new paradigm based on new principles. We need to know how the Universe is *actually* structured. We already know several major things that Darwin was not aware of, such as the Big Bang, genetics and subatomic particles. We also have the concept of 'information'. In the new explanation of life's origin being proposed in this book, 'information' is central; however, the general perception of 'information' in present day science is not that which is completely accurate. Paul Davies elaborates on a new, or better, understanding of "information" and "programming" that is needed to understand how life may have begun:

> We now need to explain, not the origin of material stuff, but the origin of information. Whereas it is good science to seek a physical process to generate matter, it is regarded as unscientific in the extreme to entertain a process that generates information. Information is not something that is supposed to come for free (like cosmic matter), but something you have to work for. This is really just the second law of thermodynamics revisited, because the spontaneous appearance of information in the Universe would be equivalent to a reduction of the entropy of the Universe—a violation of the second law, a miracle. Now, the fact is that the Universe containing information is undeniable (because it is not in thermodynamic equilibrium). If information can't get made, it must have been there at the beginning, as part of the initial input. The conclusion we are led to is that the Universe came stacked with information, or negative entropy, from the word go.[12]
>
> Might purpose be a genuine property of nature right down to the cellular or even subcellular level [and why stop there—right to the sub-subatomic level!]?[13]

12 Davies, Paul. (1999). *The Fifth Miracle: The Search for the Origin and Meaning of Life*, p. 62, 8. Ibid., p. 22.

13 Ibid., p. 22.

17

Let us explore these thoughts further: The centrality of 'information' is also the subject of Paul Davies' latest book: *The Demon in the Machine: How hidden webs of information are solving the mystery of life*[14]. One fact is that information involves meaning and intelligent design that is inescapable, not in the sense of God-of-the-gaps, but in sense of a God-of-the-origin. This is revealed clearly in the Quran where God is called *al-Fatir*, the Originator, which is one of His attributes, that is, one who sets things in motion. In fact, the word *amr* (see Quran 65:12 (in the form *l'amru*)) which means command in Arabic, is the *one* command God gave to the inception of the Universe; after this, *all* physicality in the Universe evolved. 'Information' only makes sense if there is order, pattern, teleology (and an end goal); these imply intelligence and not mindlessness or randomness.

To see how teleology arises let us examine four words that are used in the Quran for this: In the Quran it is stated that God creates (*khalaqa*), proportions (*fasawwa*), measures (*qaddara*) and guides (*fahada*)[15]. Therefore, there are, according to God Himself, only four steps to the creation: There is the decision to create. This requires knowing what you are creating and why—the intentionality and imagination: What will be the purpose and function of your creation? This requires foresight. If you, for example, decide to create a boat, you have the end goal of it being able to ply through the water efficiently, while carrying a load; that is your goal. So you will shape it in a certain way. But shaping implies that you know the dimensions and if you know the dimensions it will be created in such a way that you will be able to guide it in the water because you know that this design confers that type of motion. With respect to both biological systems, once you reach step three—'measures', it then automatically guides. For example, bacteria are God's creation that are designed as an intrinsic part of the ecosystem and biosystem until humans mess with that system, when there is a harmful spillover effect into humans. Certain bacteria have been designed by the Creator in a particular way so that they will naturally travel through the body, because of their structure. Therefore, creation, proportioning and measuring leads to the bacterial structure and function that, in turn, leads to the end goal: the bacteria's behaviour, as it were, even though they are not conscious entities. However, it should be remembered that each component of the bacteria itself

---

14   Davies, Paul. (2019). *The Demon in the Machine: How hidden webs of information are solving the mystery of life*, University of Chicago Press.
15   Quran 87:2-3.

is itself created, proportioned and measured to create the bacteria. In this way all of creation's components are automaticized, with no God-of-the-gaps, by using this procedure—development therefore happens by the same principles: creation (origin); proportioning, measuring (precision) and guiding, the last which is a result of the first three. Since there was an origin to the Universe, as the Quran itself attests with the Big-Bang verse, then we take this to be the initial creation. Following the single command of God (*amr*) all proportioning and measuring were automated, due to God's infinite knowledge, leading to 'guiding'. The whole Universe was created at the Big Bang and in that singularity there was already inherent proportion and measure, which then guided its evolution. Consider another example: The fact that plants, for example, are not conscious entities but exhibit conscious-like behaviour in seeking sunlight, for instance, means that the consciousness that guides them must be outside that system. This basic concept applies to everything in nature and therefore logically, to the totality of nature itself. This is why the type of intelligent design being discussed in this book is inescapable.

Chapter 4

Developmental Considerations

It is not accurate to say that we are created from dust in one step. Quran 3:59 implies that our creation from dust is ultimately from gaseous/dust in the sense of stellar/planetary formation, and likewise, so is Adam's creation, be it the individual Adam or every one of us generically as 'Adam'. In other words, we originate from those very same planetary dust particles as the ultimate source. This means that Adam was born embryologically the same way we were but from clay through the process discussed in Chapter 1. Jesus was also born through embryological processes and ultimately from the same cosmic source of planetary dust. The details of the early stages of Jesus' embryological creation may have been unusual, but he was not created out of dust in one step! All of us, including Jesus and Adam, were created from dust in the sense that this is the first evolutionary point for the formation of clay. Clay evolves from primal cosmic dust. The absolute origin of dust is stardust from stellar system formation processes from which our solar system formed from the accretion of that ambient dust that formed our rocky planet. No dust, no clay! In fact, in the Quran, it is pointed out that just as we were all not miraculously sprung instantaneously from the Earth, likewise were Jesus and Adam *not* miraculously sprung up from dust. Most of the Muslim world has taken the opposite meaning because of not realizing the 'time factor'. In the Quran 3:59, it is stated, prior to declaring that we are created from dust, that "with" God/"in relation" to God/"from God's perspective or sight" (*'inda*) we are created from dust. Why is this so? What is the reason for this statement concerning God, which, idiomatically, is akin to 'in the eyes/sight of God'?

> Surely, the likeness of Isa (Jesus), *in the sight of God*, is like the case of Adam. He created him from dust, then He said to him: Be , and he came to be. (3:59)[16]

16 There is, of course, no question that Man possesses "extra-animal" qualities, the origins of which are traceable inthe Quran, to the moment of special blessing upon upon Man decsribed as " breathed unto him from Our spirit" or a moment where Man acquires "ruh" by the order of "kun faya kun". The details of this requires another book in the future, God-willing (see verses 15:29 and 32:9)

God makes this statement because from God's point of view, which sees times stretched billions of years as a single point, He is able to connect vast disparate epochs to each other, because they causally flow into each other despite their separation. For example, if we have a sequence A, B, C, D E, God can truncate that and simply say A, E, leaving out the intermediate sequences. This is 'God-talk', as the time span is immaterial to Him.

We human beings are not used to thinking in such long terms and cannot see this, this being so abstract: but for God it is visually concrete. In the Quran, however, a visual interconnection of these disparate epochs is presented in one sentence. This has the advantage of getting across a true concept, but at the same time making it understandable for people with less scientific understanding. The main point conveyed is that you were created from something simpler in time. As science advances, people will discover the purposely built gaps in the Quran—which is exactly what is being shown in this book. Since our Earth evolved about 4.54 billion years ago from gas and dust, that included the building blocks of life which are now known to be present in this 'dust' and gas in space, the advent of the human being is linked in God's eyes to our creation/evolution much later on. Besides, as was pointed, the word *thumma* (then) is used for transitions from one state to another, i.e., dust, then the next stage (see for example Quran 18:37, where *thumma* signifies a long duration between phases).

In the Quran in 41:11, it states that the Universe was once *dukhanun* which then evolved into galaxies. *Dukhan* means smoke—i.e., gas and dust (nebulae). The word for dust used in the Quran in 3:59 is *turabin*. Remarkably, it is now known that these six elements, namely, hydrogen, oxygen, carbon, sulfur, nitrogen and phosphorous found in outer space dust are also the six main elements found in the dust on earth (*turab*) though the ratios of these are different on Earth than the dust found in outer space. In addition, various other compounds have been found in stellar nebulae such as:

> Scattered through the clouds are particles, interstellar dust grains that contain a core of silica or carbon-rich material surrounded by ice. The ions and molecules within a cloud can attach to these grains and concentrate. Now we have a mechanism to bring them together; otherwise, these ions and molecules would be left floating aimlessly in interstellar space. Astrochemists think that much of the chemistry in molecular

clouds happens on these grains. Each grain is a factory and, more interestingly, a miniature reactor for making organic compounds.[17]

In conclusion then, God has revealed the Quran this way so that the basic message of creation can be understood by people of all times. In the Dark Ages (at the time of the Prophet), people would not have understood creation if it were described in terms of DNA etc. It would have been a big jump to say the least. However, the way the Quran has been written (for example, they would know that *yaum* does not necessarily mean a 24-hour day) influenced thinkers to eventually, over 100 years after the Quranic advent, to postulate that that evolution has occurred, though of course they would not have known of genes, DNA and could not have hypothesized internal mechanisms. These early Quranic thinkers were the initiators of evolutionary thought.

In addition, in the Quran, it is stated that after God created the Earth (after six periods) He set His throne on the water, in order to test mankind:

> And He is the one who created the galactical systems and the Earth in
> six periods, and His throne (*arsh*) was on the water so that He might test
> which one of you is best in deed. (11:7)

Throne here undoubtedly signifies command and power from a single source: God. Setting His power through the unique life-giving properties of water signifies the emergence of life into the form of the human being who is then to be tested. If there was no water, there would be no life developing eventually into the human being and other extraterrestrial 'higher' carbon-based life, and therefore no test and no purpose for having created the cosmos. Note the importance of water, for carbon-based life:

> We know of no single organism that can be active without water, and
> we know of no form of life that can use an alternative solvent to do the
> bulk of its essential chemical reactions. The question is whether this re-
> quirement for water results from one very specific set of evolutionary
> conditions or whether it derives from something more fundamental.[18]

---

17 Cockell, Charles S. (2018). *The Equations of Life: How physics shapes evolution*, p. 199.
18 Ibid., p. 168.

This passage about water is another example of 'God-speak' that does away with human notions of time. If we were to spell it out, it would be *something like* the following, shown in square brackets:

> And He is the one who created the galactical systems and the Earth in six periods, and His throne (*arsh*) was on the water [**which then played the crucial role in the *development* of *all* carbon-based life**] so that He might test which one of you is best in deed. (11:7)

Does anyone think that human beings during the early Dark Ages could have understood that sentence added to the passage in brackets?

Many Muslim academics and non-academics buy into the problematic concept of natural selection for playing a major role in macroevolution, whereas there is no real evidence that this 'mechanism' has anything to do with macroevolution! In fact, Michael Denton, in his new book *Evolution: Still a Theory in Crisis*, which is an update of his book *Evolution: A Theory in Crisis* written in 1985, elaborates on his main point that totally blows Darwinian natural selection out of the water with a veritable torpedo:

> No matter how anomalous it may seem in the context of an evolutionary worldview firmly wedded to the notion of continuity, in the case of the enucleate red cell, the ESC, and the ORFan genes, there is not the slightest evidence that they were actualized gradually via functional continuums as Darwinianism demands....On the contrary, evidence reviewed above provides overwhelming support for the radicalist notion that a considerable degree of organic order is the result of internal causal factors intrinsic to living systems.[19]

The dual function of the word Adam in the Quran

> And certainly [like Adam] We created **you**, then We fashioned **you**, then (or moreover) We said to the angels: Make obeisance to **Adam.** So they did obeisance except Iblis; he was not of those who did obeisance. (7:11)

The word Adam, which comes from an earlier Semitic language (i.e., an earlier form of Arabic), is both used as meaning humanity, or the human, as well as the name of a specific person in the Quran. The word is used contextually, much

---

19 Denton, Michael, (2016), *Evolution: Still a Theory in Crisis*, p. 144.

like the word *samaa* (in the Quran) which means "that which is above", and can mean the whole Universe, or the sky etc., depending on the context. Verse 7:11, discussed above, specifically proves that this word has a dual function, in that *you*, that is the reader, are Adam, where Adam is used generically to represent 'Man'. In other verses, it speaks of Adam as the first human on Earth we know of, (through the Quran) with whom God had direct instructional communication. Iblis's (i.e. Satan's) refusal to bow down to Adam is symbolic of his refusal to bow down to creatures made from clay (or originated in clay as we have shown) and, in effect, he has refused to bow to us as humans, even though ordered by God to do so, and this is another important meaning of 7:11. His rebelliousness *continues* and will last till doomsday. The verse should be read, *in terms of understanding*, as follows:

> And certainly [like Adam] **We created you**, then We fashioned you, then (or moreover) We said to the angels: **Make prostration to Man.** So, they did prostrate except Iblis; he was not of those who did prostrate. (7:11).—call this sentence 'A'.

> Why is it NOT stated in the Quran that: "And certainly **We created Adam (the historical person)**, then We fashioned him, then (or moreover) We said to the angels: Make prostration to him. So, they did prostrate except Iblis; he was not of those who did prostrate. (7:11)." —call this sentence 'B'.

The reason for this is because more information is given out in a condensed form, the way the Quran has been structured in A above. Here is how the dual function of the word Adam is utilized in that structure and in the Quran, in general:

1. Iblis, in 7:11 was not told to bow *just* to Adam, the individual who appeared thousands of years ago, but to the species of *homo sapiens*, denoted by the word Adam in verse 7:11, by the pre-juxtaposition of the word "you".

2. The universal usage of the word Adam, as representing Mankind, also represents a particularization, that is, the individual Adam in the story of the garden of Eden on earth, where the word "you" is not used, and only Adam has been used. This is the true and non-mythological story

is recounted which has a profound message for moral behaviour for all times, as it occurs to two individuals: Adam and his wife.

Chapter 5

The *Ipso Facto* of Cosmobiosys

Repetition, Mutations

In the previous chapters we established how carbon-based life gets originated through clay, with the aid of water in an amenable and conducive environment/atmosphere. From this originating process, we have to account for the diversity of life over the epochs, to the present day, and in so doing, we have to tackle the question of change. From nothing, comes nothing, but the fact is that changes have to come from somewhere. In terms of biology, change is contingent upon reproduction. However, reproduction requires a continuity of the species to maintain its health, and this negates the emergence of drastic or significant changes in the species. Any dramatic change must lead to the creature's death, in the event it is said that a species gives rise to something other than itself. This is because large changes are required and mutations are deleterious, leaving the macro-evolutionary view of biological organisms as being an unproven hypothesis at best. Therefore, a so-called new species can never be proved to have arisen from a different species. Continuity in time is repetition, for if you do not repeat, you not exist, but for a living creature or a living thing, repetition can only come from the reproduction of an existing living thing. You can only repeat your kind and because of this undeniable reality, 'a different new' cannot arise from an 'existing old'.

Time Factor

There is also a time factor issue that is highly problematic and makes Darwinian and Neo-Darwinian evolution impossible. Not enough time has elapsed to produce the changes in the myriad creatures to transform into other species, both in terms of macro and molecular changes. Think of all the cells that have to change. With respect to the issue of time pertaining to the random evolution hypothesis, no person can establish the length of time required for the microbits (the original unit particles that form subatomic particles considered fundamental—see Part 4 of this book) to form to develop to relate to and to become living things, from which will be born the number and variety of all living things. The sheer volume of microbits (subatomic particles) etc. necessary to form randomly, into the correct sequences required in order to produce this type of Universe would be impossible in any finite time. But the Universe was started—it had a 'before'—so chance is ruled out at the very outset! This leads to the converse: Programming of creation, as detailed herein, which is the opposite of chance and randomness. How can random repetition get it right? With multiple random mutations we would expect disorder rather than perfection. Randomness does not repeat by definition, but to be is to repeat every time—this negates randomness. If the existing species can mutate significantly so as to be transformed, that mutation will be the death of the living thing and not result in a new species. Furthermore, where mutation is random it can never be proved that apart from one fraction or organ or tissue of the species that mutated, all other cells, molecules, tissues or network of the species also mutated, synchronously, to achieve a totally harmonious order, so as to give rise to a new species. If the new species, in other words, is not pre-programmed into reality, it can never arise or can never be.

It is, in fact, more elegant and logical that the individual living thing reflect a programmed Universe, each manifesting the individual parts as expressed through the Programmer. God did not only begin the creation of man from clay as described in Chapters 1 and 2, but all carbon-based life, that is, all carbon-based species developed from clay, replicating the developmental process of embryology to produce each new species. Therefore, it is evidential that a singular origin of each species (SOES) occurred.

Not only that, but biological objects that change, are irreducibly complex and partial changes cannot do. There is also the issue of co-ordination where ecological stability and balance is maintained and this would require co-evolution with other species. The species must be perfectly in sync with the environment. 'Evolution' as seen with Darwinian evolution, is therefore extremely unscientific. It is propped up only because it helps produce and maintain a godless society, plagued by a consumeristic and the capitalistic notion of survival of the fittest, where this falsely drawn picture serves to justify and maintain hegemonic control and practices in societies and nations that maintain a separation of Church (alleged irrational) and State (alleged rational).

Bio-Programming

In the Quran it states that: "God (Allah) has caused you [i.e. your species/ the first human] to grow from the earth as a plant (growth)" (71:17). This not only applies to the human line, but to all species, each of which have their own line, but with the logical consequence that they have the shared toolkits of the RNA and DNA as derived from the earth through the process of clay and water, facilitating life's formation, with programmed diversity to fill all niches. This necessitates that the actual process of development of all-carbon-based species in the Universe be programmed by a Programmer, the Originator of the Big Bang, wherein all laws were set and each species on Earth and indeed on any life bearing planet with carbon-based life, were sequenced to be, to come into existence from clay/water as their origin. This programming is based on physical movement of the subatomic particles (microbits) based on pathways of pressure forces. Once the toolkit is there, then the Builder begins to build the cell through programming that is based on motion and pathways created by pressure forces arising from physicalist if/then logic no wherein no God-of-the-gaps exists. The Builder is God. Whether the cell develops into a fully formed species in the cocoon/womb of an outside environment or in a human female womb is not fundamental but the presence of all the components is the key factor. Once present, development will ensue necessarily. In the book, *The Master Builder: How the new science of the cell is rewriting the story of life*, by Professor Alfonzo Martinez Arias, a pioneering researcher in developmental biology, it is shown that DNA does not build the organism but it is the cell that builds the organism through physical forces. But the cell is not conscious and this begs the question as to who the actual builder is. With Cosmobiosys we are saying that the clay produced the toolkit and then it produced the cell for each species that developed into the complete organism for each species, having from one cell to tens of trillions, depending on the species, but all originating through the non-biotic clay that served as a vesicle and nurturer of these fundamental biological elements. This highlights the primary role of physics for developmental biology, based on such physicalistic programming.

All species were therefore created from clay/water directly, as discussed in Chapters 1 and 2, in great detail. The Adams and Eves of each species, so to speak, were so created. If you find that hard to believe think of your creation from a single cell in embryology, into a full human being comprising tens of trillions of specialized cells, each one more complicated than any human machine ever designed; think of the ultra-complex panoply of processes involved. Then extend your thinking to the fast moving field of ectogenesis, where the complete human being will be formable outside the human womb, from the earliest stages. Would it be impossible for the Creator to use this process, using the womb of the earth, from clay and water? Once each species was created with male and female, then and only then (aside for reproduction by fission or parthenogenesis) was reproduction of that species possible. No species changed into any other species but were sequenced to arise at different times based on the plan of the Sustainer and in accordance with environmental changes that were also in sync with the arising of the new species. It is this sequencing process that is based on physics, at its base, and it was that which was programmed by the Creator right at the inception of the Universe that we call Cosmobiosys. Amazingly, this is also how galaxies form, in principle. If you consider each galaxy as a species, they do not arise from one another but are created uniquely separately from the same laws but have similar features. These galaxies as 'individuals' have birth, life and death. That variants of the particular biological species died or whole species died when the environment was not amenable, was a way to make some species extinct so that others would follow a plan, in the divine scheme of long range teleology, so that humans could arise on Earth, together harmoniously with other isochronal creatures that were created. This view is neither that of seven day creationism, nor that associated with Darwinian Evolution, or any of its contemporary offshoots and desperately attempted yet futile rectifications. These events, based on uniform and ordered laws, occurred over the billions of years, for the hundreds of millions of species that have arisen on the Earth.

If the first instance or beings of all carbon-based species, including Man, developed from clay/water, through the initial processes described in Chapter 1, then the first instance must be produced without the normal reproduction process of animals. Rather, the first 'Adam' of each species must develop from the earth like a plant, without male and female germ cell fusion reproduction. This is why the first Adam's creation is compared to that of a plant (see Quran 71:17, below). Many plants reproduce through self-pollination and fertilisation; however, humans cannot achieve any fertilization without another human's reproductive cells. In addition, the creation of Adam, in the Quran, is compared to the birth of Jesus or Isa as his birth was also akin to parthenogenesis, that is, without another human's reproductive cell. Therefore, this verse is alluding to such special creation for Man, and by extension, for all other carbon-based entities (i.e. the other animals). The Adam/Jesus verse cited below, shows that although the creation of the first Man was special, it was nonetheless a process and based on cause and effect, using the matter/energy (microbits) in this Universe. In other words, the development of RNA/DNA and further development of the human origination (from non-existence) in clay, followed a creation very similar to, but not identical with, the creation of Isa/Jesus and that of which how many types of plants grow. There is a strong clue here that if we want to understand further the exact details of the creation of man from clay, and, indeed, all individual species, these two creations (animal parthenogenesis and aspects of plant (asexual) reproduction) will be crucial:

God (Allah) has caused you [i.e. of your species/the first human] to grow from the earth as a plant (vegetation) (*nabatan*) [which can also mean 'rearing' as in 3:37, which implies care, nurturing and protection over time]. (71:17).

Surely the likeness of Isa [Jesus] is, near (*'inda*) [i.e., in respect of the perspective of, or in the sight of] God as the likeness of Adam; He created him [Adam] from dust, then [a word which alludes to unspecified gradualness] said to him, Be, and he was. (3:59)

Facing the Fossil Record

All the programming was set at the Big Bang and the microbits (particles) arose at particular times as set by the Creator. This Creator did not have to intervene at each stage to order the origination of species. Everything was pre-set and automated, what we are referring to as Cosmobiosys. Indeed, the fossil record supports this view 100%. There are no transitional species; the species arrive fully formed and die out or continue to today. The sequential arising of various life-forms over the billions of years have led people into erroneously believing that transformations from one species to another have occurred, even though there is absolutely no evidence for it, and even though die-hard evolutionists have been searching desperately, ever since the time of Darwin. The late evolutionist Stephen Jay Gould admitted that:

The history of most fossil species include two features particularly inconsistent with gradualism:

> 1. Stasis. Most species exhibit no directional change during their ten-
> ure on earth. They appear in the fossil record looking much the same as
> when they disappear; morphological change is usually limited and direc-
> tionless.
>
> 2. Sudden appearance. In any local area, a species does not arise gradually
> by the steady transformation of its ancestors; it appears all at once and
> "fully formed."[20]

Of course, Gould then proceeded to come up with his own theory of evolution ('punctuated equilibrium') to explain the reality of the fossil record; however, his attempt could not explain two points cited above, and has been a complete failure as no form of genetics can create the purported evolution.

Status of Cosmobiosys

The Quran, in passage 6:2, which has been discussed in great detail, in Chapter 1, shows that God did not suddenly create Adam out of clay without a process occurring in it. Adam was sequenced and programmed to arise after billions of years on Earth 70,000 years ago. The view here is that verse 6:2 is similar to the one that states unequivocally that the Universe is teeming with life; this is verse 42:29, where it is stated that: "And one of His signs is the creation of the heavens and the Earth and what He has spread forth in both of them of carbon-based corporal creatures; and when He pleases, He is all-powerful to gather them together." In 42:29, the verse deals with respect to extraterrestrial life. Here, we have a situation in which the Quran clearly states some phenomenon, but we have not, as of yet, encountered extraterrestrial carbon-based life (we deal with this topic in depth, in Part 3 of this book). On the other hand, the verse on the Big Bang (21:30) has a different status because we have concrete and ever-mounting evidences for the Big Bang. It is imminent that verse 6: 2 will eventually have the same status as 21:30, in terms of the status of knowledge in nature and in purported revelation. Then the status of the verse will become like that of verse 21:30.

The view of the mechanism of evolution then, being posited, coincides, in principle, with the record of the fossils and also with new discoveries being made in genetics. Consequentially, the view has elements of the two camps of

20 Gould, Stephen Jay. (1980). The Panda's Thumb, More Reflections in Natural History, p. 182.

non-divine evolution, with proponents such as Richard Dawkins, on one side, and 'creationism' as espoused by the Intelligent Design group such as Michael Behe and others, on the other. Biological objects that change are irreducibly complex and partial changes cannot do. Michael Behe, highlights that there is an "irreducible complexity" of myriad structures in nature. Behe uses the example of a mousetrap. All the components in a mousetrap have to be present and work in a co-operative fashion for the trap to work at all. Likewise, countless structures in biology are similarly interrelated in terms of the components of which they are comprised. Behe does not see how intermediate forms could have arisen, because the particular biological structure then would be incomplete and non-functional.

Those who oppose Behe et al, and are against any teleological arguments, claim that one can have intermediate structures that can be usefully employed in nature that are evolving towards the so-called irreducibly complex structure, and that hence Behe's arguments have no validity. In particular, they propound that evolutionary development theory can account for the evolution of such structures, and, as a result, Behe's arguments and case are invalid. The anti-Behe group states that many of the processes have redundancy. This redundancy may act as scaffolding to produce other remarkably complex and functional biochemical/biological structures. The main point to observe in all this counter-argument against Behe is that any explanation used to counter the intelligent design argument is still a process that has to be explained. For example, 'redundancy' has both a useful function and is also a process. However, instead of a God-of-the-gaps explanation, we need a seamless explanation that explains the process through laws. Behe rightly criticizes the Evo-Devo camp of Sean Carroll, where he highlights the fact that Hox genes, enhancers etc. cannot work in conjunction with Darwinian natural selection (through random mutation) to produce major beneficial changes.[21]

Similarly, the complexity and sequence of steps in the blood clotting process possess irreducible complexity and that too, after 20 years has not been debunkable by anyone, although attempts were made. Natural selection fails to explain these processes. Behe shows in his book, Darwin *Devolves* that natural selection only narrows down the possibilities and in fact goes against macroevolution.

---

21 Behe, Michael. (2007). The Edge of Evolution: the Search for the Limits of Darwinism, pp. 183-203.

The random mutation that is associated with this theorized process, wrecks everything:

The great majority of even beneficial positively selected mutations damage an organism's genetic information—either degrading or outright destroying functional coded elements.[22]

Behe states that:

> Twenty years on, [from writing about irreducible complexity with respect to the bacterium flagellum in Darwin's Black Box] there has been a grand total of zero attempts to show how the elegant molecular machine might have been produced by random processes and natural selection.[23]

Cosmobiosys as Reality

From a logical analysis of the above consideration it appears that the Sustainer of this Universe (i.e. Allah) created stages and sequences for the elastic beings He made, who require time and healthy communities for their awakening and jubilation. This reality does not involve the transformation of one creature turning into another or of one thing turning into another. Think! There is not enough time for a ladder-crawling processes to result in the splendid variety of fully formed creatures in the worlds. From the very beginning, each thing was sent forth to be what your Sustainer chose it to be; and it had to be what it was numbered to be. In the gardens and fields of your Originator, one thing was made ready for another so that in the encounters between things these would nurture forms and relationships that made growth and strengths possible for the countless lives spread far and wide. From the very beginning, everything was numbered and sent forward in its name so as to be what it was destined to be. In each lane of being, a wide spread of notes was made so as to allow for the appearance of the weak, the strong and the greater other, within each being. Those species who survived in each 'ecological city' or lane did not evolve from other species, but they themselves were the living descendants of those of the same species. That all species had a common origin from clay/water developing into genetic apparatus as described in Chapters 1 and 2 leads to a respect and

22 Behe, Michael. (2019). Darwin Devolves: The New Science About DNA That Challenges Evolution, p. 183.
23 Ibid. p. 287.

affinity where the commonality of origination and process of all other species is highlighted with respect to the human species. All current species, together with humans, are indeed stellar co-journeyers who have arrived here through Intention, up to this point, on this jewel-like planet, from the vast stretches of time and reaches of space where stardust formed into rocky planets which yielded the crucial water and clay necessary for carbon-based creatures to arise, as described in the Quran, and as observed and recorded in nature.

(This Chapter was written by Nadeem Haque and Mohammed Muslim.)

Bibliography

Alonso, Claudio S., and Wilkins, David S. (2005). "The molecular elements that underlie developmental evolution", *Nature Reviews: Genetics*, Vol. 6, No. 9.

Ahmedullah, M. (2014). "Ibn Khaldun and Karl Marx: Five Centuries of History and Two Civilisations Apart, Yet Remarkably Similar. http://alochonaa. com/2014/10/21/ibn-khaldun-and-karl-marx-five-centuries-of-history-and-two-civilisations-apart-yet-remarkably-similar/

Alakbarli, F. (2001). "A 13th century Darwin? Tusi's Views on Evolution Azerbaijan International 9:48-49.

Arias, Alfonzo Martinez. (2023). *The Master Builder: How the new science of the cell is rewriting the story of life*, Basic Books, New York.

Asad, Muhammad. (1980). *The Message of The Quran*, Dar Al-Andalus, Gibraltar.

Asghar, A. (2013). "Canadian and Pakistani Muslim teachers' perceptions of evolutionary science and evolution education Evolution: Education and Outreach 6:1-12.

Asghar, A., Wiles, J. R., Alters, B. (2007). "Discovering international perspectives on biological evolution across religions and cultures", *The International Journal of Diversity*, 6:81-89.

Asghar, A., Wiles, J. R., Alters, B. (2010). "The origin and evolution of life in Pakistani High School Biology", *Journal of Biological Education*, 44:65-71.

Attar, S. (2007). *The vital roots of European enlightenment: Ibn Tufayl's influence on modern Western thought*, Lexington Books.

Bayrakdar, M. (1983). "Al-Jahiz and the rise of biological evolution", *The Islamic Quarterly*, 27:307-315

Behe, Michael. (2007). *The Edge of Evolution: The Search for the Limits of Darwinism,* Free Press, New York.

Behe, Michael. (2019). *Darwin Devolves: The New Science About DNA That Challenges Evolution*, HarperOne, Simon and Schuster, New York.

Boulter, M. (2013). Scienceandartblog: "Early Islam. http://scienceandartblog.com/2013/09/12/early-islam/.

Bucaille, Maurice. (1983). *What is the Origin of Man? The Answers of Science and the Holy Scriptures.* Seghers, Paris.

Cairns-Smith, A.G. (1985). *Seven clues to the Origin of Life*, Cambridge University Press, Cambridge.

Caporale, Lynn Helena. (2003). *Darwin in the Genome: Molecular Strategies in Biological Evolution,* McGraw-Hill.

Carroll, Sean B. (2005). *Endless Forms Most Beautiful The New Science of Evo Devo*, W.W. Norton and Company, New York/London.

Cerdá-Olmedo, E. (2008). "Ibn Tufayl (Abentofail) and the Origins of Scientific Method European Review 16:159-167

Cockell, Charles S. (2018). *The Equations of Life: How physics shapes evolution*, Basic Books, New York.

Davies, Paul. (1999). *The Fifth Miracle: The Search for the Origin and Meaning of Life,* Simon and Schuster.

Denton, Michael. (2016). *Evolution: Still a Theory in Crisis*, Discovery Institute Press.

Daily News. (2010). *Muslims—Founders of great libraries in history.* http://archives.dailynews.lk/2010/10/15/fea26.asp.

Dajani, R. (2015). "Why I teach evolution to Muslim students", *Nature* 520:409.

Darwin, C. (1859) *On the origins of species by means of natural selection.* Murray, London.

Diamandopoulos, A., Goudas, C. (2007). "Human and ape: the legend, the history and the DNA", *Hippokratia*, 11:92.

Diogo, R., Abdala, V. (2010). "Muscles of Vertebrates - Comparative Anatomy, Evolution, Homologies and Development", Vol. 1. CRC Press; Science Publisher, Enfield, New Hampshire.

Diogo, R., Wood, B. (2012). "Comparative Anatomy and Phylogeny of Primate Muscles and Human Evolution", CRC press.

Draper, J. W. (1875). "History of the Conflict between Religion and Science", Vol 13, D. Appleton, New York.

Draper, J. W. (1876). "History of the Intellectual Development of Europe", Vol 1 (rev. ed. in two volumes).

Garstang, M. (2015). "Elephant Sense and Sensibility", *Elsevier Science*.

Gould, S. J. (2002). *The structure of evolutionary theory*. Harvard University Press.

Guessoum, N. (2011). *Islam's Quantum Question: Reconciling Muslim Tradition and Modern Science*, IB Tauris,

Hameed, S. (2008). *Bracing for Islamic creationism Science*, 322:1637-1638.

Hameed, S. (2012). "Walking the tightrope of the science and religion boundary", *Zygon*, 47:337-342.

Haque, Nadeem. (2017). *Animal Afterlife*, An IHR Preprint. https://www.academia.edu/39493564/Animal_Afterlife

Haque, Nadeem. (2012). "Future Implications of a Pre-Adamic, Global & High Ancient Civilization (Investigating the Archaeological, Textual and Quranic Evidence)", *Scientific GOD Journal*, January, Vol. 3, Issue 1.

Haque, Nadeem and Muslim, M. (2007). *From Microbits to Everything: Universe of the Imaginator, Volume 2: The Philosophical Implications*, Optagon Publications Ltd., Toronto.

Hashizume, Hideo. (September 12, 2012). "The Role of Clay Minerals in Chemical Evolution and the Origins of Life", *Clay Minerals and Nature*, Ed. Marta Valaskova and Grazyna Simha Martynkova, IntechOpen.

Hawi, S. S. (1974). *Islamic naturalism and mysticism: A Philosophic Study of Ibn Tufayl's Hayy bin Yaqzan*, E.J. Brill.

Hehmeyer, I., Khan, A. (2007). "Islam's forgotten contributions to medical science Canadian Medical Association Journal", 176:1467-1468.

Hiley, B.J., and Peat, F. David, (Editors). (1987). *Implications: Essays in honour of David Bohm*, Routledge, London and New York.

Ibn-Khaldūn. (1377). *Al-Muqaddimah, Chapter 1, Sixth Prefatory Discussion. Muslim Philosophy*, Princeton University Press. Bollinger Series, Princeton., (Trans. F. Rosenthal, 1967).

Kaya, V. (2012). "Can the Quran Support Darwin? An Evolutionist Approach by Two Turkish Scholars after the Foundation of the Turkish Republic", *The Muslim World*, 102:357-370

Kechichian, J. A. (2012). *The Father of the Theory of Evolution* Al Nisr Publishing LLC, Middle East and online. doi:http://gulfnews.com/about-gulf-news/al-nisr-portfolio/weekend-review/the-father-of-the-theory-of-evolution-1.1079209.

Khodadoust, K., Ardalan, M., Ghabili, K., Golzari, S. E., Eknoyan, G. (2013). "Discourse on pulse in medieval Persia—the Hidayat of Al-Akhawayni (?–983AD)", *International journal of cardiology*, 166:289-293

Kloprogge , Jacob Teunis (Theo) and Hartmann, Hymann. (Feb. 9, 2022 (online)). *Life (Basel)*, "Clays and the Origin of Life: Experiments", 12(2): 259.

Leroi, A. M. (2014). "The lagoon: How Aristotle invented science", Bloomsbury Publishing.

Malik, Aamina H., Ziermann, Janine M., and Diogo, Rui. (2017). "An Untold Story in Biology: The Historical Continuity of Evolutionary Ideas of Muslim Scholars from the 8th Century to Darwin's Time", *Journal of Biological Education*.

Mayr, E. (1982). *The growth of biological thought: Diversity, evolution, and inheritance*, Harvard University Press, Cambridge, MA.

Nasr, S. H. (1993). *An introduction to Islamic cosmological doctrines.* SUNY Press.

Nidhami-i-Arudi-i-Samarqandi. (12th Century). *The Chahar Maqala ("Four discourses") of Nidhami-i-Arudi-i-Samarqandi*, Stephen Austin and Sons, (Trans. Edward G. Browne, 1899).

Plotkin, Henry, (1995), *Darwin Machines and the Nature of Knowledge: Concerning Adaptations, Instinct and the Evolution of Intelligence*, Penguin Books, London.

Saniotis, A. (2012). "Islamic medicine and evolutionary medicine: a comparative analysis *The Journal of IMA 44*.

Săvoiu, G. (2014). "The impact of inter-, trans-and multidisciplinarity on modern taxonomy of sciences, *Current Science*, 106:685.

Shanavas, T. O. (2010). *Islamic Theory of Evolution: the Missing Link between Darwin and the Origin of Species*, Brainbow Press.

Shapiro, Michael D.; Marks, Melissa E.; Peichel, Catherine L.; Blackman; Benjamin K.; Nereng, Kisten K.; Jonsson, Bjarn; Schluter, Dolph; Kingsley, David M., (15 April 2004). "Genetic and developmental basis of evolutionary pelvic reduction in threespine stickleback", *Nature*, Vol. 428.

Sharma, A. (1991). "Karma and Rebirth in Alberuni's India Asian Philosophy", 1:77-91.

Shubin, N. (2008). *Your inner fish: a journey into the 3.5-billion-year history of the human body*, Vintage, New York.

Siddiqi, A. H. (1995). *Muslim geographic thought and the influence of Greek philosophy*, GeoJournal, 37:9-15.

Singer, C. J. (1941). "A short history of science to the nineteenth century", Clarendon Press Oxford.

Singer, C. J. (1957). *A short history of anatomy and physiology from the Greeks to Harvey*, Dover Publications, New York.

Singer, C. J. (1959). *History of Biology to About the Year 1900*, Abelard-Schuman, London and New York.

Starr, S. F. (2009). "Rediscovering Central Asia", *The Wilson Quarterly* (1976-) 33:33-43

Tufayl, Ibn. (2009). *Ibn Tufayl's Hayy Ibn Yaqzan: A philosophical tale,*. Translated with an Introduction ans Notes by Lenn Goodman, University of Chicago Press.

Stindl, Reinhard. (2004*).* "Is Telomere Erosion a Mechanism of Species Extinction?", *Journal of Experimental Zoology (Mol. Dev. Evol.)*, 302B, pp. 111-120.

Strogatz, Steven. (2003). *Sync: How order emerges from Chaos in the Universe, Nature, and Daily Life*, Hyperion, New York.

Wallace, A.R. (1911). *The World of Life: A Manifestation of Creative Power, Directive Mind and Ultimate Purpose*, Chapman and Hall, London.

Wikipedia. (2014). "Nizami Aruzi". http://en.wikipedia.org/w/index.php?title=Nizami_Aruzi&oldid=593787037.

Wikipedia. (2015a). "Al-Biruni". https://en.wikipedia.org/wiki/Ab%C5%AB_Ray%E1%B8%A5%C4%81n_al-B%C4%ABr%C5%ABn%C4%AB

Wikipedia (2015c) "Nasir al-Din Tusi" by scan of stamp. Licensed under Public Domain via Wikimedia Commons. https://commons.wikimedia.org/wiki/File:Nasir_al-Din_Tusi.jpg#/media/File:Nasir_al-Din_Tusi.jpg

Wilczynski, J. Z. (1959). "On the presumed Darwinism of Alberuni eight hundred years before Darwin", *Isis*:459-466

Wilkins, David S. (2002). *The Evolution of Developmental Pathways*, Sinauer Associates Inc., Massachusetts.

Wolpoff, Milford H. and Caspari, Rachel. (1997). *Race and Human Evolution,* Simon and Schuster, New York.

Zimmer, Carl. (June 2004). "How did life on earth begin?", *Discover*, Volume 25, Number 6.

Zirkle, C. (1941). "Natural Selection before the "Origin of Species" ", *Proceedings of the American Philosophical Society*:71-123

PART 2

Solving Consciousness:
Cracking the 'hard problem' of the mysterious mind-body connection

Introduction

The claimed or purported solution to the 'Hard Problem' of consciousness has been provided in writings by the authors, with the solution originated by M. Muslim, but it has never been presented in a focus way, since, for example, in the book the Microbits series, Volume 2: *Universe of the Imaginator*, the discussion was intermixed with other questions. This book seeks to remedy this situation, through a much more focused, step by step logical proof. The solution is essentially a two-step process. Any link in the chain of sequential argumentation that can be debunked would collapse the proof. We claim that the arguments are watertight and indefeasible, and we challenge the reader to show otherwise. If they cannot debunk the logic, it inevitably leads to the solution. There are two steps to showing what consciousness is, its origin and how it arises in living entities. Each of the two steps has to be flawless to constitute proof.

> **Step 1:** *Proof of the existence of God (Eternal and Infinite Consciousness) and simultaneously the exact relation of this God to space.*
>
> **Step 2:** *Proof of human consciousness as portions of that space through the agency of God.*

Before and after is an introduction to the topic and a general discussion of the findings, respectively. All this thus constitutes the 'Proof' of what consciousness is, that is, that the framework of the 'hard problem' is provided.

The Human Mind and the Issue of the 'Soul'

Of the several views on the issue of the mind/body problem, we shall discuss the three *main* categories (other categories do exist, such as Panpsychism but a critique in subsequent pages will cover that theory). There are the:

1. Materialists: Who say that there is only the brain and no such thing as the mind.
2. Dualists: Who say that there is the brain and mind, and these are of two entirely different categories of things.
3. Property Dualists: Who say that the mind is an emergent property of the brain and that they both interact with each other strongly.

The solution to the mind/body problem we introduce in this chapter fits into none of the above and defies all categories. But first, let us examine what the critics of the dualists have to say, as a preamble.

The Physicalist Trap

Philosopher of the mind, Patricia Churchland asks the following questions regarding the 'soul', which she feels is problematic. She states that:

> On this hypothesis [of substance dualism], no reduction of psycholog-ical theory is forthcoming because the former is a theory about states and processes of mind-substance, whereas the latter is a theory about the states and processes of a material substance, the brain. Each substance is thought to have its own laws and its own range of properties, hence research on the brain is not going to yield knowledge of the mind and its dynamics, nor by parity of reasoning, will research on the mind tell us anything about how the brain works. The unavailability of a solution to the manner of interaction between two radically different substances does not entail that substance dualism is false. For all we now know, fur-ther research may yet discover a solution. [24]

A staunch anti-dualist, philosopher Daniel Dennett, in his book *Conscious-ness Explained*, discusses the contrasting views on the mind:

> By thinking of our brains as information processing systems, we can gradually dispel the fog and pick our way across the great divide, discov-ering how it might be that our brains produce all the phenomena. Our consciousness does not consist in the fact that your brain is inhabited by an inner agent to whom your brain presents displays... [25]

The problem with Dennett's view is that the material that comprises the brain is solely made of atoms and ultimately microbits (for those that have not read Volume 1 of *From Microbits to Everything*, or the latest book on this sub-ject *Microbits: A New Unified Physics*, substitute the word 'subatomic particles', every time you see the word "microbits", or read Part 4 of this book), and mi-crobits cannot generate consciousness, no matter how they are arranged; at the

---

24 Churchland, Patrricia Smith.(1989).Neurophilosophy:Toward a Uniform
Science of Mind/Brain, p. 318 and p. 320.
25 Dennett, Daniel C. (1991). Consciousness Explained, p.433.

most, re-organized or complexified matter/energy can only produce different and more sophisticated mechanical, electrical, photonic etc., functions. Indeed, whatever Dennett uses to explain the self, will always remain a unified conceptual entity in its functionality that somehow acts in space to command the body, whether he calls it "multiple drafts" or whatever. Furthermore, his view cannot explain subjective experience, such as pain, pleasure and countless phenomena experienced by the unchanging unity of self. Indeed, both philosophers of the mind and philosophically inclined neuroscientists are at a loss to explain qualia. Christof Koch, biologist and cognitive scientist at Caltech in Pasadena, California remarks that:

> It is true that there's this deeply mysterious aspect of consciousness that is subjective feeling. Why should physical activity in some subset of my brain give rise to this buzz in the head? It's a logical chasm. It's non-sequitur. [26]

The problem with the thinking of many philosophers of science is that they mistake correlation for causation; they assume that the brain gives rise to the mind because of the correlation between brain processes and our conscious reactions. All explanations that seek to show that the mind is the product of the brain are trying to say that Level 2 (the mind) depends on and is a result of the activity of Level 1 (the nervous system). However, the activity in Level 1 is basically the motion of particles. Now no matter how those particles are re-arranged and/or move, they cannot create Level 2. Only physical functionality is changed, that is all! The reason why even quantum mechanics as the new physics or the further advancement of quantum mechanics will never be able to solve the mind-body problem is because it still deals with subatomic particles and is forever trapped in Level 1. This is what I refer to as *The Physicalist Trap*.

Colin McGinn, philosopher at Miami University comments that:

> I do sympathize with [mathematical physicist] Roger Penrose... I think his view is a little too conservative in a way... [in that]... quantum theory applies to non-psychological phenomena, non-conscious systems, so it's unlikely that it will give you an account of conscious systems. [27]

---

26 CBC Radio. Ideas: The Matter of Mind: Parts 1 and 2. Aired in 2002.
27 Ibid.

Furthermore, indeterminism does not exist in the laws of nature. This erroneous assumption is the result of assuming that reality is formed by perception. It arose as a counter-reaction to mystical doctrines in the form of Logical Positivism. Nothing special lies behind quantum mechanics, in reality. Level 1 comprises of atoms and subatomic particles, essentially in motion. As stated above, a complex arrangement of motion gives nothing but a mechanical/electrical/chemical/biological function based on that configuration of complexity, and that complexity still remains in Level 1. In the mind-body problem, then, the observer or witness always exists. Those who look at the bottom-to-top solution of the mind emanating from the brain cannot prove that the particles that comprise the brain are the observers, taken collectively, because no matter how complicated their motion and interaction, they cannot rise above the category of being merely the interaction of particles!

In this vein, let us go through the following arguments of philosophers of the mind, where Patricia Churchland and John Searle ideas are flawed, from a number of angles, which we shall now discuss in depth. Firstly, Searle says that: "... we had this debate a century ago about life... [e.g.] you've got to have a "vital spirit", an élan vital. And now we can't even remember it." The analogies these philosophers are drawing to criticize dualism are incorrect: The phenomena of light, which was puzzling a century ago, lay in the explanation of Level 1—the motion of particles etc., to produce light. Those who could not understand 'light', immediately 'jumped the gun' and erroneously took light to be something that belonged to Level 2. The issue of 'vital spirit', is more complicated, however: Although knowledge of DNA etc. shows us what the building blocks of nature are, the physicalists provide no ultimate explanation for what it is that causes their precise motion to precise locations to produce precise organisms or biological structures, for precise functions. It cannot be plausibly explained by chance (i.e., no mind behind/ laws)! The criticisms spouted by Churchland, as a result, are erroneous, for these thinkers take the invalid example of light and the unresolved example of vital spirit. In fact, explaining consciousness is a different kettle of fish entirely, since it pertains to explaining qualia, that cannot be lumped with light or vital spirit. Colin McGinn, had expressed the view that a 'new physics' (which we discuss in Part 4) would be needed to explain consciousness:

Now the physics you'll get there will presumably be very different from the physics we have now, because the physics we have now isn't a theory of the conscious world at all. It's a theory of the non-conscious physical world. So whatever "physics" we have which applies to consciousness will have to have very different laws and different principles, different explanatory ideas if it's going to account for the specificity of consciousness. But it seems to me that, yes, we do basically need a new physics, that is to say, a new overall theory of the natural world.

Let us see how the view being presented in this book solves the mind/body problem through an entirely 'new physics'. In other words, let us now attempt to solve consciousness.

Proof of the Existence of God

ABSTRACT: The eternal Imaginator must exist. Without eternity and imagination, nothing can come into being.

Key Words: proof, existence, GOD, sesamatic, relatiological, "STOP" argument.

Introduction

It is fashionable these days for many intellectuals to say that there is no God or that the existence of God cannot be proven logically. The reason for this is that all the previous arguments for the existence of God have been found to be less than satisfactory in one form or another by the logicians. This had led many religious people to retreat from logic and to claim that the issue of God is a matter of the heart and not of the mind. This, however, cannot be true. In this section I will prove the existence of God in a way that cannot be disproven by any logician. You need to know whether God exists or not. If God is a phantom, as some people say, then this life has no meaning in itself; and all the dreams and structures of mankind, including this very journal, are nothing but babbles of miserable dreamers. Fortunately, God is. The simplest way of resolving the issue is to ask a series of basic questions as follows. First, do human beings exist or not? No one can rationally prove that we do not exist. Any person that argues that we do not exist disproves himself or herself by the very fact of the denial. Non-existent beings do not speak. We exist because we cannot deny it without being stupid or mad. Since we did not make ourselves, it follows that something made us. This is also clear. Let us refer to the thing that brought us into being as our Cause. Since we all agree that we have a Cause, the question can never be whether our Cause exists or not, rather what the nature of this Cause is. Let me reword the whole thing. Some people call this Cause "God". So, if we replace Cause with God, we can see that questions as to whether God exists become nonsensical. The real issue is never whether there is God but what kind of God are we talking about. Inevitably, when we speak about God's qualities we use words which are all too human. But as the question of God is a human question the answer to it must be in human language. The point to be made is that if this

Cause (of our existence) were named "God" this naming of the cause cannot be said to change the nature of the cause or the fact that it is. At this point then, the disputes about God become no more than disputes about God's attributes. You should keep in mind that even the so-called religious do not unanimously agree on the attributes of God. There are thousands of contradictory statements from different religions and from different sects about what God is. We are all atheists about the God of those that we do not believe in. So, in effect we are all atheists and we are all believers. It all depends upon which God you are talking about. We are now going to look at a more detailed argument for the existence of God.

How do things come into being? By things coming into being I mean the way in which children, for example, are born for the first time into the world. Prior to your birth, something was here. For the sake of simplicity let us say that your parents caused you to be here. And continuing with that logic let us say that your parents' parents caused them too to be here. Let us also take the position that it has always been like this, namely, one or more things uniting to cause another thing to come into being, and that thing too causing something else to come into being and so forth. When it comes to the question of the origin of all these changes, there are only two possibilities. One is that matter is forever and has been changing forever. This would mean that there is no beginning point or time for this change. The other possibility is that matter had a beginning and that changes have not been forever. This would make God the creator of all things. I do not wish to go into definitions of God at this point. For now, though it is important to keep in mind that the philosophers have not proved that change is eternal. What they have said is that it is possible that matter is eternal and has been changing forever. The significance of the argument about change is that if matter has been changing forever then obviously, there would be no need for a God. If it has not, then we turn to God.

Has matter been changing forever? One undeniable thing about reality is change. Billions of people now living were not here—say, 200 years ago. In addition, we also know that there were millions and millions of people before we came here and that these are no longer here. Every day, more newcomers are added to the mix. More may come after we are gone. Where do all these people come from? From the logic of the philosophers, the only answer must be that we all come from eternally changing matter. According to this position, everything that is happening is simply matter changing from one state to another. But is it? When the philosophers say that matter has been moving forever, they imply that the changes have no beginning. There is no point in space or time where these changes began.

The fact, however, is that changes are by definition, successive. In this world, we see that all things have not arrived at once. Some things come before others. Our parents, for instance, came before us and we come before our children and so on. But then if, as the philosophers say, changes of matter have no beginning or a first step, how can they explain the successions that are all over the place? Successions characterize our world. To get a subsequent step, you require a prior step. Where there is no beginning step, there can be no succeeding step. The problem is that if our changes had no beginnings as the philosophers say, we could never have arrived here. That which has no beginning cannot have succession. If you can think of changes as sequences, you can easily see how it is that if you don't move from '1', you can't get to '2'. Without a first change, there can never be a subsequent change.

Let me explain things in a different way. Matter is a collection of limited things. The fact that we are each able to move from one position to another shows clearly that we are each limited. For when you are endless, you move not, as you are everywhere already. The fact that everything in space moves proves that everything in space is limited. Indeed, the very possibility of multiple things is conditional upon each thing being limited. To have more than one thing, each thing must be limited. To be limited, however, is to have a fixed position in space. You cannot be limited and have no place. That which is said to be limited but has no position in space is nothing. Now, matter is a collection of limited things. Let us assume for a moment, with the philosophers, that matter had been here forever. That must mean that each part of matter has always occupied a position in space. There are only two ways by which matter could have been present in space. One is by way of what we call rest and the other is by way of what we call motions. Therefore, matter has either been moving or resting forever. To change, however, is to move from one position to the other. A change only occurs when a thing accelerates or de-accelerates (or deceleration) from a state of rest or from a rate of motion in space. When matter is at a constant rate of rest, or motion, the manner in which it changes is to accelerate or decelerate from that position. Acceleration, deceleration, divisions, and multiplications, are the only things that define change. Where matter is before the change occurs is its "from" position. Where it ends after the change is the "to" position. Changes are no more than "from" "to", etc. If, therefore, matter has been changing, it could only have done so by moving "from" "to". Here is the crux of the matter. Every change is between the "from" and the "to". The "to" is always subsequent. No matter what you think of "forever", a subsequent position is not and cannot be forever. What is important to remember is that acceleration or deceleration is always after the "from" position. The "from" is always before the "to". The fact that the "to" comes after the "from", clearly shows that the "to" has not been forever. But then you need the "to" to have change. If therefore, the "to" has not been forever, then necessarily, changes, cannot and have not been forever. That is just another way of saying that every change must have a beginning. So, clearly, this shows without a doubt then that this changing world had a beginning. To see this with clarity we need to answer the question of infinite regress with respect to change, where some philosophers deny a beginning. This leads us to the "STOP" argument.

The STOP argument

One of the easiest ways of figuring out that matter has not been changing forever is this: Let us convert time into distance so that we can see changes as movements in distance. In this respect, to say that matter has been changing forever would be the same as saying that it has been moving forever. In other words, if we assume with the philosophers that the changes had no beginning, then no one can point to any point in space and say, "here is where it started". As I said earlier, however, we know that changes are successive. What we have now was not always here. If one thing is certain, it is that we have a past. Yesterday is not today and today is not tomorrow. One comes after the other. Let us call the present the "now". But because we have yesterday, we know that the "now" was not always here. It has come from somewhere. Let us build an imaginative STOP sign for matter in the "now" and then try to send matter back from the STOP sign to where it came from. Do you think that if matter started returning to where it came from, it would ever arrive or reach the end? The answer is absolutely not. This is because no matter how far and how long matter moves back, there could never be an end position for matter. This is because, according to the philosophers, its changes did not start anywhere. But the fact is that if you don't start anywhere, you don't end anywhere. The problem is that the distance between our STOP and where matter came from is the same for matter, whether it is coming or going. Therefore, if it is impossible for matter to reach home or to any beginning point of its changes, it must follow that matter could never have arrived at this present STOP from there. If matter is here, therefore, that must show that matter has not been changing forever. It had to start somewhere. Once again, I show conclusively that matter's changes had a beginning.

Could matter on its own have "caused" its beginning changes? We know that matter has not been changing forever and must have had a beginning. Still, we must ask ourselves whether matter could have caused these changes. Again, let us assume with the philosophers that matter has been around forever. Since we are not adding God to the mix, matter would be the whole of reality. If this is so, then every change that we see in matter today, must always have been a possibility of matter. That is, matter should always have had all that it needed to make human beings, for example. The question then is, if all that was needed to make a human being, always existed in matter, why did we only arrive recently? Why weren't we born before the time that we were born? What's with the delay? Let us break it down. Suppose a quality or quantity "x" is what is needed to finalize the making of a human being. If this "x" were not a part of eternal matter, matter could not subsequently acquire it. If reality didn't have this "x" then "x" did not exist and there is no other place to get "x" from. On the other hand, if this "x" was eternally present in matter, then changes should have occurred long before they did. Let's say that a thing, call it "M", is at position "1". Let's call this "M1". When M moves to position "2" it becomes "M2". Clearly, before M moved to position "2", position "2" already existed.

As I mentioned before, an object in a constant state of rest is said to change only when it decreases or increases its rate of speed. An object that increases its speed expands its positions in space or reaches more of its possibilities. The opposite is true. An object that decreases its speed contracts its positions and reaches less of its possibilities. Hence, if the original state of matter was that of constant rate of the highest speed of motion for example, then the type of change that we would have seen in this world would have been one of contraction or of de-acceleration. Contraction, however, is the opposite of births and growths. The type of changes that we see in this world are expansive rather than contracting. If matter had been de-accelerating from an original state of motion, we would not have had an expansion, but the contraction of the Universe or of life. Birth or growth is the result of an acceleration from a position of no birth (rest) to a position of birth (motion). It represents a grab of one or more of matter's possibilities. This, therefore, shows that if matter had been forever, its 'forever' state would not have been that of the highest speed of motion but that of rest. But matter cannot be in a 'forever' position of rest. If something is in space, it must move. The limited cannot rest. It has nothing to rest on. If to be matter is to move and if we are saying that matter could only have begun its motions from rest, then we are saying that matter did not exist before it moved. The first movement was existence. For matter and change are interchangeable. Just as the changes that we see have a beginning, so too does matter. The only relevant observation about this is that prior to the move, there was a gap between position "2" and M. Since M is complete as M at position "1" before it moves, position "2" is not M, but M+ or M- depending on the situation. Let us say that "x" is the quality whose presence necessarily enables M's movement from position "1" to position "2". If "x" was a part of M before the move, then M could not have rested at position "1" since "x" necessarily results in movement from position "1" to position "2". Thus if "x" is the facilitator of the change from M1 to M2, it must be external to M. Where M stands for matter, this clearly shows that the "x" that made the first change possible was not eternally present in matter. It is only when the "x" is not inherently present in matter that we can explain the delay in the actualisation of matter's possibilities. But then once you admit that something outside of matter caused its changes then you must admit that there is more to reality than matter. Or, in other words, whatever caused the changes that we see is not matter. What is it then? The only answer is God. I will get to that in a moment. Another fact that shows that the "x" of changes is external to matter is this. Before each change occurs, it is preceded by the possibility of the change. Before a child is born, children must be possibilities, outside of, and independent of, a particular parent. It is neither the parent nor the child that makes the child possible but "childrenability" independent of the parents. It is only when the parents participate or fulfil the conditions of this "children-ability" that a child can be born. But then you must agree that these conditions are not something that the parent dreamed of. Nor is it possible for the parent to fulfil the conditions and not have the child. Similarly, a car moves, but it is not the car that makes motion possible. Motion in general exists as possibility in space, independent of, and external to, the car. The car moves only when it fulfils certain conditions for motion. A particular function is always subsequent and external to an independent antecedent possibility of the general function. This is true of everything or every function in space. No individual thing makes any of the relationships or positions that define, limit and shape its presence.

As matter is no more than these individual things in relationships, it follows that neither matter as individual pieces nor matter collectively as a whole has anything to do with the very positions or "principles" in space that enable matter to be, move and change. It is never our mere quantities that change us, but our relationships in space. The problem is that the principles or relationships that we are subject to, are independent of each thing. The principles that make relationships possible must precede the relationships. Since all changes are relationships, this must mean that the cause of these changes must be external to the subjects of the change. In other words, in itself nothing can change on its own.

In order to make the foregoing even clearer, think about this. To change is to divide, add or multiply the relationships or positions of a given thing. Every activity in space can be given a certain number. This way, if for example, we replace all matter with numbers, we can still divide, add and multiply things. That is, we do not need actual matter in order to have changes. It is never so much matter, as much as the order of space that necessarily results in what we call changes. The fact that you can imagine the possibility of change without the necessity for actual matter shows once again that the principles of change or the order that causes change is not matter, but something else. What is it? Before I answer the question of what it is that causes changes, let me answer a question that is probably on everybody's mind. It is this: Is matter eternal? Someone could argue that even if changes had a beginning, still, is it not possible that matter itself had no beginning? The answer is: not a chance! Time is a measure of events in sequence. Forever means an infinity of sequential events. Where there are no sequential events, there is no time. Where all the events happen at the same time without any sequence, those events are for all purposes one and not successive enough to be time. Now, changes are the same as the events of time. Since we have already seen that these changes have not been forever, that must mean that there are not enough events to give an infinity of time or forever. Because matter does not have enough changes or events to constitute forever, matter cannot be said to have existed forever. Time is not a place. It is a number of events. So, if those events do not add up to forever, matter could not have been around forever. You cannot be in a time that does not exist. The clear conclusion then must mean that matter had a beginning.

Another angle: If you are not moving, you do not exist in space. When you are limited, you must move. You cannot be limited and be completely at rest. But then whenever you move, you must rest and then move and then rest. It does not matter how fast or how slow you move, if you move a hundred times, you must stop a hundred times. But these moves and rests or the 'froms' and 'tos' are what we call changes. As we have already seen, however, matter has not been changing forever. This must mean that matter has not been moving forever. But then to be matter is to move or to change. Therefore, if matter has not been changing forever, that must mean that matter itself has not been forever. Let me explain things from a different position. It is impossible for matter to be, without motion. This is because the only thing that does not move is that which is either limitless or prevented from moving by something else. This is true of all limited things, big and small. But there is no one thing in space that is so powerful and so far-reaching as to stop anything from moving forever. That must mean that sooner or later, everything in space moves. In space, rest without motion is fiction. We don't see matter at rest anywhere. Every part of matter moves and is moving. To be matter is to move. But to move is the same thing as changing. If, therefore, matter been around forever then, it would have been changing forever. Since we have already seen that all changes have a beginning, it must follow that matter has not been around forever. This must mean that matter was born at the moment when motions or changes were born! What I am saying is that there is no difference between matter and change. To change, is to be matter. To be matter is to change. Since changes have a beginning, matter must have had a beginning.

Space as the Creator of Matter and the Infinite Enabler of Change

If matter itself had a beginning and if matter is not responsible for change, what is the obvious and the only alternative? The answer is "space"; that limitless, indivisible eternity in which everything is and which is the prerequisite for every presence, movement, division, multiplication and change. That ever-present space which you can never imagine as being absent anywhere, anytime, is the creator, container, mover, organizer and planner behind everything. In one of my previous books, I showed that Albert Einstein was wrong in talking about the "curvature" of space. (this is also discussed In Part 4 of this book). Only a limited thing curves. This confusion has had the effect of giving people the idea that "space is matter". Neither was Descartes right when he talked about space as an "extension" of matter. Space is not like a shadow. It does not extend from anything. Space is independent of matter. It is, and can be, without matter. It is matter that needs space. But space itself does not need matter. We can imagine a matterless space but not a spaceless matter. By space I am not referring to positions or areas. These are fractions in space. Space itself is that objectless constant without which no limited thing can be. It is that vast expanse through which we move. But space alone cannot be sensed, limited, divided or grasped in any manner. Matter is derivative from space as music is a derivative of plays. If we are the music, space is the musician. When the singing stops, the music stops. But although the song is from the player, the musician is not the music, and the music is not the musician. It is the constancy of space that gives each thing its presence and stability. It is also the limitlessness of space that allows for that 'extra' room that enables all possible movement. A full space has no new tenants. But then when you think about it, you would see that all changes are mathematical propositions of pluses, divisions, and multiplications. These are all functions of limits. And these limits are divisible or multipliable as a result of infinity. It is the logic of this infinity that gives us the logic of all relationships, mathematics, included. We do not change then because we are a given quantity. We change only because we are not made to rest and cannot be at rest in space. And because the logic of space and of our limits forces us to move, we become the spaces that we occupy. All changes in matter result from this "relationizing" in space. Without space, nothing can move, be or change. It is space, therefore, that enables change and nothing else.

Willful and Imaginative Space as reason for delay in changes

But then we must ask, if all changes were always possibilities of space and if space has always been around forever, then how can we explain the delays in changes? I pose the same question that I gave to matter, to space. If space were like matter, namely, mindless, then naturally, it too could never explain the delay in the changes for the same reasons that a mindless matter cannot explain the delays. For the sake of argument only, let us assume for a moment that space is mindless. If space and matter had been around forever, then between the two of them, changes should have occurred long before they did. This is because between the two of them they should have all that they needed to make changes. The only explanation that the human mind can give for delay in changes is purposeful delay. Nothing else can explain delay in the actualisation of possibilities except will, wishes or desire. Think about it. A mindless reality cannot maintain a distance between its possibilities and its actualities. With the mindless, what can be, is what is. It is only a willful, imaginative, singular space that can delay the actualisation of its potential. Nothing else can do it. Only a reality that has wishes can say for example, "I want humans now," or "I can have humans, but not yet". There can be no other reasonable alternative for explaining how the eternal gives rise to the temporal except where the eternal is imaginative so that changes occur, not as changes of the eternal itself, but as the manifestations of the eternal imagination or will. If you think that this is not true, try to coming up with the temporary from a mindless eternity!

The Necessity for God

Let us look at the problem from another perspective. Everything that exists has always been here or has come into being as a manifestation of a pre-existing potential of reality. What is clear, however, is that all those things existing right now are the result of changes. Nothing in space has been pre-existing in the same form, function and position in space. This must mean that all that exists today must have come into being as a manifestation of the previous potential of reality. Let us call this reality X. The first question is, "is X too, the result of change or is it eternal?" Every change is preceded by a previous position. Where there is no prior position, there cannot be a subsequent move. We have subsequent moves, therefore, there must have been a first move. But if there is a first move, it could only have come from a position before movement, i.e., the eternal. So, whatever gave rise to change must have existed before change. The eternal is that which always was; is and will be. Every change requires and depends upon a constant. Without such a constant, there cannot be change. The problem is that to be eternal is exactly that, namely, to be "forever". But forever what? A thing cannot be said to exist unless it is a fixed quantity or quality. Since one thing cannot be said to be and not be at the same time, when we say that there is such a thing as the eternal, we are talking about an everlasting "something". This something must either be mindless or mindful. The mindless is that which is not aware of itself and has no ability to think, imagine or wish for things. The mindful on the other hand, is aware of itself and can think, imagine and wish for things.

A Mindless Eternal can never change

A mindless eternal can never account for the emergence of the temporary. This is because however you look at the issue, the first move is either a function of automatic processes or one of will. If the eternal is mindless, the only way to explain the first move would be to say that time was always a potential of the eternal and that at some point the potential became active. Active or not, passive to active or vice versa, is a form of change. Change can only occur in one of two ways; through automatic force or willful force. Since we are talking about the mindless, the only possible way for change to occur is by way of automatic force or processes. To be eternal is to exist before time. Where there is no time, there can be no movement, changes or processes. Before time, there are no processes, but only X. You cannot have processes before you have time. So, the first change could only have come from within X itself. Keep in mind that before the first change, X is the only reality and has no other source or power to influence it to change. Now, whatever X was immediately before the first change, it had been the same eternally. Since X is the only reality before change, nothing could have come from anywhere to cause any change in X immediately before the first move. Since there is no external force or event to change the eternal, the mindless eternal could never have changed from within itself and thus could not have changed at all to give us time. A good reply might be that the first change was a unique event and that it occurred spontaneously. Spontaneous or not, a change is a break away from a previous position. Adding the term spontaneous to the change does not take away from the fact that we must still explain what it is that enables the eternal to break away from its eternal self. You might reply that the change must have occurred as a result of continuing processes or events in the eternal until there was a critical mass and then voila!, time. If this were true, this situation would be much like what happens when water keeps on eroding the soil under the foundation of a building slowly but steadily until one day the foundation gives way and whole building collapses. Or like what happens when you keeping on loading straws onto a camel until you break its back from overload. The problem with this explanation however, is that it is baseless. All processes require time. Indeed, the processes themselves are time. So, we cannot logically say that time was happening or that changes were occurring before the first change or the first time occurred. Given that we are talking about the first time or the first change, arguments about processes, etc., cannot apply. Another reply might be that there could have been something else that caused the eternal to change. Earlier on in this section, I had stated that, and now repeat that: if this were so, that thing too would have to be eternal. This is because that which does not exist before time does not exist at all, so as to cause any change before time. But then if the thing that caused the eternal to change were also eternal, that would not help us very much. For the second, third or even the trillionth eternal would also have the same problem that the first has, namely, what is it that made the eternal change? If one eternal cannot account for the birth of time, the trillionth of them cannot either.

Inexplicable delays

Another problem is that there has been a delay in our births. When we are talking about the eternal, all the pieces that are needed to make us must have been there forever. If something was missing, the eternal could not subsequently get it from anywhere. So, if all the ingredients were there, and if time was no problem, then all things that could have occurred in the eternal should have occurred long before they did. The mindless cannot delay the consequences of its nature. We know that because the eternal has existed forever, whenever the first change occurred, it could have occurred much, much earlier than it did. Since it is the eternal that gives rise to time, all of us could have been born a very long, long time ago rather than now. Even if we agree for the sake of argument only that the eternal needed time, still, the eternal has had forever into the past. Whatever time you consider can be extended into the past infinitely so that we should have been here a very long, long time ago, say a trillion, trillion, trillion years before you were born. Why now? What's up with the delay? Let me illustrate. When fire and dry wood meet in dry conditions, the wood necessarily burns. The wood cannot say to the fire, "wait a minute, don't let me burn right now". When two and two come together, they have no choice but to burn. You can think of a million other things like that. So, if all the ingredients that are necessary to make human beings, for example, were always present in the eternal, then we should have been here a long time ago. Even if for the sake of argument only, we were to say that the eternal needed time, still, given that it was the eternal itself that created time, it could always have done it long before it actually did it. Since neither missing pieces, external factors, nor time can explain why changes occur in the eternal, it must follow that as long as the eternal is mindless, it can never give rise to change, and it can never account for the delays in our births.

Voluntariness as the only correct answer

Since we have eliminated the mindless as a possibility, the only answer is voluntariness. The temporal arises from the eternal in the same way that in the human realm, creative works arise from reality. That is, through the will and imagination. In the human realm, it is through "fiction" and "imagination" that we can temporarily escape the clutches of nature without changing our nature. The reason we are able to do that is that we have minds that can willfully "fabricate" unreality. The interesting thing is that although the imagined or the fictional may not be a part of reality, it can become temporarily real when we real beings pay attention to it. It is our willful construction of the forms and our attentiveness to the subject that makes our creative works a part of reality sometimes. Similarly, the temporary can arise from the eternal only when the eternal has the capacity to wish for or imagine something other than itself. When the eternal has wishes and imagination, the first change can occur as a matter of will. Only this will can explain the break in the eternal. But for this to happen, willfulness must be a part of eternal nature. As for the delay, it can be explained as the prerogative of the eternal will. It wills what it wants when it wants. In this respect, even though it does not move, the eternal must be by nature, an unceasing imagination so that the changes can arise, not as changes in the eternal itself, but as manifestations of the unceasing wishes. But how, you ask, can the eternal have imagination or wishes, when it has no time or does not move?

Imaginative Will

The imagination of the eternal is contained in its will. We do not have two separate things, namely, the will and the imagination. What the eternal is, is an imaginative will. This is at once, the imagination and the ensuing action that we call time, creatures and change. The will can be turned on or off for specific goals or projects. When the will is turned on, all the goals of the will come into being. It is the contents of the will as they manifest, that I refer to as the imagination. When the will is not turned on for time, or for subjects such as ourselves, the eternal is "emptiness". Note, however, that this is a relative term to mean the absence of all those things that come to play, when the will kicks in.

Because the eternal is emptiness, it is one. You cannot have two or more eternal "emptinesses". It must be one. Whenever the will kicks in, there is "fullness". Again, this is a relative term to mean the presence of those things that were not eternally present in the emptiness. Because this emptiness is eternal, you should know that having creatures cannot add anything to the nature of the eternal. What changes when creatures are born is not so much the eternal itself as much as its attention. Creation then is a form of self-sacrifice or an act of selflessness. The creatures are like guests. Before the creatures come, the attention of the eternal is of itself. When the creatures come, the attention shifts somewhat to the creatures, to the extent of their presence in the eternal presence. In this regard then, creation is a favor upon the creatures and a loss of quiet on the part of the creator. Naturally, the things that come into being as a result of the will of the eternal were always possibilities of the eternal. But before these possibilities are willed into being, the eternal is in a state of itself only. However, you should know that the possibilities of the eternal are strictly those of will only. The possibilities are not independent "somethings" that exist in the eternal before time. Only the eternal is present before time. Other things come into being only when the eternal wills in a particular way. Like thoughts, creatures come into being only when the eternal "thinks" about them or imagines them. If you can imagine the creatures as the "thoughts" of the eternal, they are real to the extent that the eternal continues to hold these thoughts. When the thoughts cease or when the imagination stops, like characters in the eternal dream, we all disappear just as we were before the imagination.

God's Being

But what kind of existence is this, you ask, if to be eternal is not to do anything? The short answer is that you and I cannot imagine how it must feel like. We can never be eternal, nor can we ever be emptiness. Nevertheless, "doing" something always involves a change of position or pursuit of a goal. If you can pursue a goal but choose not to, then not doing anything becomes the "do". Being without acting is a form of doing because it is a state that is maintained by a will that could act otherwise. But anyway, we all do stuff because we want to get this and that. When we do not need anything or when we do not want to get anything, we do not do anything. Sometimes, it is enough to be and not to do anything. Being alone and having silence is sometimes better than company and noise.

A similar thing applies to the eternal. It does what it wills when it wills. Being eternal, it does not need the temporary for its being. The temporary can never add or take away anything of substance from the eternal. Therefore, the eternal can never need to create. It can only want to create. When it does not want to create, it does not. It is that simple. This explains why you and I appeared "just like that." Remarkably, it is the nature of the will that although it can lead to action it does not have to. So, while the eternal has the capacity to wish for this and wish for that, the eternal is not under any necessity or compulsion either from within itself or from without, to act or to act continuously. This explains why there can be a moment where there are no objects or time at all. But given that the presence or absence of time is subject to the eternal will, the whole thing is elastic so that the eternal can have cycles of creatures, no creatures, then creatures and then no creatures and so on forever. Why and when some creatures come into being is not a matter of necessity at all, but only a matter of the wishes of the eternal. In effect then, all creatures exist at the pleasure of the eternal.

Where does God come from?

This eternal being that wishes things into being is what I refer to as our God. But speaking of origins, we may as well ask the same question about God. Because God is the everlasting reality from which all things come, the question is of the same order as "where does everlasting reality come from?" The answer is that reality cannot come from unreality. Since God is reality, the real answer to the question is "God comes from God". Or in other words, He was always there. The only thing that "comes" from somewhere is something that is not everlasting. Because God is everlasting, He cannot come from anywhere. It is mind boggling to admit that there is a being such as God that has been there forever. But if there were no such thing as a forever 'something', nothing could have been. I admit that it is difficult to imagine a Being that does not come from anywhere, right? But if you think that this is amazing, what about us? Are you not amazed that some time ago, you were not here and then one day, boom!, here you are and tomorrow you may be gone just like that? We are all the imagined or the desired beings of God.

Conclusion

So, in conclusion, whether things evolve from the simplest to the complex does not at all prove or disprove the existence of God. Evolution merely describes the relationships that exist between limited and changing things that have a beginning, for which a creator is required. Besides, evolution depends upon time and space and cannot explain the origin of time and space. The origin of these things cannot be accounted for by evolution and for that matter, by any process alone. Life can only be explained by one everlasting person that we call God. Matter is, by definition, temporary and limited. Every limited thing changes and has a beginning. All changes must come from the eternal. There can only be one eternal. This is God. It has been proven logically that God is irrefutable as the everlasting source of all things that exist through this 'His' will and imagination.

Addendum

Those who opine that: "Evolution, explains the origin of everything in space. So, God does not exist," should carefully consider the following, in conjunction with the preceding proof: Where do you begin refuting the aforementioned thesis? Let us break it down. In this case, there are two parts to the statement. The first part is that "evolution explains the origin of everything". The key term here is 'evolution'. What is it? Let us assume that from your research on the matter, you find out that "evolution is the theory that all things result from a process of nature wherein the simple gives rise to the complex; and the weaker gives way to the stronger, so that in the long run, only the fittest survive". What we learn from this then is that evolution is the name given to a process of change. The first question that you must ask is, whether it is true that evolution "explains the origin of everything". Never assume that just because it says so, it must be so. Where are the facts in support of this statement? If there are no facts to back the assertion, still, you must ask whether this conclusion is one of those intellectual necessities that we discussed earlier? In other words, is the statement so clear that it cannot be refuted in a logical manner? If the facts do not support the position, or if the statement is not necessarily true, then naturally you cannot affirm that the statement is true. For now, though, let us look at several possibilities in terms of the facts. You might be surprised to hear this, but often, the bolder the claim, the more baseless it is. This is because if all fallacies are the same, why create a small fallacy when with the same effort you can get away with a great one? But

I digress. For the sake of brevity, we will assume that there are facts in support of evolution, but we cannot assume that all the facts point to the conclusion that the author seeks to make. If this were so, that would mean that the facts are inconclusive, and that the conclusion could be true but needs more work. Or that the statement could be false, again with more facts. But how much evidence would you need in order to know whether the claim is proved conclusively? A clue is in the statement itself. Because evolution is supposed to explain the origin of "everything", the evidence must cover "every" thing. If the argument were that evolution explained "some" things, then partial evidence in respect of those things would suffice. When you are dealing with a theory of everything, it must be able to explain everything. If a theory of everything leaves out some things that it cannot explain or account for, either toss it out as a lie or put it into quotes as a partial truth. Now in this case, you should know that whatever they say about evolution, evolution itself depends upon time and space. This is because evolution is a process; and every process needs time and space. Without time or space, there cannot be movement and change. The problem, however, is that no matter how you look at it, evolution can never account for the origin of either time or space. Nobody in his or her right mind can tell you that in the beginning there was no time or space, but only evolution. Then evolution said, "let there be space; let there be time" and voila! Time and space were born. For if space did not co-exist with evolution or pre-exist evolution, then evolution could have had no place in order to be. If time did not coexist with evolution or pre-exist evolution, then evolution could have had no moment in order to be and to move or change anything. Remember that space and time are the primary conditions for positioning and for movement and change. So, if evolution could not have created either space or time, then naturally, evolution simply cannot account for "everything". As such, it is clear that the statement that evolution explains everything is false. At best, the statement is an exaggeration. For the sake of argument, however, let us ignore what I have just said about time and space for a moment and proceed as though evolution does in fact explain "everything". If this were so, then obviously, the first part of the statement "Evolution, explains the origin of everything in space" would be correct. But wait a moment. Just because the first part of the statement is correct would not mean that therefore, the second part of the statement, that: "So, God does not exist," too, must be correct.

Do not get into the habit of saying that just because things are together, they are necessarily related such that what happens to one must necessarily happen to the other. What happens to one tooth does not necessarily happen to another, even though they are in the same mouth. What you would have to do then would be to see whether because everything came from evolution, it follows that God does not exist. In order to see whether the second portion of the statement is true, we must find out the connection between the two statements. For it is possible that God created evolution or that God co-exists with evolution. Think. In order to resolve this, we must find out whether evolution is something that has no need for another such as a creator or God, or whether its nature is such that it does require another or a creator in order come into being. The first question then is: "Where does this process of evolution come from?" It does not matter that everything that you see may have come from evolution. We must still ask whether evolution itself had a beginning or if it is everlasting. If evolution is everlasting, then logically, it would not need to be created or initiated by anyone or anything. If, on the other hand, it turns out that evolution had a beginning, then it cannot displace God at all. Before we can talk about God we must define the term. God is "one, everlasting, limitless person that created all things by will". The question is this. If everything came from evolution as alleged, does that then prove that God does not exist? Well, let us see. The first thing about evolution is that it is not a thing such as a table or a chair that occupies a limited position in space. Evolution is not like a tree, an animal or a star. Evolution in fact is not an object. It is just the way people describe the relationships that exist between things. Because evolution is not an independent "something" that is out there, but the way things relate to each other, it is in effect, "nothing". Thus, when some people argue that things happen through evolution, all that they are saying is that things behave in a certain way. To explain action, however, is not to explain energy, origins, time and space. So, at best, evolution is no more than the logic of the relationships between things that are already present in time and space. Evolution does not and cannot explain where these things come from in the first place. Because evolution is not something that exists independently of things and because it does not explain the origin of things, it would be a fallacy to conclude that when every change is traceable to evolution, that therefore, it must mean that God does not exist. Even when we assume for the sake of argument, that evolution explains why things turn out the way they do, still, that would not prove one bit that evolution itself is everlasting or that God does not exist. For evolution to be everlasting, it must be independent of all the things that it affects and must have no beginning. The problem, however, is that as I said earlier, there is no animal called evolution. If you are not out there someplace, somewhere as something, you are nothing at all, let alone be everlasting. What about the possibility that things have always been evolving and that there is no need for an independent "something" called evolution? The answer is that to evolve is to change. Where there is no beginning to that change there cannot be a post beginning. Where there is no "1", there cannot be a "2". Since we have subsequence, it must follow that the changes must have had beginnings. The result is that there can be no such thing as a "change forever" or "always evolving". These are oxymorons. Any which way you look at it, the result is that neither evolution nor the subjects of evolution can be everlasting. Both evolution and the subjects of evolution must have had beginnings somewhere. You would agree of course that anything that has a beginning must have come from something other than itself. You cannot give birth to yourself. As a consequence, even if evolution explains the origin of everything in space, it cannot explain the origin of reality, or of the origin of evolution itself. Translation? Even with the best arguments and facts in support of evolution, it would be a fallacy to rule out God. So far, we have seen that evolution has not eliminated and cannot rule out God as the possible originator of things. But does that necessarily mean that there must be a God or that God must be the creator of all things? No! In order for God to be the originator of things, we must be able to prove first that He exists and second that He is the creator of things. This, we must be able to do independently of the weaknesses of the theory of evolution. It is possible that God does not exist or that He is not the creator of all things. Never assume that just because one option is false that therefore, its opposite must be true. God too may fail as an answer. Just because the first alternative might not work does not mean that the second must necessarily be correct. Just because evolution is not proved as the originator of things does not mean that we can take it for granted that God is the originator. The Sesamatic or Relatiological Proof discussed above, provides us with a solid answer.

The above discussion shows that by necessity there is an infinite space that is a conscious space, an imaginative, thinking space within which we are situated as finite imagined products shaping reality. It establishes that consciousness is in space—in objectless, containerless space.

Short Version of the Relatio-logic Proof of God's Existence

Here is a short version of the proof in point form.

CLAIM: The Theist's claim is that a God exists, who is a non-anthropomorphic conscious being and is unlike anything in creation, countering the Atheist's contention that only matter (or energy) exists within space for eternity. The following is a proof of the Theistic claim:

1. Let Matter = X
2. Let X exist for Eternity
3. Let X also be L (limited), since all matter is limited in dimensionality and rests on nothing, so it continuously moves.
4. The limited L has motion M because it is limited.
5. All motion leads to unique NOWS.
6. If point #5 cannot happen due to perennial matter it never will because according to the postulate of the atheists there is only matter that can do this.
7. But if point #5 can happen, then why at time T, rather than any preceding time T-1 (in other words, why the delay?)
8. So matter cannot have caused the unique NOWS, as it cannot cause a delay that logically exists.
9. A delay can only happen by intention.
10. Matter does not possess an intention,
11. The only other option is Space (S), because there is only Space and Matter to consider.
12. So Space is not part of the causal change (chain) but is the causeless cause of the causal change (chain).
13. But then space must possess an INTENTION.
14. Therefore, Space is Conscious, Formless, Timeless etc., and SINGULAR.
15. Also matter X must have started at a unique point (STOP point)
16. If it did not, we would not be here in the unique NOW.
17. Reason: if the stop point was an infinite distance away, the cause-and-effect relationship creating the NOW would never ever reach us.
18. Analogy: If you lived an infinite distance away you would not be here, where you are; therefore, you come from a finite distance designated by a STOP point, at the other end.

19. Likewise, if matter had a STOP point in the past, which it must, then matter did not once exist (in other words, it had a definite origin).

20. But Space was always there and is not subject to this restriction. Therefore, Space is the only other alternative.

21. If one says that this Space was created and emanates from a different type of space (a different dimension etc.) that always existed out of which this Space was created, then that other-dimensional space would be the starting point and it would have a beginning, begging the question as to how it got there, unless it was the creator (objectless space), for which it would possess properties in #14. But if that other-dimensional space was part of another space, which, in turn, came from another space, definite, then the Universe would not have a starting point and would not now exist, applying the STOP point argument, but then neither that type of space, nor matter, could have created the Universe, and so the Universe would not exist. As proved in point 14, again, therefore, Space must be the unique basis plane that constitutes a Singular, Indivisible Conscious Entity as the Imaginator of all.

QED: The Theist's claim is, therefore, demonstrated to be true, by proving the impossibility of the atheist's assertion.

Note: This proof is valid even if it is erroneously claimed that 'space' was created with the Big Bang from yet another angle: there is the violation of the conservation of energy if space is expanding simultaneously with the Big Bang, a fact that is currently being ignored or swept under the carpet by contemporary professional physicists and cosmologists. This is discussed in great depth in Part 4 of this book.

Let us now move to showing how our consciousness derives from this.

Chapter 2

Portion of Space

In the last section we saw that there is a conscious entity that **must perforce exist** that is conscious, self-aware and intelligent, that is eternal and has imagination, for without this, our Universe would not exist. It was also proven that the space of that consciousness is space itself—objectless space, and that we humans are a product of the thought of that consciousness. In a sense then, we have to realize that God is Existence itself, and if God did not exist, neither would existence and that this state of non-existent existence would be perennial. So, if space is consciousness it leads to the following particularities concerning how and where our individual consciousness relates to that space and how it develops.

The particular consciousness or experiences that we have as human beings is shaped by our brains and bodies. But consciousness as a whole is independent of brains and bodies. It is space that is conscious. We come conscious when we come into space and become portions of this space. What is important to remember is that no particular number of microbitic (subatomic particle) arrangements is required in order to be conscious. It is only necessary that you be present in space in order to have the potential for consciousness.

When I say that consciousness is space, I mean by that all portions and parts of space are conscious. So, when we are born, into space, we are automatically born into consciousness. However, what you become aware of, depends upon what you are. Having a brain gives you a particular awareness. But you do not need a brain in order to be conscious. Given that it is space, but not the brain that gives us consciousness, not having a brain, does not necessarily makes you unconscious. Not having a brain gives you a brainless consciousness. Of course, in our present condition, you will never know how it feels like to be without a brain. But that does not mean that therefore, brainless objects have no consciousness. I will get into more detail about this below. For now though, what is important is that the reason we are able to personalize our awareness and claim it as "I" is the fullness that a particular presence brings to a particular portion of space. Let me explain. Imagine a conscious space before our births. Let us call this space "empty" for the sake of convenience. The type of consciousness that this space possesses is solely that of itself or of the emptiness. It is the presence of things that result in divisions. Where there is no thing or event, there is unity. Thus, pre-time or pre-events consciousness is undivided and hence one. Also, it is passage of events that give rise to pasts and futures. So, since this space has no events in pre-time it does not allow for the possibility of past and future. Now whenever an event is born, it necessarily occupies a portion of space equal to its limits, number, capacity, extension or function.

Given that every portion of space is conscious, that portion of space that the event occupies is also conscious. With the presence of the event, the previously "empty" portion becomes filled to the extent of the event. What we call the person or the individual or the sense of "I" is born, when the given portion of space becomes exclusively occupied with the repeating or continuing activity what we call the body. You can see then that should the attentiveness of awareness on a given body break for one reason or another, the person would no longer be conscious of himself or herself. It is this perfect fixation of attention or perfect link between consciousness and a particular event that enables the fractionalization of the otherwise universal or indivisible consciousness. This divides the body or event. It necessarily results in the "privatization" of the "public" space. It is also this perfect fixation of attention on a particular event that gives rise to the multiplicity of times in an otherwise indivisible unity of presence. In fact, it is this "private" sphere that we call the person. The whole process of the relationship between consciousness and events is akin to acting. But here, it is more serious, more perfect in a sense of necessity. It is only the perfect possession or ownership of a given body by a portion of space that can enable the unity that we call a conscious body.

Obviously, that portion of consciousness that now refers to "I" existed before the body was born. And naturally, when the body dies, consciousness still remains as a portion of space. In between, however, this previously "eventless" consciousness gets to be or have a body. Given that the body is temporary, it must follow that this type of consciousness is also temporary. The interesting thing is that after the birth of the body, space changes forever. For when the body is no more, still, what the body did, remains in the "memory" of the portion of space that the body occupied. If you are not clear about this, think of the portion of space that the body occupies as time. Let us say that a person lives for 40 years. Now assume that time is conscious so that every moment or fraction of this time remembers everything that you did in that moment. If you look at it from this angle, you can easily see how it is that even when the person is no more, the person remains in time. The birth of the body and its resulting events, forever change the contents of the consciousness of space. If you can think of space as a wall, births are paintings. They leave permanent portraits in these walls. This is one of the facts of immortality. I will discuss this in more detail later. How, you ask, do we know that consciousness is a property of space? As I write, there are at present billions of human beings, fish, birds, insects and other animals on earth. Everyone of these beings is conscious at the same time. But each species is made up of a different quantity of microbits (subatomic particles). Compare. And certainly, when it comes to the brain, different species have different brains. So, if consciousness were a property of the brain, then only those with the same or similar brains should have it. Those with different brains should have different consciousnesses. But there is no such thing as different consciousness. In reality, there are endless arrangements of microbits (subatomic particles). The numbers differ greatly from species to species and from one Universe to the other. Yet, all beings that have biofluidic motions, regardless of how many or how fewmicrobits (subatomic particles as described in Part 4 of this book) there are. They can be equally aware or present, provided that they have the same GRC (General Rate of Consciousness, which is discussed on pages 99 to 100   and extensively in the book *From Microbits to Everything: Universe of the Imaginator*[28]). Granted that some beings are more complex than others; still, complexity is not the definition of awareness.

Quantum Lights

Complexities are accessories to life. In this world, the being that is only milligram in weight is no less aware or present than the being that is a billion kilos in weight. Consciousness, like time, or presence, is the same for everyone, pea-brain or not. In addition, there are other lifeforms that do not have heads with brains in them like ours and yet they too are conscious. This, therefore, necessarily means that consciousness does not depend upon the brain or upon how big or small you are. The point, however, is that if two beings with different rates of motion or two beings with two different quantities of microbits, can be

---

28 Haque, Nadeem and Muslim, M. (2007). *From Microbits to Everything: Universe of the Imaginator: Volume 2: The Philosophical Implications.*

equally conscious, then it must follow that consciousness does not arise from any particular speed or any particular quantity of matter. If consciousness were caused by, say, 1 speed of GRC or conditional upon a certain quantity of matter, then those with 2 speed of GRC should not be able to have it. Continuing with the example, if consciousness were fixed at say, 2 then those who are not 2, should not have it. But then if both 1 and 2 give rise to the same consciousness then that must mean that consciousness does not depend upon either 1 exclusively or on 2 exclusively. This is because if consciousness were dependent upon any number then only that number should give rise to it and not two or more different numbers. The fact that in our example, 1 and 2 can cause the same phenomenon shows that the phenomenon is not dependent on either 1 or 2. But then if it is not dependent upon 1 or 2, it cannot be fixed at any other number either. For any number other than 1 or 2 were the exclusive cause, then neither 1 or 2 could have caused it either. The fact that different arrangements of matter from the small to the large exhibit consciousness, therefore, proves that consciousness is not dependent on any particular arrangement of matter. Now reality is made up of different arrangements of matter and space. Therefore, if the arrangements of microbits are not the causes of consciousness, then the only other cause for consciousness must be its presence in space. However, presence in space is just another way of saying that it is space that gives them consciousness.

Of course, one could argue that consciousness is not independent of from matter, but that simply, different numbers give rise to the same consciousness. But if so, then the numbers become irrelevant for the purpose of causation. Every number is unique and if despite their uniqueness, every numerical arrangement of microbits from 1 to 2,3 or 4 give rise to the same thing, then we have to move beyond the numbers. In a nutshell, awareness is neither dependent upon the number of microbits that form a life-unit nor upon the speed of the microbits at any given place. Reality is made up of only numbers (of microbits) and space. If, therefore, the microbits do not give rise to consciousness, then it must follow that consciousness must come from space. Besides, it is more elegant that the consciousness of all be one than to have endless beings making up their consciousnesses as they go. Unity of source gives us unity of world, unity of communication and unity of experience. Given that each person is unique, if every person made and carried his or her own consciousness, each consciousness would be unique. This would not only be ugly from a system's point of view, it would pose an in incorrigible communications problem. How do you propose that each unique consciousness could invent the necessary language to communicate with the trillions and trillions of other unique consciousnesses out there across countries, planets and galaxies?

In order to understand consciousness in carbon-based and other type of particle-based beings in the Universe, we will be using the concept of GRC a great deal. For the purposes of this book, simply remember that there are processes occurring in your body at light speed and not simply at electron's speed. In other words, light is pulsing in your body at the velocity c, in a particular way. This velocity helps to make an object conscious. In other words, all conscious entities have a GRC—the general rate of consciousness. Below this rate is the GRP—all objects have a GRP—that is a general rate of presence. In GRP objects, light speed of photon activity is not present, or it is not being channelled through the organism in the particular way at that speed to achieve consciousness. In order to understand what is happening: A photon is not really an object that travels from A to B; it is a particle type that occupies the whole Universe (indeed photons are overabundant) and it is the energy hv that gets transported as adjacent photons collide into each other and transmit this 'energy'. This resolves the wave particle duality because photons do cause waves but themselves are nonetheless particles. As an analogy, if one saw a 'wave' in a soccer stadium it would be foolish to think it is some type of wave; rather it is individual spectators moving in a particular way to make it seem that there is a wave. It is this back-and-forth oscillatory motion upon disturbance and the transmittal of the energy in a point like fashion that gives the illusion of the photon travelling from A to B. We are now equipped to answer the question of what and where is consciousness, by the process of elimination.

Let us now discuss expanding the number and variety of the conscious: The above has several consequences. First, all provided that it is arranged biofluidically (cyclically) at a minimum of the speed of light, c, any number of things can be conscious as we are. It does not matter what material that life-unit is made of. Even stones would think and speak if arranged properly. While the contents of consciousness may be unique, according to the events taking place in there, consciousness itself, like presence, is not unique. It is the same across reality. Second, consciousness itself, does not rise and fall like the events that are the contents of consciousness. Because consciousness is space, it is capable of aligning itself with endless speed possibilities of microbits from the slowest to the fastest. Because events are different from space, what happens to events does not necessarily happen to consciousness. That is to say, that when the event that forms the contents of a particular portion of consciousness stops, consciousness does not have to stop with it; and does not, in fact, stop. As I mentioned briefly, the person is born when consciousness takes the form of the activities of the body within its presence and focuses on them exclusively to the point that it becomes one with the body. You may think of consciousness as a perfect actor. It completely identifies itself with the events in its presence by focusing on them to the exclusion of all else.

On the issue of the Self: As you know, no two persons can occupy the same position at the same time. Every person's birth, position and capacities in space are unique. Also, the variety of circumstances is such that although we all live in the same world we do not usually have the same experiences. Even when we share the same things, the uniqueness of the person is such that all experiences get filtered; and reality presents itself uniquely to everyone.

For everyone of us, our identity as a person is maintained by the fixity of our GRC (General Rate of Consciousness) and the uniqueness of our positions in time. Also, the activities of every person from the date of birth to death can be traced as a number. So, in theory, it should be possible to trace every step of the person.

We have established that consciousness exists independent of matter and particles as the plenum and cause of the creation of matter and particles/energy. We have established that this consciousness is the space in which all resides as a matter of irrefutable logic. However, the question remains as to how our body and consciousness relate to each other, the mystery of the mind-body connection. How does consciousness arise in the body? In this part of the book we shall be answering this question, definitively.

Self as body (SAB) model

There are two views of the self. One view is that the self is the result of the total activities of the body at any given time. According to this view, the self is not an independent quality separate and apart from the works of the body; it is simply the body at work. As long as there is a living body, there is a self. When the body dies, the self too dies. If this view is true, then death is the end of the human being. The only way to regain the self, following death on earth would be a regrouping of microbits exactly as they were before. But even if rebirth were possible, the same individual could not be duplicated.

This is because the individual is a product of a given time, place and fortunes of birth. Since time and circumstances are unique the same experiences cannot be duplicated. Therefore, if the self were the activities of body, none of us could ever return as we are. This view then shatters all dreams of another life. But is it true?

Self as Driver (SAD) model

An alternative view to the above, is that the self is not the activity of the body but that it is separate and apart from it. According to this view, the self and the body exist in a relationship that is much like that of a driver in a car. When the body is active, the self is the director. But when the body breaks down, the self simply steps out and continues elsewhere. Let us explore this model. If the self is separate and apart from the activities of the body, it must either be inside or outside the body. Let us first discuss the possibility of the self being outside the body. In the discussion below let microbits = subatomic particles; those readers who have read Part 4 first, would know exactly what is meant by this term.

The Self Outside the Body model

If each person has his or her own self, then logically, the self must be limited. If it is limited, then the self must be made of microbits. If this microbitic self is not inside the body but external to it, the problem is that being outside the body, these microbits must move at a speed that is far greater than that of the body. Things that move at different speeds do not stick together. Whether as one or as many microbits, therefore, if the mircobitic self were outside the body, we would have a situation where, because of the differences in their speed and therefore, time, the self could be on Mars for example, while the body could be in Mecca. Furthermore, if these were outside the body, given that its GRC (General Rate of Consciousness) would be faster or higher than that of body, we would have a situation where it could be conscious of events taking place at a higher GRC while being simultaneously conscious of events at our GRC. The self would thus have multiple consciousnesses and be two or more different beings at once. Clearly, not only do we not have multiple consciousnesses; it is unnecessarily messy. This would also be a negation of the individual and for that matter of moral, legal, intellectual and spiritual responsibility.

The Self Inside the Body model

Let us suppose for a moment that the self is in the body. As discussed earlier, if there is a self inside, it should be different than the rest of the cells that makeup the body. The reason why the cells move at their GRC is because of the number of microbits in them. The cells are multiplications of microbits. We already know that in order for two or more things to be together, they have to move at the same speed. Clearly then, in order for the microbitic self to be in the body, it too must move at the same speed as the cells. The problem, however, is that the self cannot move at the speed of a cell unless it is a cell. But a cell is a cell is a cell. We know that conception begins with cells from parents. If there is a mircobitic self, it must already be apart of these foundational cells. If it is a cell, it is simply a cell. It is no different from any other cell. Every minute or so, billions of these cells are spilled around the world without consequence. On the other hand, if the self is not a part of the cells that form the embryo, then it is impossible to see how it needs to be a cell in order to run the body and yet it does not form a part of the cells that make up the body. In addition, cells die from time to time. The new ones that go into the body are the cells of other living things that we consume as food. No cell forms a part of the human body that is not from a parent or from food. If there is a microbitic (subatomic particle) self then it must come from food or from the parents. First, if it is from food or from the parents, its speed must be that of its parents and hence no faster than that of the parents. Second, whether from parents or from food, if there is a microbitic self, it must be capable of being identified in the body as an irreplaceable and undying group of cells. For how can it be in charge if it dies while the body is still running? I am not at all discounting the possibility of permanent cells. But whether it is permanent or temporary, if the self is a part of the body, it is the body. Whether or not they are the building blocks that hold the entire structure together, foundational stones are still stones. So, if the self is inside the body, this leads us to a position that is not different from that of those who say that the body is all that there is. But let us assume for a moment that there is a permanent group of cells that form the self, and this automatically passes on. In this respect, if it is the self that gives life, or if life depends upon the presence of this self, then all life forms should have it too. There is an even more intractable problem with this model. It is this. This model tends to disprove that which it seeks to prove. Human consciousness is what it is because of our uniqueness as humans. So, if we are forced to conclude that the self is made from some microbits, then upon cessation of motion at our present speed, the human consciousness must cease. If it is said that the self continues after death, the rate at which this self moves, independent of the body, must necessarily be different. This would mean that the self that continues post-death, does not and cannot have human consciousness. This necessarily gives rise to discontinuity of the person. Or in other words, permanent death.

Self as Space (SAS) model

If you have followed this argumentation carefully, it is clear that the answer to the question of self was already self evident when I explained that consciousness is a property of space. If we define ourselves by our consciousness and consciousness is space, then naturally, we are portions of space. But don't worry. It works, so it does not matter where the self is. At the end of the day though, nobody cares so much about the self as much as we care about continuity. The question is not whether there is a self but whether we can continue to believe and be as conscious as we are, preferably if not in a better world, in a place that is no worse off than here. But is there the particular consciousness or experience that we have as human beings that is shaped by our brains and bodies? Consciousness as a whole is independent of brains and bodies. It is space that is conscious. We become conscious when we come into space and become portions of this space. What is important to remember is that no particular number of microbitic arrangements is required in order to be conscious in the sense that consciousness is not from microbits themselves. It is only necessary that your microbits be present in space in order to have the potential for consciousness and their particular arrangement will give you consciousness. When I say that consciousness is space, I mean by that all portions and parts of space are conscious as proven earlier. So, when we are born, into space, we are automatically born into consciousness. However, what you become aware of, depends upon what you are. Having a brain gives you a particular awareness. But you do not need a brain in order to become conscious. Given that it is space, but not the brain that gives us consciousness, not having a brain does not necessarily makes you unconscious.

Not having a brain gives you a brainless consciousness. Of course, in our present condition, you will never know how it feels like to be without a brain. But that does not mean that therefore, brainless objects have no consciousness. I will get into more detail about this below. For now though, what is important is that the reason we are able to personalize our awareness and claim it as "I" is the fullness that a particular presence brings to a particular portion of space. Let me explain. Imagine conscious space before our births. Let us call this space "empty" for the sake of convenience. The type of consciousness that this space possesses is solely that of itself or of the emptiness. It is the presence of things that result in divisions. Where there is no thing or event, there is unity. Thus, pre-time or pre-events consciousness is undivided and hence one. Also, it is passage of events that give rise to pasts and futures. So, since this space has no events in pre-time it does not allow for the possibility of past and future. Now whenever an event is born, it necessarily occupies a portion of space equal to its limits, number, capacity, extension or function.

Given that every portion of space is conscious, that portion of space that the event occupies is also conscious. With the presence of the event, the previously "empty" portion becomes filled to the extent of the event. What we call the person or the individual or the sense of "I" is born, when the given portion of space becomes exclusively occupied with the repeating or continuing activity of what we call the body. You can see then that should the attentiveness of awareness on a given body break for one reason or another, the person would no longer be conscious of himself or herself. It is this perfect fixation of attention or perfect link between consciousness and a particular event that enables the fractionalization of the otherwise universal or indivisible consciousness. This divides the body or event. It necessarily results in the "privatization" of the "public" space. It is also this perfect fixation of attention on a particular event that gives rise to the multiplicity of times in an otherwise indivisible unity of presence. In fact, it is this "private" sphere that we call the person. The whole process of the relationship between consciousness and events is akin to acting. But here, it is more serious, more perfect in a sense of necessity. It is only the perfect possession or ownership of given body by a portion of space that can enable the unity that we call a conscious body. Obviously, that portion of consciousness that now refers to "I" existed before the body was born. And naturally, when the body dies, the consciousness still remains as a portion of space. In between, however, this previously "eventless" consciousness gets to be or have a body. Given that the body is temporary, it must follow that this type of consciousness is also temporary. The interesting thing is that after the birth of the body, space changes forever. For when the body is no more, still, what the body did, remains in the "memory" of the portion of space that the body occupied. If you are not clear about this, think of the portion of space that the body occupies as time. Let us say that a person lives for 40 years. Now assume that time is conscious so that every moment or fraction of this time remembers everything that you did in that moment. If you look at it from this angle, you can easily see how it is that even when the person is no more, the person remains in time. The birth of the body and its resulting events, forever change the contents of the consciousness of space. If you can think of spaces as a wall, births are paintings. They leave permanent portraits in these walls. This is one of the facts of immortality. I will discuss this in more detail later.

How, you ask, do we know that consciousness is a property of space? As I write, there are at present billions of human beings, fish, birds, insects and animals on earth. Every one of these beings is conscious at the same time. But each species is made up of a different quantity of microbits. Compare. And certainly, when it comes to the brain, different species have different brains. So, if consciousness were a property of the brain, then only those with the same or similar brains should have it. Those with different brains should have different consciousnesses. But there is no such things different consciousness. In reality, there are endless arrangements of microbits. The numbers differ greatly from species to species and from one Universe to the other. Yet, all beings that have biofluidic motions (photonic oscillatory motions), regardless of how many or how few microbits they are comprised of, and they can be equally aware or present provided that they have the same GRC (i.e. the specific pattern of biofluidic motion). Granted that some beings are more complex than others; still, complexity is not the definition of awareness. Complexities are accessories to life. In this world, the being that is only milligram in weight is no less aware or present than the being that is a billion kilos in weight; a tardigrade is as conscious as a blue whale. Consciousness, like time, or presence, is the same for everyone, pea-brain or not. In addition, there are other lifeforms that do not have heads with brains in them like ours and yet they too are conscious.

This, therefore, necessarily means that consciousness does not depend upon the brain or upon how big or small you are. It is the organization of the brain or equivalent structure that accesses the same plenum of consciousness that gives that entity personalized consciousness. The moot point is that if two beings with different rates of motion or two beings with two different quantities of microbits, can be equally conscious, then it must follow that consciousness does not arise from any particular speed or any particular quantity of matter. If consciousness were caused by, say, 1 speed of GRC or conditional upon a certain quantity of matter, then those with 2 speed of GRC should not be able to have it. Continuing with the example, if consciousness were fixed at say, 2 then those who are not 2, should not have it. But then if both 1 and 2 give rise to the same consciousness then that must mean that consciousness does not depend upon either 1 exclusively on 2 exclusively. This is because if consciousness were dependent upon any number then only that number should give rise to it and not two or more different numbers. The fact that in our example, 1 and 2 can cause the same phenomenon shows that the phenomenon is not dependent on either 1 or 2. It is the arrangement and motion of different numbers of microbits, that produce GRC and consciousness.

Therefore, if it is not dependent upon 1 or 2, it cannot be fixed at another number either. For if any number other than 1 or 2 were the exclusive cause, then neither 1 or 2 could have caused it either. The fact that different arrangements of matter from the small to the large exhibit consciousness, therefore, proves that consciousness is not dependent on any particular arrangement of matter. Now reality is made up of different arrangements of matter and space. Therefore, if the arrangements of microbits are not the causes of consciousness, then the only other cause for consciousness must be their presence in space. However, presence in space is just another way of saying that it is space that gives them consciousness.

Of course, one could argue that consciousness is not independent of matter, but that simply, different numbers give rise to the same consciousness. But if so, then the numbers become irrelevant for the purpose of causation. Every number is unique and if despite their uniqueness, every numerical arrangement of microbits from 1 to infinity can give rise to the same thing, then we have to move beyond the numbers. In a nutshell, awareness is neither dependent upon the number of microbits that form a life-unit nor upon the speed of the microbits at any given place.

Reality is made up of only numbers (of microbits) and space. If, therefore, the microbits do not give rise to consciousness, then it must follow that consciousness must come from space. Besides, it is more elegant that the consciousness of all be one than to have endless beings making up their consciousnesses as they go. Unity of source gives us unity of world, unity of communication and unity of experience. Given that each person is unique, if every person made and carried his or her own consciousness, each consciousness would be unique. This would not only be ugly from a system's point of view, it would pose an in incorrigible communications problem. How do you propose that each unique consciousness could invent the necessary language to communicate with the trillions and trillions of other unique consciousnesses out there across countries, planets and galaxies?

Expanding the number and variety of the consciousness described above has several consequences. First, provided that it is arranged biofluidically at a minimum of the speed of light, c, any number of things can be conscious as we are. It does not matter what material that life-unit is made of. Even stones would think and speak if arranged properly. While the contents of consciousness may be unique, according to the events taking place in there, consciousness itself, like presence, is not unique. It is the same across reality. Second, consciousness itself, does not rise and fall like the events that are the contents of consciousness. Because consciousness is space, it is capable of aligning itself with endless speed possibilities of microbits from the slowest to the fastest. Because events are different from space, what happens to events does not necessarily happen to consciousness. That is to say, that when the event that forms the contents of a particular portion of consciousness stops, consciousness does not have to stop with it; and does not, in fact, stop.

As I mentioned briefly, the person is born when consciousness takes the form of the activities of the body within its presence and focuses on them exclusively to the point that it becomes one with the body. You may think of consciousness as a perfect actor. It completely identifies itself with the events in its presence by focusing on them to the exclusion of all else.

On the issue of the Self

As you know, no two persons can occupy the same position at the same time. Every person's birth, position and capacities in space are unique. Also, the variety of circumstances is such that although we all live in the same world we do not usually have the same experiences. Even when we share the same things, the uniqueness of the person is such that all experiences get filtered; and reality presents itself uniquely to everyone.

For everyone of us, our identity as a person is maintained by the fixity of our GRC and the uniqueness of our positions in time. Also, as I mentioned earlier, the activities of every person from the date of birth to death can be traced as a number. So, in theory, it should be possible to trace every step of the person.

Self as Body (SAB) Model

There are two views of the self. One view is that the self is the result of the total activities of the body at any given time. According to this view, the self is not an independent quality separate and apart from the works of the body, but it is simply the body at work. As long as there is a living body, there is a self. When the body dies, the self too dies. If this view is true, then death is the end of the human being. The only way to regain the self, following death on Earth would be a re-grouping of microbits exactly as they were before. But even if rebirth were possible, the same individual could not be duplicated. This is because the individual is not only a product of a given GRC but also the person is a product of a given time, place and fortunes of birth. Since time and circumstances are unique the same experiences cannot be duplicated. Therefore, if the self were the activities of body, none of us could ever return as we are. This view then shatters all dreams of another life. But is it true?

Self as Driver (SAD) Model

An alternative view to the above, is that the self is not the activity of the body but that it is separate and apart from it. According to this view, the self and the body exist in a relationship that is much like that of a driver in a car. When the body is active, the self is the director. But when the body breaks down, the self simply steps out and continues elsewhere. Let us explore this model. If the self is separate and apart from the activities of the body, it must either be inside or outside the body. Let us first discuss the possibility of the self being outside the body.

The Self Outside the Body model

If each person has his or her own self, then logically, the self must be limited. If it is limited, then the self must be made of microbits. If this microbitic self is not inside the body but external to it, the problem is that being outside the body, these microbits must move at a speed that is far greater than that of the body. Things that move at different speeds do not stick together. Whether as one or as many microbits, therefore, if the mircobitic self were outside the body, we would have a situation where, because of the differences in their speed and therefore, time, the self could be on Mars for example, while the body could be in Mecca. Furthermore, if the self were outside the body, given that its GRC would be faster or higher than that of the body, we would have a situation where it could be conscious of events taking place at a higher GRC while being simultaneously conscious of events at our GRC. The self would thus have multiple consciousnesses and be two or more different beings at once. Clearly, not only do we not have multiple consciousnesses; it is unnecessarily messy. This would also be a negation of the individual and for that matter of moral, legal, intellectual and spiritual responsibility.

The Self Inside the Body Model

Let us suppose for a moment that the self is in the body. As discussed earlier, if there is a self inside, it should be different than the rest of the cells that makeup the body. The reason why the cells move their GRC is because of the number of microbits in them. The cells are multiplications of microbits. We already know that in order for two or more things to be together, they have to move at the same speed. Clearly then, in order for the microbitic self to be in the body, it too must move at the same speed as the cells. The problem, however, is that the self cannot move at the speed of a cell unless it is a cell. But a cell is a cell is a cell. We know that conception begins with cells from parents. If there is a mircobitic self, it must already be apart of these foundational cells. If it is a cell, it is simply a cell. It is no different from any other cell. Every minute or so, billions of these cells are spilled around the world without consequence. On the other hand, if the self is not apart of the cells that form the embryo, then it is impossible to see how it needs to be a cell in order to run the body and yet it does not form apart of the cells that make up the body. In addition, cells die from time to time. The new ones that go into the body are the cells of other living things that we consume as food. No cell forms apart of the human body that is not from a parent or from food. If there is self then it must come from food or from the parents. First, if it is from food or from the parents, its speed must be that of its parents and hence no faster than that of the parents. Second, whether from parents or from food, if there is a microbitic self, it must be capable of being identified in the body as an irreplaceable and undying group of cells. For how can it be in charge if it dies while the body is still running? I am not at all discounting the possibility of permanent cells. But whether it is permanent or temporary, if the self is a part of the body, it is the body. Whether or not they are the building blocks that hold the entire structure together, foundational stones are still stones. So, if the self is inside the body, this leads us to a position that is not different from that of those who say that the body is all that there is. But let us assume for a moment that there is a permanent group of cells that form the self, and this automatically passes on. In this respect, if it is this self that gives life, or if life depends upon the presence of this self, then all life forms should have it too.

There is an even more intractable problem with this model. It is this. This model tends to disprove that which it seeks to prove. Human consciousness is what it is because of our unique GRC. So, if we are forced to conclude that the self is made from some microbits, then upon cessation of motion at our present speed, the human consciousness must cease. If it is said that the self continues after death, the rate at which this self moves, independent of the body, must necessarily be different. This would mean that the self that continues post-death, does not and cannot have human consciousness. This necessarily gives rise to discontinuity of the person. Or in other words, permanent death.

Self as Space (SAS) model

If you have followed this paper carefully, it is clear that the answer to the question of self was already self evident when I explained that consciousness is a property of space. If we define ourselves by our consciousness and consciousness is space, then naturally, we are portions of space. But do not worry. It works, so it does not matter where the self is. At the end of the day though, nobody cares so much about the self as much as we care about continuity. The question is not whether there is a self but whether we can continue to believe and be as conscious as we are, preferably if not in a better world, in a place that is no worse off than here. But is there continuity of life from here?

Chapter 3

Implications of the Proofs

As discussed in Chapters 1 and 2, the mind is not made of particles but is the transfocation of the objectless space of the consciousness of God. In Chapter 1, M. Muslim proved the Universe to be the Imagination of God and, as such, His space. The solution to the mind-body problem is linked directly and seamlessly to this proof. Once this proof is comprehended, everything else flows and one can easily see how and why human consciousness can arise only as a result of and within another pre-existing higher consciousness and that taking all fundamental points into consideration, this is the only possible solution. It is indeed impossible to solve the consciousness problem unless the unique line of argument we are presenting is understood and followed. Here is an analogy to see why: Let us assume that there is an alien expert on bird flight from Planet Zeton that has no water; he is also someone who has never seen any fish. He comes to Earth, goes to an aquarium and in the distance he observes some fish 'floating', according to him. He finds this singularly remarkable because he notes that the aerodynamic design of fish is not commensurate for sustained flight. In other words, he does not realize that the fish are floating in water since he does not have a notion of water. This 'water', analogously speaking, is the all-pervasive objectless space of God (God's mind and being) from whom our consciousness is drawn and sustained, as a result of His creative will. God makes His space accessible to microbit based structures and, as such, these structures become portals, as small wills. Furthermore, if God does not will His space to be accessible by microbitic structures, then no matter how they are organized, such objects would not become sentient, for He is the one who, as it were, empowers a character who He has created to see through eyes, hears through ears and thinks thought, as an imagined finite creation within His infiniteness. But when He wills such accessibility, then such structures have to be organized in a particular and precise way in absolute space to be a gateway for the expression of limited intelligence-cum-consciousness. Such a process is that which comprises fractionalization (the initiation of creation of other subwills within the Will of God) and transfocation (the simultaneous sustenance of the wills into various bodies that are comprised of particles as they become portals for objectless space where the property of Consciousness lies). In this chapter, we shall explore and elaborate on this concept at greater length. We have, thus far, seen that as the particle-based body interacts with objectless space, hitherto defined, it is effused with consciousness, which we called transfocation. Consequentially, our new explanation is indeed physicalist to a large extent, since we are saying that the body becomes a content for consciousness; it gives the appearance of being solely the result of a particle comprised body. However, it is actually a portal for objectless space, wherein resides the property of Intelligence and Consciousness, as it is not the particles which really give rise to consciousness, but fractionalization and transfocation within the space of God, that is, of God's mind, as discussed in the previous chapter.

In reality, the materialists are correct in saying that if the mind is in the brain or is an emergent phenomenon, and if body and brain do indeed stop functioning, then we shall cease to exist. However, the problem of the continuation of life after death, does not even arise when we are dealing with consciousness being the property of space. Let us explore this concept further. How exactly does consciousness/will arise? Intelligence is a property of space, since we are in the Mind of God, and God's essence and being pervades absolute objectless space since it is that space; but then how exactly do other intelligences arise? When a microbitic (subatomic particle-based) structure is created and that body becomes more complicated, as it develops, it is able to become a portal of that ultimate consciousness of the Creator that the Creator has willed to be accessible to all creation within that space of His consciousness. However, the level of consciousness depends on the level of the organism's biological complexity. The biological body, in other words, interacts with objectless space (i.e., the mind of God) in a limited way and thereby gains limited consciousness. In other terms, the biological object becomes conscious at a certain stage and develops a particularized personality of self because it is imagined to form, as a creation and not pantheistically, from the ultimate will of God: indeed consciousness can only arise from the Consciousness. This consciousness that sentient entities possess is not part of God, because God creates the biological object with His imagination and, as such, it is His creation, for imagination is a form of creation. The other important factor is that our consciousness is initialized in terms of knowing its relation to the Creator. There are two analogies that can be used to describe the generation of consciousness: a series of flutes of different sizes are laid out in an extremely windy place—each one produces a different sound, based on its complexity. It becomes conscious, metaphorically, upon producing the sounds. Or yet another analogy: molecules permeating space are accessed by the vocal chords, producing the voice; different types of vocal chords produce different sounds, whilst being in the same space.

Why memory is not stored on carbon-based bodies

In order to realize what consciousness really is, let us examine a tiny creature. There is a flatworm worm called Planaria which, when its head is cut-off, grows another head, and when its tail is cut off it produces another tail– in fact when it is cut in two, one gets growth from both ends and you get two 'new' Planaria. These creatures break themselves up in order to reproduce (reproduction by fission). Now when this type of experiment on severing the Planaria was first conducted in the 1960s by J.V. McConnell, it was discovered that if this flatworm is conditioned by exposing it to a light source where there is a change in overhead illumination designated by Conditioned Stimulus (CS), followed by weak electric shock, designated as Unconditioned Stimulus (UCS), the worm contracts itself in a longitudinal direction as a Conditioned Response (CR). Learning occurs when it anticipates the shock before it is given and curls up, after simply having been exposed to the CS. Now when the worm is cut up in half, two worms are produced: one with a new head, and the other with a new tail. When these new worms are reconditioned, both the 'new head' worm and the 'new tail' worm appear to remember their previous conditioning: The worm with the new head has retained a great detail of 'information'; something which was not expected since the new head never received the initial conditioning. Given this anomalous situation, scientists have speculated that the worm's memory is distributed throughout the body, since they believe that the molecules in terms of neurons, RNA or what have you, could contain memory in the form of engrams or structures recorded somehow on the biological components. However, these conjectures fall flat with this organism: The experiments on Planaria prove that memory is not stored on neurons, because the neurons were in the brain part of the creature and the brain was in the head, and the new head Planaria, that is, the one with the head that had been amputated, never received any training/ conditioning. Indeed, the researcher in one of the latest studies, concludes—in the report comes to a conclusion which is strikingly at odds with what is generally considered to be the 'official position' of a purely materialistic scientific perspective– that: The finding that organisms derived from the anterior and posterior regions or a trained organism retained the same amount of memory was significant because it suggested the hypothesis that memory is non-neural.

The use of classical conditioning in Planaria is used to investigate a non-neural memory mechanism certain in parts of the brain or nervous system and that these then change shape and form connections etc. This experiment, or indeed any other experiment so far, does not prove that memory is retained in the biological structures. Besides, if memory is stored and the neurons/other cells and structures hypothesized for memory storage, they are in a dynamic state of either disappearing or changing shape, how do we, for example, retain fixed memories. As biochemist and philosopher Rupert Sheldrake states:

> Not only have the hypothetical memory traces proved to be spatially elusive, but their physical nature has also remained obscure. The idea of specific RNA "memory molecules" was fashionable in the 1960s but has now been more or less abandoned. The theory of reverberating circuits of electrical activity... cannot explain long-term memory. ... If memories are somehow stored in synapses, then the synapses themselves must remain stable over long periods of time: indeed, the nervous system as a whole must be stable if it is to act as a memory store. Until recently this was generally assumed to be the case... . [29]

Sheldrake goes on to explain that the brain, in terms of the functioning of the nervous system, is more dynamical than once thought and he highlights some experiments to illustrate this. Even at the molecular level– with the exception of DNA—as Francis Crick points out, there is a turnover of molecules within a few days, weeks and certainly no longer than a few weeks. Steven Rose, the world-renowned expert on research into memory, states:

> So was Hebb right: is memory biochemical or synaptic? But this is where the paradoxes begin, for neither in the chick nor in mammals does the memory 'stay' where the initial synaptic changes occur. If the specific region of the changes in the chick brain is removed a few hours after the

---

29 Sheldrake, Rupert. (1988). The Presence of the Past: Morphic Resonance and the Habits of Nature, pp. 165-166.

learning experience, the memory surprisingly, is not lost. [All emphasis is ours].[30]

Rose goes on to recount how a patient, whose hippocampus was removed—which is involved with learning and memory– could remember events of his life up to the time of the removal of the structure; however, he could not retain memories of immediately fleeting events and hence learn new things. Keeping in mind the view that is being advocated in this book regarding consciousness: how can the Planaria's behaviour be explained? Are two Planaria souls created by God upon cutting the worms in two? Here is the answer: Since the whole body of the worm experiences consciousness in absolute space, for both the top and bottom half of the worm, when it is cut in two, then two worm personalities are created which, up to that point of being cut, retain the same memories (i.e. experience of previous conditioning). This is because both halves of the single worm which is cut has more or less the same accessibility to the property of consciousness in absolute objectless space, the brain merely being a switchgear to generate the activity of the senses of seeing, hearing etc. If a human being were cut in half and if the bottom half produced a new torso and head and the top half sprouted new legs etc. then the 'new head' human would not remember anything because the bottom half of the body would not have been accessing the consciousness that is the inherent property of absolute objectless space. The human body in other words is not symmetrical with respect to such accessibility as is a creature such as Planaria due to the nature of the structuring of the microbits. Memory then, both short or long-term, is not stored in the brain. It is not stored on or in any particle in this Universe. Ultimately, everything that has happened or will happen is indeed already written and exists in the mind of God exactly as it happens or will happen to its minutest detail, but it is only He who lets the sub-wills in His mind access that which He wills. The basic mechanism for this is the GRC as discussed previously. General human memory is a narrow and low-level access to the personal record. The access to one's personal file in the record depends on the focus and what one pays attention to and if one has brain damage to a particular area etc., such personal records cannot be built up, and one only operates in the moment, with short-term memory. This is because that particular part of the brain is responsible for accessing the record and its

---

30 Rose, Stephen. (2006). The Future of the Brain: The Promise and Perils of Tommorow's Neuroscience, p. 160.

malfunctioning severs its connection with the record. The continuous, albeit limited, access to the records is necessary for the notion of self-hood, learning and mental growth, accountability, and the very practicalities of living. But how then does all of this explain qualia? Essentially, since all consciousness exists by the will of the divine Consciousness within which it operates, the ultimate qualia are witnessed because they are imagined to be witnessed/experienced by the Consciousness of God within each created and sustained 'consciousness.'

The Transfocation Explanation of Consciousness

In Part 2 of this book, we claim to have advanced a solution to the Mind-Body problem. One of the key features is our emphasis on what we normally term matter, energy and mind which was tackled in part through our model of physics and 'where all supposed 'matter' and 'energy' is derived from microbits (the unit particle out of which everything in the Universe is made; for the purposes of argument, for those who have not read up on microbits as discussed in Part 4, 'subatomic particles' as a substitute will do), thereby rendering our model not subject to dualism. That is because we have a view interrelating mind, matter energy and space that is unique and holds the answer resolving consciousness. In any event, our 'model' is uncategorizable, as it is not based on materialism idealism, pantheism, panpsychism etc. Uniqueness itself, however, may not necessarily be the truth, but the explanatory power of a model/concept is what needs to be critically examined. We attempt to categorically show why it is not substance dualism by focusing on some key concepts. In addition, my colleague, Zeshan Shahbaz, has also clarified in what we are going to call the Transfocation Model of Consciousness (TMC) in a diagrammatic form:

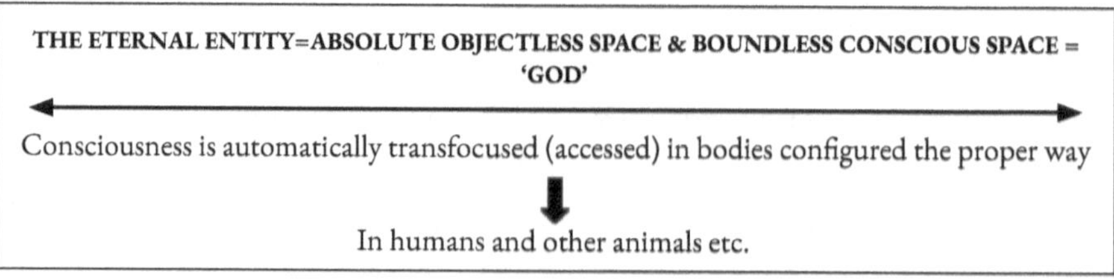

Figure 2: How consciousness arises in created beings.

Understanding consciousness in humans is directly dependent upon our understanding the existence and nature of 'God'. This God is a personal conscious being and as the Quran states: there is nothing comparable to 'Him' or

'It'. Instead of 'It' I will refer to this God as 'Him', but this in no way purports to imply any anthropomorphic projections, whatsoever. We are not part of God's essence; rather, we are part of His sustained creative thought, that is, His imagination. After death life is in another lighter body, created after death, according to the Quran, and this ties in with innumerable Near Death Experiences (NDEs) of a 'subtle' body.

Access to consciousness can be understood by this analogy: The way consciousness arises is that if you want to listen to CBC radio, for example in Canada, you have to tune in to that frequency of station which is FM 99.1. Similarly, after death, your 'number', as it were, is retained and your new body (rapidly evolved body—which grows from outside to inside—the reverse of the embryological process) accesses that number and there is a continuity of life. God has numbered everything in that sense. We use numbers for tracking, knowing the amount and matching things and so does God. The essential process is that there is an interaction between the particles (i.e. the brain) and the 'soul' because they are essentially thought constructs of God; matter and energy are made of particles which are sustained and arranged by God's thoughts alone and our individuality fractionalizes from the Creator and 'attaches' to the particular body; it is a pure limited thought from the infinite mind and space of God. So we have thought (the fractionalization and transfocation of thought from God) on one level, interacting with a thought structure on another (i.e. the brain). Both are commands to "Be" that arise from the same thought. Therefore, our view cannot be termed as classical Idealism because the 'whereness' of God is absolute objectless space which is a precondition for any temporal existence; and if temporal existence is created and becomes conscious there is no category problem.

The STOP Argument

A mind must exist and direct the Universe because of the two facts which we prove that pertain to the notion of 'delay' in creation; and the STOP analysis which deals with infinite regress that also has been presented earlier. So, once it is established incontrovertibly from these two interrelated points there is this one infinite mind that is co-extensive with space and is this space itself, where the major error has been made to think that this 'space is created', we are then inexorably led to realize that nothing can be outside this mind. We are then also led logically to believe that matter, energy and the human mind too are thought constructs of *the* Mind. Indeed, we should not be sidelined into thinking that 'matter' and 'energy' are not thought constructs. It only stands to reason that the Source of all must be independent of all and that the created implies a creator, meaning that the creator cannot logically be anything in essence like the created. Indeed, as we probe the depths of the submicroscopic, we are becoming more sophisticated to know that an atom is not like a billiard ball and by extension, particles are not 'hard macro-objects' like this.

What is a solid?

When one understands what a solid is, and that is only explained properly and logically in our Microbit Model (i.e. that all particles are groupings of the unit particle that originated in the Big Bang, discussed in Part 4 of this book) then the notion of Idealistic or Dualistic category problems disappear, because all are seen as thought constructs in the Mind and Space of God, that is, as an organization of temporal and contingent space within an atemporal and non-contingent space. Therefore, at the base of it, we are not part of God as the pantheists would say. This is where a mistake is being made by many. We are simply commands of God in that sense and this is what all the Prophets of God, from Adam to Buddha to Muhammad came to reveal and this is why we are all brothers/sisters and one family, and our current divisions are due to greed, power, envy, jealousy, prejudice—an immature outlook on an immature planet. Hopefully, we can assist in showing the right way to all humankind to bring it to true maturity. This is the highest goal. And for this, we must seek the help and guidance from this type of God, because 'He' is not nothing, but no thing.

A General Explanation of the Solution

I think the mind-body problem is solved only in the following manner:

1. God and objectless space are synonymous—so God is pure consciousness and is not made of particles.

2. We have shown in Part 4 of this book how all particles are derived from one type of particle (we call it the microbit). All contact is made at that level; indeed, all other particles are a grouping of that particle. We have not reached this phase in physics. We are, in fact, too backward experimentally to show it empirically at this point; hence there is silence about the solution Muslim and I have for unification. Energy is nothing but the ef-

fort required (measured) to move these particles and they are all conserved because they do not disappear; there is no loss of energy when seen and defined this way.

3. These particles are nothing but thought structures with rules. They interact to give us so called matter and energy, including momentum; there is no violation of causation or energy. One of these complex conglomerations of particles is the brain.

4. The mind is just a fractionalization from the consciousness of God. It is not made of any particles and as such it is a will of the Willer (God). It uses the biological body like a portal.

5. Because the biological body, sustained by the thought of God and made of an immense grouping of microbits (up to the level of molecules and thence neurons etc.), it is structured in a particular way and the fractionalization is able to read the 'images' produced by the brain (i.e. ultimately the sustained microbits that make up the brain in terms of neurons). So, the material of 'mind' and 'body' (as 'congealed' mind) is basically of the same stuff. It is like a laser reading a DVD—the result is an image. In the case of the fractionalization/transfocation of God's consciousness, it reads the, metaphorically speaking the 'grooves', in the brain, like the needle reads the grooves of a record. The result is various senses and sensations.

The Brain as Switchgear

The brain is therefore only a switchgear; it does not generate consciousness but consciousness 'reads' the brain and wills neurons to move etc. The reason why unification has not been achieved in the West aside from what I am expostulating, is because they were trying to unite the forces, not realizing that it is not a matter of uniting the forces; when you have one type of particle, all physics and biology become united. Secondly, when there is only God and His imagination, the eternal and imagination, there is no problem with qualia or the interaction between mind and matter, because both are mind products and mind products can interact. They are mind products of God. One product (the fractionalization) is the user, the other (the body/brain) is the used. The materialists are trying to fuse user and used and that is why they cannot solve the 'hard problem' of consciousness. The dualists are separating user and used and they cannot bridge the gap. The pantheists have a problem because they are depersonalizing a personal entity albeit formless entity we call God. If God was not a person none of us would have individualities and personalities. Our thoughts are within the thoughts of God. God is the Reality and absolute and we are not absolute; but we are indeed thought products of the absolute and hence His creation. This is why our view is different from pantheism and monism. We are not part of God, but part of His thoughts. If He stopped thinking of us now we would vanish.

I have answered the charge of Idealism, leveled at me in this discussion, based on the indubitability of God's existence using the Sesamatic/Relatiological Proof and the Teleogenic proof for God's existence as opposed to mindlessness as the basis of existence. Consciousness is the property of objectless space and has to be because of the proof of Transcendence of mind over matter and energy. The body is accessed by the 'portion' of objectless space when it (the body) reaches a critical threshold in its structure. We have shown why there is no duality and the concept of 'soul' as envisioned by the traditional thinkers is profoundly incorrect in terms of the details of what transpires after death, though the idea of consciousnesses continuance is correct. There is no separation at death of the soul because the soul is not a phantasm co-existing with the body—it is the property of space itself; the body continuously accesses it because that consciousness is all pervasive. Certainly, this view is not dualistic in the usual sense; neither is it monistic. It is something totally different and probably unclassified, as of yet, by mainstream.

Life After Death

To clarify our position on life after death processes, which I term ADE (After Death Experience):

1. There is no astral body associated with the grosser body and embedded within it while the person is alive. On the contrary, a new body is actually created that then becomes the transfocation of one's thought which 'went back' into the consciousness of God; actually, it is always there once He (God) willed its existence, but it is just focused on particular bodies that He wills. That is why we call it transfocation or fractionalization of consciousness. So, our view overcomes dualism.

2. At the same time there is life after death and our view shares with the view that there is a subtler body; it is not exactly like ours in terms of

visage but similar and of course it is made of lighter particles—smaller groupings than quarks (i.e. it is just a different grouping of microbits according to our physics model).

3. God is separate from creation but at the same time all creation is within God; that is because creation is a thought of God and not the essence of God, so it is not exactly monistic either. For these three reasons the outlook we are describing is unique but we can see traces of it in all major scriptures as they exist now. Because of the reasons above, it shares something from monism, dualism, and scientific/atheism but it is none of these. I think investigators will soon find concrete evidence of NDE (more rigorous experiments are now under way). Indeed, it has become clear from innumerable testimonies now that the mind can be transferred out of the body and see things during 'brain death'/heart stoppage, and that those who return speak of floating above or outside their bodies and explaining what they see concerning the activities and statements of nurses and doctors who are trying to revive them[31]. In addition, those who have met an accident together see each other in their subtler body. This will render the field wide open and I think we (using the Transfocation Model of Consciousness TMC) have the capacity to explain all of it.

There is only one absolute reality that is not made of particles etc., that is, God. All matter and energy are just sustained thought products of that absolute consciousness we call God who is a Person and not some amorphous nothingness. In trying to determine what happens after death we ruled out a co-existing astral type body associated with our biological body from logical considerations. However, the exact mechanics of re-creation or *telemorphogenesis*, which we call this process, is a matter of detail and not crucial for moral and ethical purposes, in most cases. The other aspect of our work that connects with all this has to do with realizing that there is only one type of particle out of which everything is made in absolute space. We termed that the microbit. It forms all quarks, gluons etc. What I mean is that all particles are groupings of microbits. So, God creates the most complex from the simplest; there cannot be anything simpler for creation than absolute space and only one type of particle and God therefore shows

---

31 Lommel, Pim Van. (2011). *Consciousness Beyond Life: The Science of the Near-Death Experience*, Harper-One, Reprint Edition.

maximal diversity from the most minimum, and therefore really how great and glorious He truly is as a Personal Being who is not like anything that we know of; in other words God is Incomparable. Currently the whole of fundamental physics is supporting itself on false premises and is simply being propped up artificially. It is bound to and will collapse, and especially, hell will break loose, as they say, when it is realized that all these so-called fundamental particles are not fundamental after all. The true nature of space and particles will then be realized and this is bound to make it easier to understand what may be seen as abstract or without "empirical evidence" right now though it is perfectly logical. Both particles (matter and energy) and consciousness will then be seen as interacting commands issuing from God or the mind of God. Here, neither the word duality, nor monism can be applied, because neither one of them captures the dynamics of what I am talking about. The truth of the matter is beyond both monism and dualism.

To understand why there is no dualism in our scheme of understanding consciousness I want to discuss the concept of this Universe being the Inverse-Dream or Negative-Dream of God. This concept reveals many aspects of the Universe hitherto not fathomable. It helps us see why the Transfocation Model of Consciousness, that is being advocated must be the reality and why there are no dualistic or materialistic problems associated with it. We shall now discuss the Inverse-Dream: Let us take this step by step to answer the charge of inescapable dualism that is leveled against us: firstly, everyone knows what a dream is. We all dream while asleep and some dreams are so vivid that we wonder whether they have really happened out there in space outside our minds! Now in these dreams, which are propelled by our consciousness while asleep, we see people who are conscious. These people in our dream-state have a 'body' and a mind or soul. There's no duality in the dream and no one in his right mind would question how the interaction between the mind and the body of the person in the dream occurs: The actors in the dream are conscious in the dream. Now their consciousness within the dream is dependent on the consciousness of the Dreamer (that is, you as the Dreamer). However, since the Dreamer is asleep, we call it a Dream. But what is the Inverse Dream? God is the ever-awake and is in no need of sleeping! Yet just as in our sleeping state we have a vivid world created inside us in our dream, analogously, a vivid creation of reality is created in the space of God, which is His mind, which is the infinite objectless space or plane that exists. Just as in our dream, where the body of the subject in our dream is a thought product, and the consciousness in that person in our dream is likewise a thought product, there is no dualism, in the sense of the interactability between mind and body, because they are at the level of the sleepers imagination, albeit imagination generated while asleep (i.e. the dream), so too is there no dualistic problem in the reality we see in this Universe when it comes to our body, soul and qualia. They are all at the imaginational level of the Inverse-Dream of God, who is Awake; our Universe is therefore a product of His ever Wakefulness.

Let me address more technically why there is no explanatory gap: The mechanism for experiencing redness according to the Transfocation Model of Consciousness (TMC), results in the external environment mapping into neurons via 'senses', which are 'read' by consciousness in that portion of space interacting with the brain/nervous system. That consciousness is transfocated by the eternal Consciousness as it interacts with the neurons that are themselves mind products of that Consciousness (God).

Concerning Idealism, ultimately only the mental aspect exists but this is not from the human perspective or human generated; to the contrary, it is a generating mentality originating and sustained by the Imagination of an infinitely conscious entity that has created the entire Universe. In addition, the physical aspect is really a conglomeration and interplay of thought structures in which a single particle, which forms the basis of all particles, is willed into existence and is sustained, in the sense that a rule is given by the will of God that certain regions of space are populated by this particle (the microbit) which is like a submicroscopic minuscule region in the space-mind of God; this particle (the willed-by-God always moving spherical minuscule region of space) is deemed to exist in the mind of God and also imagined to be impenetrable by other like particles; from this impenetrability (again willed/imagined) issues forth our notion of solidity of particles as groupings of this particle and hence with rules of interaction (again imagined by God) whereby higher order structures are formed, eventually resulting in the 'biological body'. In this sense then, I think that according to the Transfocation Model of Consciousness (TMC), that provides the solution to the problem of consciousness, we are first of all conscious because our consciousness is borrowed from God who is the infinite space of consciousness. That is where consciousness comes from and it is a consequence of the proof presented, concerning God and space (in Chapter 1).

Remember that consciousness has similar problems as those faced by the property of intelligence and design and purpose engrained in the structures and processes of the Universe, which the atheists deny, even though they cannot escape it in terms of the use of language. What I mean is that teleology pervades in the language itself: for example, I have a book that is a purely technical one (*The Mechanical Design of Organisms*), in which the authors apologetically state in their introduction that the biological organisms they are investigating are 'designed'. They know this implies teleology, but state that they cannot escape such a description because of the precise nature of the structure of the organisms to fulfill their goals (and of course a design implies a designer). You see, if you have a carpet which is of the wrong size, there will always be a bump in it. No matter how much you try to squash the bump to flatten the carpet, the bump will inevitably show up elsewhere. Same with the problem of intelligence and hence consciousness in the Universe; the problem keeps getting shifted. Therefore, if we try to explain human consciousness, we are entering the same problem. If one says that particles possess both consciousness (a mental aspect) and materiality, one assumes consciousness to prove consciousness; it is a circular problem. Furthermore, the aforementioned statement is an assertion and not a proof. Also, words such as 'selection' imply a selector and hence consciousness. If there is a material mechanism for selection that leads to or causes the selection, then one has not proved the origin of consciousness. On the other hand, if there is a conscious selector it begs the question as to how consciousness got there in the first place and becomes an assumption that one is trying to prove; hence circularity. Some thinkers have tried to use Darwinism to explain consciousness. However, Darwinism is facing severe problems in its own field (in my view fatal problems) see (*What Darwin Got Wrong* by Fodor and his colleague[32]) let alone trying to apply it in the area of consciousness. Likewise with string theory. String theory is so far-fetched and has assumed so many dimensions and different dimensions— depending on the version— dimensions for which there is no proof, that it cannot even be applied to consciousness studies with any solid footing, whatsoever. String theory was concocted, for example, to get rid of the infinity problems in physics. Nature does not have such problems; only humans, who concoct inconsistent and incomplete theories. It is true that consciousness and matter

---

32 Fodor, Jerry, and Piatelli-Palmarini, Massimo. (2010). *What Darwin Got Wrong*, Farrar, Straus and Giroux, New York.

must have the same type of properties. The TMC does have that feature—but I won't call it monism because that tends to detract from a personal God and conveys a wrong concept. To explain qualia, which is the experience produced in consciousness, the microbits (particles) in the body get inputs from the environment, as for example seeing the colour red, and that occurs in specific parts of the brain or brain structures. Exactly what the structure(s) are (or is), will be determined by more investigations into the brain. Different structures will produce different colour experiences because that is the way the fractionalization (our consciousness is, as extracted from God, by God's will itself). I will draw an analogy: If you had a sheet of paper, that paper would have a particular quality; so it would react in a specific way to pastel colouring, water colouring, or blots of ink thrown on it, in terms of the diffusion of the paint etc. It is a material that reacts in a particular way to other materials being cast upon it. Likewise, this fractionalization which is our individual consciousness, in every creature with nervous systems, will react to specific neural structures in a specific way. So a command to see redness, blueness does not have to be given each time. A translation does not have to be done each time, just as for a piece of paper we do not have to intervene to get various types of patterns on it, in terms of how the paper 'accepts' the material being thrown upon it. It is really a global command that the fractionalization will react in fixed ways to an indefinite number (from our perspective) neural motions. So, you can see that from a simple worm to man, we are all united in a common thread of this fractionalization, impinging on each type of biological entity. The more the sophisticated arrangement of microbits (or subatomic particles, after a particular pattern of placement) the more our functions available and hence knowledge obtainable etc. and the build-up of our self etc.

The principle behind the mechanisms is God's Imagination, that is, the Eternal One's Imagination. The rest are details and not an explanatory gap. *Without Eternity and Imagination you will have nothing.* There has to be an Imaginator and hence an Ultimately Conscious One from whom all consciousness is a derivative, by will, and hence a creation. "Thought sustained structures" is merely another name for Imagination, but it is an imagination that becomes a secondary reality, whereas God is the Prime Reality. In this way the 'Hard Problem of Consciousness' is softened, in the sense of solved but with details to be worked upon. But first the proof of such a singular intelligent all-pervasive entity must irrefutably be shown; second, the relation of that entity as being collinear in ontological existence with space must be identified; thirdly, our accessibility to that space to draw upon consciousness must be logically explained (avoiding dualism), and finally if there is some scripture that itself flawlessly points to that, it is a bonus (i.e. the Quran). Lastly, our scientific research should then start informing us of the details of this framework, through the cognitive/brain sciences and other research yet to come, particularly through particle physics and our understanding of the true nature of the photon, which is crucial to a further understanding of the difference between consciousness and non-consciousness.

How are certain material bodies conscious? The Eternal Consciousness 'will' certainly created/designed bodies to access this 'made accessible consciousness'—the 'accessed' consciousness by the individual bodies translates into the Self. This entire system demonstrates that there is a law operating that only certainly fashioned bodies or bodies in a certain state are able to become receivers of the 'accessible consciousness'—'accessible consciousness' being the result of the Eternal's/Primer Mover's will (thus making our consciousness contingent on time, because accessible consciousness was willed at a point in time) and together are contingent on the Eternal. A dead body is one that no longer has the ability (i.e. failure of vital organ [heart, brain, etc]) to receive or access the 'accessible consciousness.'

Conscious Robots

We discuss here how our system supports conscious robots and how to make them, in principle (it is connected to photons). Essentially, we are just structured in a particular way to access consciousness, that is all, and then we make the public space of consciousness, private. Not only that, but it is not necessary to be carbon-based for consciousness, for an equivalent system could do this. This has been dealt with on page 75 where we discuss the issue of the real nature of the photon, the GRP (General Rate of Presence) and GRC (General Rate of Consciousness) mechanism that distinguishes between consciousness and non-consciousness. Also the real nature of the photon was also discussed in our book *Microbits: A New Unified Physics* in depth, as to what it really is, and once the photon is really understood, it becomes obvious that light does not have any dual nature/paradox etc. This needs a change in the understanding of physics itself, or even if they (Western science right now enmeshed in incommensurable quantum mechanics and relativity) cannot do so, if our ideas on microbits and 'space' become known then they might be directed more to the photon and its role in sustaining both life and consciousness and will no doubt (in my view) move towards the realization of what the photon is and how it moves; this is step 1. Step 2 is: once this is known then the correct engineering neural networks can be designed that mimic or are analogous to the human structures that convey biophotons/photons. Once this happens the machine (like our biological body, which is nothing but a special machine built up of cells) will access consciousness which is a particleless property of space itself and become conscious itself. It is accessible because "God" (this formless entity that has existed for eternity) who is this space of consciousness, allows such specific dynamical structural configurations to access consciousness; their specific pattern/threshold arrangement and motion is a specific key which unlocks consciousness. Anything below that critical pattern level will not be conscious (the demarcation between GRP and GRC). It was because of all this that our view is not dualistic and therefore dualism is not a stumbling block because of matter and energy and a mysterious thing called the soul. There is no soul as such, but there is still a continuation of life and our identity. Once we realize the property of objectless space and the housing of singular Consciousness of which we are fractionalizations, the puzzle is resolved. We are too far behind right now as humanity but what we are saying is that explaining consciousness is like trying to explain aerodynamics to 9th Century villagers in Europe. Yes! You can fly, but first the structure has to be configured to enable the proper forces (lift/drag) to act on the object to give flight. If you have the wrong materials and concepts of gravity and forces, you cannot put something heavier than air into flight. Likewise, the structure (brain/nervous system) has to be created (like the plane) knowing the correct principles (like the forces) to be able to become the key that unlocks consciousness which is a property of objectless space itself and which then will indubitably lead to the flight of consciousness! I would suggest starting with simple organisms such as a worm, which according to our view is a conscious entity. The chemical and electrical activity of the neurons has to be mapped and studied and also the photonic activity which exists needs to be studied very carefully. One has to understand the new physics Muslim and I are talking about, plus Muslim's explanation of the GRC and GRP. Then one has to replicate all of this. Once done, the created entity will necessarily exhibit consciousness. After this, more complex organisms can be designed, eventually, over the many centuries leading to the creation of conscious androids. The iPhone did not arise in a day and to stone age man it would be like magic. Similarly, consciousness is like magic to us but there are ways of creating entities that will possess it.

This view entails that God created energy (particles) from His mind and sustains them. We do not know exactly how, but some rules are being sustained that segment space into regions that we call particles and the intractability of all these particles is so structured as to give the semblance in His imagination of solidity. There is nothing like the particle-based 'essence' of God and God is not therefore comprised of anything in this Universe; He is not part of His Imagination, but His imagination is a transient part of Him—and we are in this Universe which is finite and one of His transient Universes. This is indeed only one of many separate Universes that He has created as an eternal being. On the meta-level, Muslim and I know that He has these periods of creativity and then silence—what I mean is that this happens through 'serial' but probably separate Big Bang and Big Crunches and perhaps other co-existent separated Universes in His space of Imagination. We do not know of course how long this creative venture has gone on from the meta-time perspective. But it is not difficult to see that His existence naturally led to His creation of Universes. Once these Universes started rolling God was not the same God as He would have been had He never created. He wants us to know Him and is giving us clues but not the complete answers. He wants us to do work and come close to Him (no matter what our circumstances; and this is what He really admires). He wants those who achieve this level of sincerity and dedication to be in His company connected to the concept for which the whole Universe was created. (AWE stands for Acknowledging, Welcoming and Embracing God). This is what life is all about, what consciousness is, where it comes from, and where it is headed to!

Bibliography

Fodor, Jerry, and Piatelli-Palmarini, Massimo. (2010). *What Darwin Got Wrong*, Farrar, Straus and Giroux, New York.

Haque, Nadeem and Muslim, M. *(2007). From Microbits to Everything: Universe of the Imaginator. Volume 2: The Philosophical Implications, (Vol. 2),* Toronto: Optagon Publications Ltd.

Haque, Nadeem and Muslim, M. (2011). "New Proofs for the Existence of God (Part II): The Cosmological Applications of the Sesamatic Proof", *Scientific GOD Journal*, 2(2), 105-132.

Haque, Nadeem, and Banaei, M. (2011). "New Proofs for the Existence of God (Part III): The Teleogenical Proof", *Scientific GOD Journal*, 2(2), 102-104.

Haque, Nadeem. (January 2014). "The Ultimate Reality Sustaining the Cosmos: A New Emerging Synthesis", The International Journal of Philosophical Physics, Volume 1, Issue 1, pp, 26-28.

Muslim, Mohammed. (2011). "New Proofs for the Existence of God: Part 1: The Sesamatic Proof", *Scientific God Journal*, Volume 2, No. 1.

Lommel, Pim Van. (2011). *Consciousness Beyond Life: The Science of the Near-Death Experience*, HarperOne; Reprint edition.

Rose, Stephen. (2006). *The Future of the Brain: The Promise and Perils of Tommorow's Neuroscience*, p. 160.

Sheldrake, Rupert. (1988). *The Presence of the Past: Morphic Resonance and the Habits of Nature*, Vintage Books, New York.

PART 3

Extraterrestrials in Islam
The Extraordinary Quranic Evidence of Extraterrestrial Life in the Universe

How many ETs did God create ...is it Endless? Was there a 'time' when God was not creating and doing nothing but only thinking?

They have not made a just estimation of [the power/greatness of] God... (Quran 39:67)

Foreword

In academic circles, when the captivating question of the possible existence of intelligent extraterrestrial life is debated, the validity of religions, which view humans as the only intelligent or superior species that God has created, is seriously undermined. Mistakenly, Islam is included in this list of "undermined religions". However, rather than undermining Islam, the possible discovery of extraterrestrials would actually reinforce and dramatically confirm that which is already contained in the Quran. In this book, we provide an overview of the Islamic perspective on this subject.

The question of the existence of earth-like planets and higher forms of extraterrestrial life has come to the forefront with the discovery of thousands of earth-like exoplanets. This has added some 'spice' and suspense to the perennial existential question of whether we are alone—the answer to which will indubitably have profound consequences for humankind. In this book, it is proven that the existence of Extraterrestrial Life is teeming and scattered in the Universe, according to the Quran. Several key verses are deconstructed and discussed, to prove this point. We examine the meaning of *Dabbah* and the remarkable concept of *Earth Clusters* by delving into Islamic terminology and context, by which it will be illustrated that the Quran postulates trillions upon trillions of earth-like planets in the cosmos, and higher forms of sentient carbon-based life.

We also examine the possibility and difficulties of travelling to the stars— possible mechanisms, and the Quranic view and encouragement of the exploration of outer space. In addition, we discuss the origin of life and the Quranic view on this subject, and the prevalence of equivalent laws on other Earth-like planets, to show how the Quran posits both the uniformity of laws and their automaticity, thereby eliminating further the erroneous concept of God-of-the-gaps. We then examine the special case of the Sirius star system, the ETs of Sirius, and the remarkable Quranic reference to this. Related to the origin of life, the discovery of Quranic view of Earth's unique geophysics is discussed by one of the authors—is discussed using key concepts behind two Arabic words and how it connects to the puzzle of the origin of water on earth. The generalizability of this discovery in the Quran has implications for all earth-like planets in the cosmos, not currently realized by researchers. The book also presents views on the implications of these for world religions, and, in particular, it will be shown that rather than detract from Islam, the discovery of ET life and earth-like planets will confirm the Quranic statements. The totality of the analysis drives home the point concerning the erroneous anthropocentric views that engulf not only Muslims but rest of humankind too, and shows how this is to be replaced by concepts such as the *supracommunity* and *affinity* discussed in the author's other book—*Ecolibrium*[33].

The exact nature and parameters of human uniqueness have always been present in the Quran but were not paid much attention to. The discovery of ET life will underscore all this neglect. In a nutshell, it is revealed that the assessment of ET life and Earth-like planets and their mention in the Quran, further illuminates the inextricable unity of science and religion, its singular methodology and utter inseparability.

---

33 Haque, Nadeem; Masri, Al Hafiz B.A., and Banaei, Mehran. (2021). *Ecolibrium: The Sacred Balance in Islam*, Beacon Books, Manchester.

Chapter 1

Recent Discoveries of Earth-Like Planets: A Brief Overview

How many civilizations are there in our galaxy, that are transmitting signals? In 1961, Astronomer/Astrophysicist Frank Drake came up with an equation to estimate this, that was prepared for the first meeting for the SETI Institute on this topic. The equation comprises the following terms and is known as Drake's Equation:

N = this is the number of communicable <u>civilizations</u> in our galaxy.

R_* = the average star formation average rate of the Milky Way.

f_p = fraction of stars having <u>planets</u>

ne = the average number of planets that can potentially support <u>life</u> per star that has planets

f_l = the fraction of planets that could support life where it actually develops at some stage.

fi = the fraction of planets with life that actually end up developing <u>intelligent</u> life (civilizations)

f_c = the fraction of civilizations that develop a technology that is able to transmit signs of their existence into space

L = the length of time for which such civilizations transmit detectable signals.

$N = R_* f_p n_e f_l f_i f_c L$ = the estimated number of civilizations that could communicate with us

Due to many unknowns, which we can only guestimate, right now, the equation is more like an inspirational and teaching tool to make one aware of the possibility of advanced alien life.

Detection of Exoplanets

There are five primary methods for determining exoplanets[34]: Radial velocity; the Transit Method; Direct Imaging, Microlensing and Astrometry. The following is a cursory introduction.

Radial Velocity

The exoplanet 51 Pegasi b was discovered using this method. When a planet is pulled by its gravitational field, it wobbles, the star and planet orbiting a common centre of mass. The wobble leads to the star being blue-shifted (moving toward) and red shifted (moving away from the observer) called a Doppler shift in technical parlance. Most of the earlier discoveries of exoplanets were determined using this method.

Transits

When a planet passes in front of a host star the starlight is dimmed for the observer. The time between the starlight's dips depict the orbital period of the exoplanet.

Direct imaging

In this method, optical imaging, using light from the planet, can reveal an exoplanet's existence. One of the problems is that light from the star may block light from the planet. To circumvent this problem, filters are used. 40 planets have been found so far using this method.

Microlensing

Over 70 planets have been detected using this method. When two stars happen to align, the star which is closer bends light, causing an initial smooth increase in brightness and then decrease. If there is a planet orbiting the closer star there will likewise be an additional bending causing a spike.

---

34 "ESA Science & Technology - Exoplanet detection methods", Exoplanets, ESA, https://sci.esa.int/web/exoplanets/-/60655-detection-methods

Space based telescopes

Space based telescopes were literally instrumental in the discovery of exoplanets. They observe continuously and without the earth's atmosphere. Recent ones include CNES Convection, Rotation and Planetary Transit mission, CoRoT (2006 to 2013), and NASA's 2009 Kepler which monitored 150,000 faint stars and discovered thousands of exoplanets. By combining the results of observations and surveys using different techniques, we are able to build a representative picture of the diversity of exoplanets and planetary systems. With the new space probes that are being sent after Kepler spacecraft, we will no doubt find more Earth-like planets and more about their composition. In addition, just prior to the publishing of this book, the almost $10 billion James Webb telescope was sent orbiting into space at Lagrange Point 2. The James Webb telescope will be able to obtain larger images of exoplanets. It will use a coronagraph, which impedes bright light from a star so that the dimmer brown dwarfs, planets and dust clouds can be imaged. Further similar space telescopes will be launched in years ahead. The number of Earth-like planets found has burgeoned from just a handful in the 1990s to several thousand at present. This detection will grow to perhaps exponentially in the next hundred years and will increase the likelihood of contact in some form, or at the minimum, a discovery of the signature for advanced ET life, using a variety of our advancing technological probing tools.

Interstellar Visitor—Alien or Natural?

On Oct. 19, 2017, an unusual object in space was spotted by the University of Hawaii's Pan-STARRS1 telescope, funded by NASA's Near-Earth Object Observations (NEOO) Program. This was the first *interstellar* object, as determined from its trajectory that was detected by astronomers. They gave it the catchy name "Oumuamua", which means, in Hawaiian, "the visitor who comes from afar first" (in short a scout).[35] Although it is not yet proven (that is, it is not 100% certain) that this is an artificial spacecraft or probe sent from another civilization, or some of its technological debris, there are strong indications that it could be alien-made, rather than being a natural object due to its unique features and motion. Avi Loeb, a leading astrophysicist from MIT, was a principle

---

35 Adam. Mann (March 14, 2019). *Space.com*, "Oumuamua: The First Interstellar Object", https://www.space.com/oumuamua.html.

investigator into this object. He has written a book devoted to Oumuamua and its possible ET origins. He states:

> These are certainties, and they allow us to declare confidently that the first three of Oumuamua's identified anomalies—its unusual orbit without a tail [i.e. natural comets have tails], its extreme shape [ten times longer than its width], and its luminosity—make it statistically different, by a large margin, from all other objects catalogued by humanity....[Combining all these unusual features it] is now a one-in-a-million object.[36]

Given the high probability that Oumuamua is of extraterrestrial origins, as Loeb stresses, a view with which I completely agree, scientists need to be better technically prepared to probe such an object for the next incursion into our solar system.

Why have they not visited us?

I have quipped half-jokingly with my colleagues that because of the abysmal behaviour of many humans on Earth, if an alien were told to come to Earth to find intelligent life, upon landing, he might think that his friends had played a bad practical joke on him! Why, though, seriously speaking, have the aliens not visited us, unless some researchers, including the late former Deputy Prime Minister of Canada, Paul Hellyar[37], top class researcher Timothy Good, maverick scientist Bob Lazar, Colonel Philp Corso etc. are correct in saying that we have already been and are currently being visited by ETs, and that this has been covered up by various dubious government departments, in particular, in the US government. According to many, the recent 'Tic Tac' unexplained aerial phenomenon incident is being considered by many as a genuine alien aircraft because its maneuverability is literally out of this world; we have nothing like it. It is quantum leaps ahead. However, others believe that these UFOs are based on secret technology that has been developing since at least WW2, as a parallel dark program of funds diversion by 'the elite'. Or, alternatively, that it is a combination of the two (back-engineered from fallen alien craft, particularly the Roswell incident).

---

36 Loeb, Avi. (2021). *Extraterrestrial: The First Sign of Intelligent Life Beyond Earth*, p. 61.

37 More than ten years ago, I met Paul Hellyar at a conference and informed him of the Quranic view as well as providing him with the first version of the article I co-authored on ET life and the Quran. He was very receptive. Sadly, he passed away in 2021, at the ripe old age of 98.

We cannot, using the Quranic methodology of proof, accept these UFOs and UAPs (Unidentified Aerial Phenomena) as being FACT because of their *inconclusive* nature. However, if we, therefore, reasonably assume that no aliens have visited us now or in history, then we are faced with another problem, that is, the Fermi Paradox, which is the following: Our galaxy has been around for 10 billion years or so. Indeed, it is a profound question as to where everybody is. There are several possibilities:

1. They can visit us but are not visiting or interfering: we are not worth it.
2. The ones in our local area do not have sufficiently advanced technology (light speed).
3. Those much farther away may be more advanced but are too far away to communicate or travel.
4. They have been sending signals but we have not read them or cannot interpret them.
5. We are the only advanced lifeform in the galaxy.

In my view, the most plausible explanations are #2 and #3. #4 is a possibility. #1 and #5 are implausible. In fact, I would venture to say that #5 is almost an impossibility.

The Unique Islamic Position

By 2037 latest, with the launch of the Habex Space telescope, life may be discovered (see: https://www.jpl.nasa.gov/habex/), reinforcing the Islamic position further. The Islamic Epistemological Perspective (IEP), properly understood, embraces or should embrace the Quran with the Universe in an intervolved way, where *the Quran is akin to being a written Universe* and *the Universe in akin to being a visual Quran*. Muslims with such an integrated perspective would believe in the Quranic evidence with equal weight as something found in nature. For them, the existence of such life on other planets would be a fact. This is what this part of the book is about—an epistemological analysis on this question, the discovery of which would be ranked in the top tier of all discoveries made by humans, ever. It may not be too long before we see the concrete reality of this existence, shattering our narrow ontological, epistemological, and theological views, and once again vindicating the Quran. Let us now delve, in the following chapters, into the 'meat' of the evidence of Extraterrestrial Life in the Quran.

Chapter 2

The Novel Concept of Earth Clusters in the Quran

People of Earth, your attention please... This is Prostetnic Vogon Jeltz of the Galactic Hyperspace Planning Council... As you will no doubt be aware, the plans for development of the outlying regions of the Galaxy require the building of a hyperspatial express route through your star system, and regrettably your planet is one of those scheduled for demolition. The process will take slightly less than two of your Earth minutes. Thank you.—From The Hitchhiker's Guide to the Galaxy, by Douglas Adams[38]

I have known about the existence of life in the Quran since the mid-1980s but never put pen to paper, until 2006, when the article *Extraterrestrials in the Quran*, was published in a local Muslim newspaper, *The Ambition* (Asma Warsi being the Editor) with my colleague, Zeshan Shahbaz. It was then, in 2015, when an edited, revised and expanded version was published in the international magazine, *Nexus* and subsequently translated into various European languages, by the dynamic publisher, Duncan Roads[39]. In that article, some perplexing puzzles were resolved. You see, remarkably, in the Quran, it is stated that Earthlike planets (other 'Earths') exist, which consequently means that they are hospitable to life. However, one needs to study the language in the Quran carefully to realize the full extent of this fact. The foundation for understanding the existence of ET life in the Quran is understanding the verses which are popularly translated into English as 'seven heavens'.

In connection with the following passage, it is important to note that the number seven (*saba* in Arabic) is often synonymous with "several" or "many", but it may also mean "exactly seven". The Quran (65:12) says: **"It is God who has created seven heavens [*samawati*] and of the Earth their like."** How is this "of the Earth" that the Quran speaks of, like the seven heavens? The word

---

38 Adams, Douglas.(1979). *The Hitchhiker's Guide to the Galaxy*, Pan Books, Chapter 3.

39 Haque, N.; Shahbaz, Zeshan. (August—September, 2015). "Extraterrestrials and Intraterrestrials in Islam", *Nexus Magazine*.

sama (plural *samawati*) refers to "that which is above" and has a contextual nature. In the Quran (67:3) and (71:15) it is stated that God created the seven heavens, one above the other. In addition, the "lower heaven" mentioned in 37:6 comprises planets (*kawkab*), indicating that the "lower heaven" or literally "the lower of that which is above" points to a type of grouping—in this case, the grouping of planets around one star, i.e., the solar system.

Taking this linguistic and contextual evidence, we realise that "seven heavens" consequently refers to the hierarchically clustered way in which the Universe has been structured. For example, we live in our solar system, and, of course, beyond our cosmic neighbourhood abound multitudes of other stellar systems. These stellar systems may be clustered, i.e., "bunched up" in terms of their relative proximity to each other. A cluster of these clusters of stars forms a galaxy, where our galaxy alone contains up to 400 billion stars (it could be 200 billion— no one knows for sure). But these galaxies themselves are also clustered, and these clusters of galaxies are likewise also clustered, i.e., they form superclusters. Astronomers estimate that the Universe contains roughly 100 billion to trillions of galaxies (it is unknown). If this "of the Earth" is like the seven heavens, then it means that there are clusters of Earths as well, e.g., Earthlike planets orbiting nearby stars. This being the case, there would be countless Earthlike planets in the Universe. It is worth noting that the Prophet Muhammad also mentioned the plurality of Earths: "...Say: O God, the Lord of the seven heavens and whatever they cover, Lord of the Earths [*al-aradina*] and whatever they contain..." [Emphasis added.]—Quoted by al-Tabarani in his *al-Kabir and al-Awsat*.

Earth Clusters

Clustering is clear from these verses:

> ... [God] who has created the seven heavens (*saba samawati*), one above the other (*tibaqan*). (Quran 67:3)

> Have you ever wondered how God created the seven heavens (*saba samawati*), one above the other (*tibaqan*)...? (71:15)

Here then, are the seven clustered levels:
1. Our Solar system.
2. Cluster of stars—galaxies
3. Cluster of galaxies—galactical cluster/groups.

4. Cluster of galactical clusters/groups—supercluster of galaxies.

5. Cluster of Superclusters: which I will dub: Supraclusters.

6. Cluster of Supraclusters, that I will call: Megaclusters.

7. Cluster of Megaclusters—i.e. the whole Universe.

We have reached level 4 in our exploration of the structure of the Universe. More research and better telescopes will show further clustering, up to the 6th level, we surmise, the 7th being the 'Universe bubble' itself. In the Quran then, it is being indicated that there are levels above level 4.

So, what are Earth Clusters? This refers to the "of the Earth" being like the seven "that which are above" (the galactical clusters).

In order to understand this, one needs to equate some identities in the Quran:

- Since "of the Earth" (X) is like "seven heavens" (7Y), let X=7Y from 65:12.

- ... [God] who has created the seven heavens (*saba samawati*), one above the other (*tibaqan*). (Quran 67:3)
  or re-stated: ...who has created the 7Y, one above the other.

Do a substitution in the Quranic verses to gain insight:

- ...who has created X, one above the other   (since X=7Y)
  Since X = "of the Earth" the verse becomes:

- ...who has created 'of the Earth', one above the other
  ...who has created Earthlike planets, one above the other (since "of the Earth" = with Earth properties = Earthlike planets"), where Earth is a generic term in this context

We see that the statement about Earth in Quran 65:12 becomes equivalent to the statement about the Earths and mirrors the galaxies. The galaxies are in clusters and, therefore, so too are the Earths.

The Number of Life Bearing Exoplanets and Galaxies

How many planets are there? UC Berkeley and University of Hawaii astronomers have concluded from data analyzed so far from Kepler data that about 20 percent of sun-like stars have possible habitable Earth-sized planets. According to this calculation it is further estimated that almost 200 billion stars in our galaxy alone exist, with 40 billion like our sun, and that would yield about 8 billion Earth-size planets in the Milky Way. In fact, it has been discovered through Kepler that almost all stars are orbited by planets, with 17 percent of them having Earth-sized planets in an orbit less than that of Mercury.[40]

A Fascinating *Speculative Calculation* using the Quran

There are numerous mathematical features in the Quran, all of which are checkable by anyone. Two are discussed in connection with the Sirius Star System. Is there information in the Quran to determine the number of Earthlike exoplanets? Get ready for dealing with mind bogglingly large numbers! If you take the Quranic passage 65:12 and calculate as follows: 65^{12} you get 5.7 zetta, rounded off, or more precisely:

5.68800906E21

or that

5,688,009,060,000,000,000,000

From this stars' quantity estimation, we cannot determine the total number of galaxies in the Universe until we get more data on the number of stars and the average number of stars per galaxy. In addition, with our ever-advancing probes we will start gaining a better estimate of the number of exoplanets with the possibility of life on them, or actually find life!

The above attempt using the Quran to quantify the unknown is a great lesson in humility, in terms of both knowledge and the vastness of creation. In this case, unlike other 'scientific verses' in the Quran, we cannot use the Quran to be certain about the numbers, unless it is somehow shown from within the Quran itself that 65:12 can be used to determine the number of Earthlike planets; using this verse numerically, is indeed speculative, but also most intriguing. As stated above, I have a strong feeling it does refer to the total number of Earthlike planets, but that does not constitute proof. Indeed, if anything, this speculation shows our paucity of knowledge, but, at the same time, what is highlighted, as a result, is the stark fact that our Universe is unfathomably vast, and that the number of life-bearing planets must likewise be incredibly great.

---

40 "22% of Sun-like Stars have Earth-sized Planets in the Habitable Zone - Universe Today", *Universe Today: Space and Astronomy News*, https://www.Universetoday.com/106121/22-of-sun-like-stars-have-earth-sized-planets-in-the-habitable-zone
See also: "Nearly All Sun-Like Stars Have Planetary Systems"
https://www.Universetoday.com/99309/nearly-all-sun-like-stars-have-planetary-systems

Chapter 3

Dabbah—Carbon Based ET Life forms[41]

We Are Not Alone!

According to the Islamic perspective, we are certainly not alone. The Quran (chapter/surah 42, verse/ayah 29, i.e., 42:29) states:

> And among His signs is the creation of the heavens and the Earth, and whatever corporeal creatures [*dabbatin*] that He has dispersed in both of them. He is able to gather them together when He wills [*idha yashao*].

There are several points that need to be elaborated upon with respect to this key passage. First, in the Quran the word *dabbatin* here refers to an entity that is comprised of and/or evolved from water, and it is stated that God has created every *dabbah* from water (*dabbatin min ma-in*) (see 24:45). The word *dabbah* also denotes any sentient, corporeal being capable of spontaneous movement. Second, this passage states that life in this Universe is widespread. Third, it portrays that one day, sometime in the future, we will communicate and/or meet with extraterrestrial beings and that this will be one of the signs of the Creator—signs of design, wonder and power which reflect the Intelligence that originated the Universe and its stellar inhabitants. The reason why the statement regarding the gathering of corporeal entities in this Universe relates to an event *in* the Universe itself, rather than in the hereafter, on the day of judgement, is because when the Quran states elsewhere (e.g., 10:45) that there will be a gathering of entities in the next life, it does so in respect of their gathering unto God or an equivalent. *Dabbah*, are therefore essentially carbon based/water sentient life forms. However, in this particular passage (42:29), the gathering of life-forms is not between them and God but between themselves, gathering from a dispersed state. Furthermore, when the word "signs" or "sign" is used, it means that the sign at some point will be realised or seen by human beings in this life. For example, in the Quran (10:92) it is stated that the pharaoh who chased Prophet

41 This Chapter is drawn partially from the article: Haque, N.; Shahbaz, Zeshan. (August—September, 2015). "Extraterrestrials and Intraterrestrials in Islam", *Nexus Magazine*.

Moses will be preserved in his body as a sign for those who come after him. Indeed, the bodies of both Rameses II and Merneptah remain preserved today in the Egyptian Museum in Cairo as a sign for us, as has been discussed in detail by the Dr. Maurice Bucaille in his now famous book *The Bible, The Quran and Science*. I have visited the Museum and seen these mummies with my own eyes, and they indeed are well preserved! If the creatures in the rest of the Universe will be a sign for us, we must, at some point in space and time, realise it, concretely. Let us hope that these entities are not as insensitive as Douglas Adams' "Vogons", quoted at the beginning of this part of the book, or as duplicitously cunning as the aliens in a now classic Twilight Zone episode who visit Earth purportedly to serve man. Unbeknownst to the simple Earthlings, "to serve man" actually meant literally "to serve man on a dinner plate", as opposed to being in service for man!

Michael Denton, a biochemist and author of several books on directed evolution, in his film "Privileged Species"[42] explains that out of all the elements, discovered so far, carbon, because of its 'self-replicating' bonding stability with itself and other elements, is the ideal building block for life: more than 65 million carbon compounds have been found so far. No other element in the Universe so far has been found with these unique properties. Stars are carbon factories—so the Universe full of stars is a carbon-based life producing factory. For example, stars produce carbon but a resonance state of 7.68 MeV in the carbon-12 nucleus has to exist as discovered by Fred Hoyle in 1953. No such resonance—no 'us' down the road! Hoyle was an atheist but candidly admitting that it looks like there is a super intellect behind all this. This leads to the interesting question as to whether the stars after the Big Bang were anticipating and planning life? Does a star have a mind to organize itself to have a specific resonance to produce complex life in the future? Believing so would be akin to paganism. Also, it crushes atheism to smithereens where they may say that life on Earth is a chance product—a fluke out of the quadrillions upon quadrillions of stars that have no life. When carbon and water-based ET life (*dabbah*) is found, then it will entrench in our minds the realization of the existence of a universal conditional law that makes it even harder to explain that life is a chance happenstance:

---

42   A film by Michael Denton: "Privileged Species: How the Cosmos is Designed for Human Life." https://privilegedspecies.com

> Do those who cover the truth not see that the rest of the Universe and the Earth were one piece, and We (God) suddenly (rapidly) ripped them apart and made every living thing (*shayin hayin*) from water (*min al-mai*); will they even then not—through confirmation —believe? (Quran: 21:30)

This verse on life in the context of the Big Bang equates *living things* with *dabbah*; linking to the other verse of *dabbah* being dispersed, it is reinforcing the fact that life thrives throughout the Universe. Concerning Earth:

> He (God) has appointed, precisely established and positioned the earth [both the planet as a whole, and the earth's crust itself] for the maintenance and development of sentient life forms [both humans and nonhumans]. (55:10)

Some people have confused beings in the *samawati* as being birds or angels. One of the reasons why many Muslims are not aware of these details about extraterrestrial life is because they have assumed that when the Quran declares beings in the "seven heavens and the Earth" as worshipping God, these passages refer to the angels or birds. However, interestingly enough, there are two mentions which tell us that there are entities other than the angels or birds that are in the "heavens". Surah: ayah 24:41 factors out birds, whereas 16:49 mentions angels separately and factors them out of the group "corporeal creatures", as follows: "For, before God prostrates all that is in the cosmic systems as well as on the Earth—corporeal creatures [dabbatin] and the angels...."

These beings on other star systems are solid-bodied, as stated in the Quran, in 13:15:

> And unto God [alone] falls in prostration whoever is in the cosmic systems [*samawati*, i.e., on planets in the tens of billions of galaxies] and on the Earth, willingly [e.g., good human beings and extraterrestrial beings who follow God's laws] or unwillingly, as do their shadows in the mornings and afternoons.

The fact that shadows are being cast implies that they are in the form of physical matter, rather than some type of subtler energy.

Chapter 4

The Special Case of the ETs of Sirius

Extraterrestrial Life and Sirius: A Scientific-Quranic Perspective
By Bassel A. Reyahi
Introduction by Nadeem Haque

Bassel Reyahi's book on Sirius and the Quran is a truly groundbreaking work that is currently available only in Arabic. In Arabic, it is entitled: *Najm al-Shirá fī al-Qurān al-Karīm : wa-Innahu Huwá Rabb al-Shirá: mujizāt Qurānīyah jadīdah*, published in Beirut : Dār al-Bayāriq ; Ammān : Dār Ammār, 1998, al-Tabah, 218 pages. Efforts are underway to have in translated into English. In the meantime, the following is an edited (by Nadeem Haque), brief summary of some of the salient points in the book, by the author (Reyahi) himself. There are plans to not only translate the book into English, but to also expand it, with respect to further new discoveries from the Quran and remarkable statements connected with the early Muslims, in relation to the topic of extraterrestrial life and extrasolar planets. We hope to, therefore, update the summary in the very near future.

Book Summary, by Bassel Reyahi:

This book is about Sirius in the Quran. Sirius is the only star mentioned in the Quran explicitly by name. It has two divisions: Part 1 deals with some basic astronomical information on related topics such as Procyon (another similar star system, the search for extrasolar planets, etc.). The chapter on Sirius contains comprehensive information on the star for both specialists and non-specialists. The second part is further divided into chapters that examine Sirius in the context of current scientific knowledge and enquiry. In addition, I engage in a speculative analysis with respect to future advances that might be made concerning our knowledge of this star system. Prior to the publication of this book, the subject of Sirius in the Quran had never been written about comprehensively before, other than an article I wrote in 1997 for a local newspaper. Also included in the second part, are two chapters on other scientific signs in the Quran that have a deep bearing, one way or another, upon the subject of Sirius. What follows is a very brief summary of the main points in the book. Astrophysical Details of the Sirius System Sirius, also called the "Dog Star", is the brightest star in the night sky having a visual magnitude of -1.46 (its absolute magnitude is 1.43). It has been one of the most studied and observed celestial object through the ages. Of the ancients, the Egyptians observed its helical rising to time the flooding of the Nile. In modern times, Sirius was one of the first stars for which a parallax was determined and thus opened up the Universe for further quantification. The current value of its parallax is 0.3777" which translates to a distance of 2.648 parsecs or 8.63/8.61 light years. Fredrick Bessel, when following the proper motion of Sirius, which was determined to be wobbling, inferred around 1844, the existence of an unseen companion. In January 31, 1862, the famous telescope maker Alvin Clark visually discovered Sirius B, also known as the "Pup", with a newly made 18 ½" refractor. The companion of Sirius A was very faint and its mass was determined to be about that of our sun, while the Sirius A mass was found to be about 2.15 times that of our sun.

It was also found that the distance between Sirius A and Sirius B ranged from 7 to 20 a.u., completing one revolution around their barycenter in a period of 50 years. In 1914 W. Adams of Mount Wilson Observatory, obtained the first spectra of Sirius B and estimated its surface temperature to be about 8,500 K degrees, which is a little less than the 10,000 K degrees of Sirius A itself. Adams concluded that for Sirius B to be as hot as it is, though very faint, while at the same time having a mass of the sun, it must possess a very high density. This conclusion came with the onset of the general relativity theory which predicted that a star of such a high density should have a measurable gravitational redshift. In 1919, the gravitational redshift of the sun was measured during a total solar eclipse mission, led by Eddington. Thereafter, in 1924 Adams measured the redshift of Sirius B to be 30 km/s, agreeing with general relativity theory and, in retrospect, validating the high-density state of Sirius B. In the 1930's, Chandrasekhar calculated that such densities as those of Sirius B are possible and could be maintained without the star collapsing to a singularity, according to the models being used, by what is called electron degeneracy pressure. Such stars with degenerate cores were named white dwarfs. For many years, only two white dwarfs other than Sirius B, were known. Since then, anything significant regarding Sirius A or its companion has been in refining existing data, but no new revolutionary observation has been made. In the early 1940's, Marshak showed theoretically, that Sirius B's size was less than half of that calculated previously. In 1971, a study based on new spectra of Sirius B, Greenstein, Oke and Shipman, then all at Caltech, oblivious to Marshak's results, reached similar results in that Sirius B's size is less than that of the earth, and gravitational redshift was calculated to be more than twice the value calculated decades before, by Adams (about 81 km/s). Later on, George and Carolyn Gatewood of Alleghany Observatory made a thorough examination of the data on Sirius and its companion. They published a paper entitled: "A Study of Sirius" (APJ, vol. 225, No. 1, pt. 1, 1978). Most of the relevant data adopted in this book summary, is based on the Gatewoods' paper. The surface temperature of Sirius B as reported by both the Caltech team and the Gatewoods was found to be at least three times what was previously known (about 30,000 K). This high value was derived through many methods, including ultraviolet and x-ray observations from space.

A survey by the ROSAT space observatory indicated the scarcity of hot white dwarfs, that is, ones as hot, or hotter than Sirius. This scarcity is unexplained and needs to be investigated. Many ancient records, including Ptolemy's Almagest, refer to Sirius as a red star. This has perplexed modern astronomers, for Sirius is, and has been, at least since the astronomer Al-Sufi's time in the 10th Century C.E., a white-blue star. No current astrophysical explanation is possible with current astrophysical models. A change has certainly transpired on this binary star system due to a collapse of Sirius B, but according to current theories this could not have happened thousands or even tens of thousands of years ago but happened 120 million years ago. However, due to our lack of knowledge on the evolution of stars, on limited data and modeling assumptions, such historical records should be taken seriously.

Background Information: Quran and Science

For Muslims, the Quran is the revelation of God (in Arabic: Allah) sent down to Mohammed in the early 7th century C.E. The Quran, which millions of people read every day, is exactly the same book which Mohammed and his followers recited fourteen centuries ago. This fact is so solid that even the most critical scholars who are no friends of Islam (the Orientalists) acknowledge this. Among the lesser-known things about the Quran is the abundance of scientific signs within its pages. In fact, many astronomical facts and signs pointed to, in the Quran, remained obscure for centuries until they were discovered scientifically. To take an example, the creation of the Universe from one compact entity (the Big Bang), is referred to in a chapter 21, verse 31, saying; "Have not the unbelievers seen that the heavens and the earth (i.e. the Universe) were one compact piece (*ratq*) which We (God) suddenly exploded (*fatq*) and that We made every living from water". Also, according to the Quran, the Universe is a closed one which will be folded into a 'singularity'. This is stated in the same chapter, verse 105: "The day when We (God) shall fold up the heaven (the Universe) like a recorder rolls up a scroll: as We started the first creation (from one compact piece), so too shall We repeat it. It is a promise that We shall fulfill". The above remarkable scientific statements of the Quran are just a few of many mentioned in it that pre-empt recent scientific discoveries. The Muslims had not understood that their scripture had foretold the basic Big Bang model, for example, until scientists theorized about the Big Bang, and it is the same for other such advanced Quranic statements about science, etc. A lot has been written on the subject of scientifically pre-emptive verses of the Quran. Some Western scholars have also deeply researched the subject, most notably a French physician named Maurice Bucaille in a book titled "La Bible, la Coran et la Science" published in 1970s. However, Muslims and Non-Muslims alike only dealt with already discovered scientific facts. Little attention has been paid to stellar astronomy and none has dealt with Sirius in the Quran.

The Discoveries in the Quran

From childhood, this writer has always been interested in astronomy and absorbed and fascinated by the fact that the Quran has foretold astronomical facts which scientists discovered many centuries after its purported revelation. This is why my interest in astronomy and simultaneously, in the Quran, increased. Naturally, I had always tried to expand my knowledge beyond the frontiers of knowledge, and through this process I made some minor discoveries of the scientific signs in the Quran. However, in 1985, I started a thorough and systematic search in the Quran, recording all the verses which I felt pertained to astronomy, hence accumulating hundreds of verses on the subject. By studying these verses very deeply, I have been able to make many discoveries. However, by far the most important concerns the star Sirius (Al-Shiira). What follows is a brief account of the chain of discoveries made about Sirius in the Quran. Before starting, however, some background information is presented which will hopefully facilitate a greater understanding of the nature of the Quran, and therefore, of its connection to Sirius. The Quran is divided into chapters, each called a surah. In all, there are 114 suras. Each one has a name, which is usually derived from the main subject dealt with in it, and each consists of verses (a verse is called an ayah). The shortest chapter is only 4 verses, while the longest is 289 verses. The number of verses is preserved intact, as has every single word in all verses, since the time of Prophet Mohammed. However, a very minor disagreement in this regard has occurred which stems from the following: Each chapter of the 114 chapters (except one) starts with the verse "In the name of Allah (God) the Beneficent, the most Merciful" which is called in Arabic bismillah verse. Because of the repetition of the bismillah verse at the beginning of every chapter, and because the numbers we use in counting the number of verses were not used then, some Muslims, after the Prophet, thought that this verse, bismillah, is only an opening of the chapters and is not to be counted as part of the total count of the number of verses in a particular chapter. Others, however, maintained that it must be counted. The latter opinion is more logical, since the bismillah verse is indeed a verse and therefore cannot be left out of the verse count. Accordingly, the verse count that we are adopting here is that which counts bismillah as the first verse of each chapter in which it appears, the only exception being chapter 9, the reason for which is not pertinent to the discussion at hand and is connected to an entirely different topic. In this article the verse number will therefore include "Bismillah verse" as verse number 1. Therefore, for example, if I state a verse in the Quran about water, which is usually cited as chapter 24, verse 45, it will instead be referenced as 24:46, in order to be more logical and consistent. The verse of Sirius (Al—Shiira) and the catastrophic collapse of a star. In verse 50 of a chapter 53 named "Al-Najm" (the star), it is stated that: "And He (God) is the Lord of Sirius".

The first scientific sign we deduce here is from the number of the verse —50—which we found to be an implicit indication to the revolution of Sirius' system of 50 years. This has a support from another "fact behind number" also now well-known in the Quran. In Chapter 57 called "The Iron" and in verse 26, God reminds humans of His graciousness to them in "sending down iron which has an immense strength and benefits to humans". We all know the significance of the number 26 to Iron, in that it is its atomic number, which is unique for each element! This is the only place where the word Iron is mentioned in the Quran, other than the chapter's title, where this verse occurs. We also know that

57, the chapter number, is the atomic weight of one of the isotopes of iron. This same verse is also indicative of the fact that iron is the most stable element in nature, since it is the end point of nucleosynthesis in stellar cores! In the opening of the chapter "The Star", God swears by "the star when it has collapsed". By studying this verse within the context of the whole chapter and from many correlations in the Quran, it has become obvious that the collapsed star relates to Sirius, mentioned in verse 50 of the same chapter! Sirius, of course, harbors in its system the collapsed star, which was discovered only in the last century, which has since been known as Sirius B, or simply the companion of Sirius, the technical details of which were discussed above. The binary stellar system has two risings and two settings: In the Quran Chapter 43, "The Ornaments" and in verses 37-40, God warns that "...he who will become blinded to our words, We shall attach to him a devil as a companion, who will detract them from the right path whilst they think they have been going straight, until when he [that is, the blinded one who became the devil's companion] shall come to Us, he shall wish that the distance between him and his companion would have been as the distance between the two rises (sun-like rises). That day there will be no avail for them. They will share the same punishment". Two rises, and two sets, certainly occur in the horizons of planets—habitable or not—in a binary star. Therefore, the distance between the two rises is an expression of the distance between the two stars in such a system: the source of the two rises.

Previously, scholars of Islam interpreted the two rises as the rises of the sun in its solstice points, among a few other explanations. Such an interpretation is falsified in that: the devil and his companion, though having similarities, are no doubt two different entities. So, the source of the two rises must be two and not one, a condition only two stars can fulfill, but not one like our sun. God is "the Lord of the two risings and Lord of the two settings" as stated in verse 18, of the chapter "al-Rahman" (the Merciful). In studying the verse of Sirius and the above mentioned verses, I came upon a very important fact in that most verses in the Quran bearing the numbers 18, 39 and 50 usually have meanings related to the verse of Sirius and the "two rises" verses. Furthermore, the word "companion" or expressions meaning "double" appear in many verses numbered 18, 39 and 50. For example, in verse 50, chapter 51 it is stated that "We have created pairs of everything". In conclusion, the two rises are an indication of the existence of planets—likely habitable—in binary star systems, in general. However, in particular, they imply the existence of a planet in the Sirius system, likely a habitable one, though with life on it being extinct due to the collapse of Sirius B. In the next section, I will discuss my reasons for this astonishing conclusion.

Extrasolar Planets and the ETs of Sirius

The plurality of earths in the Universe is explicitly stated in many verses of the Quran. Verse 13 of chapter 65, "The Divorce" says: "It is God who has created seven heavens and of the earth their like. His command circulates among them so that you will know that God is most able to do anything, and that God has encompassed everything with His unlimited knowledge". The seven earths are understood here as belonging to the same group, like a cluster or the galaxy and by no means stands for the number of Earths (habitable planets) as being only seven; there may be millions upon millions of them spread throughout the Universe. Moreover, creatures (*dabbah*)—whose life is dependent on water are mentioned in the Quran as being dispersed in heavens and earths. In the Chapter 42, "Al-Shoora" (the Counsel) God says in verse 29: "of His signs is the creation of the Heavens and Earth (the Universe) and of whatever creatures ("dabbah") He has dispersed in them". Dabbah is defined in another verse (Chapter 24:46) in the Quran where it states that God has created every dabbah from water...". This in turn excludes the angels and jinn from this definition. The Sirius verse, "and He who is the Lord of Sirius", is sandwiched between two groups of verses, each of which has a collective meaning of God's Lordship of living and cognitive creatures there. However, from the second group, one can conclude that such creatures were destroyed, receiving the same type of fate as the humans on earth—indicated in the verses that deal with the tribes of Aad, Thamud, the people of Noah and the people of Lot.

Other correlations of the existence of an extinct inhabited planet of the Sirius system are drawn from the many verses of similar numbers as the verse of Sirius and the verses of the "two rises" (numbers 18, 39, 50). Of particular interest is the civilization of "Aad" in which its destruction is described, directly following the verse of Sirius. Also in many other related verses (having numbers, 18, 39 and 50). "Aad" is distinctively mentioned. From these correlations I have concluded that the collapse of the Sirius companion into a white dwarf and thus the destruction of its habitable planet could likely have occurred at the time of the civilization of "Aad". One of these verses that clearly supports this notion says: "We destroyed Aad, Thamud and the people of ar-Rass and many civilizations in between." (verse 39 of the chapter 25, Al-Furqan). It is well-known that those civilizations were consecutive and contiguous to each other in time; so here on our planet very few other civilizations existed between the time periods stretching from the rise of Aad to the demise of ar-Rass, thousands of years ago. This being the case, the only meaning that can be attached to those civilizations stated as being "many" in number, could not have been a reference to those civilizations on Earth at that time, because many not many existed. However, because of the relevance of this verse to the verse of Sirius and the fact that Sirius has been chosen to be mentioned in the Quran as a sample of the countless stars in the Universe, then those "many civilizations" destroyed must be a reference to the many civilizations on the planet of Sirius, which ended with the collapse of one of their two stars, that is, the collapse of Sirius B.

A clue to the Red Sirius Mystery

All of this gives credence to the ancient records which has Sirius recorded as a "red star". Such information, on Sirius being red, need not be firsthand, as a result of observations corresponding to the specific epoch when they were recorded. Rather, such a stellar description could have probably been passed on from one civilization to another, until it reached Ptolemy in the second century. So, what about Aad? Aad is the first major civilization that flourished right after Noah's flood. This was a massive, though localized catastrophe, according to the Quran, that happened thousands of years ago. Aad is said to be buried under the sand dunes of the "Empty Quarter" in the southeast Arabian peninsula. One of their cities, "Iram" is described in the Quran as follows: "Do you not consider how your Sustainer dealt with the tribe of Aad, and with the many columned Iram, the like of which had not been created in the cities before." (Quran 89:6) An almost prehistoric civilization described in such an enigmatic way creates its own intriguing mystery! Recent excavations in Oman revealed a site named "Ubbar" which many wrongly assigned to the city mentioned in the Quran. Although "Ubbar" could have been a site in the domain of Aad, it does not seem to fit the majestic Iram. More thorough excavations are needed to reveal the true identity of the 'Aadites'. Indeed, discovering Iram would certainly validate the story of the Quran, for no other ancient record has ever mentioned Aad, including the Old Testament, other than the discovery in 1970's of an ancient Sumerian clay tablet excavated from the site of an ancient city called Ebla, in which it is recorded that the people of Ebla traded with a city called Iram, some 4,500 years ago. This Quranic correlation was first reported in *The National Geographic Magazine*, December 1978, "Ebla", (pages 730 to 759) and is not known to have existed in an any other literature or writings in the world, other than the recently discovered Eblan tablet. If Iram itself is ever discovered, it would be indeed amazing to find tablets that bore information relevant to Sirius, which many of the ancient Arab tribes used to worship! And if we ever visit the Sirius binary star system, will we find the remnants of the civilizations on that long extinct planet?

Postscript by Nadeem Haque

I have had many hours of discussion with Basel Reyahi. One of my aims has been to get his work translated into English; until this happens readers who do not know Arabic will have to be content with his concise though brief edited summary, concerning the main points/discoveries.

After reviewing his evidence carefully, I have come to the conclusion of its veracity and add the following points, that have been discussed with Basel: This is what may have transpired: On the Planet orbiting Sirius B, the civilizations worshipped the stars and not the One God and became corrupt, much like the Arab tribes who worshipped Sirius A and, at the time, Sirius B, which was not a white dwarf and would have been visible. These civilizations got destroyed at the same time: the ones on Earth and the ones on the planet of Sirius B. The evidence for some Arab tribes worshipping the two stars comes from the verse 51 of Surah (Chapter 16) where it was said:

16:48 Have they not considered how the shadows of everything Allah has created incline to the right and the left, totally submitting to Allah in all humility?

16:49 And to Allah alone bows down in submission whatever living creatures exist in the rest of the Universe and on the Earth, as do the angels—who are not too proud to do so.

16:50 They are conscious of their Lord above them, and do whatever they are commanded.

16:51 And Allah has said, "Do not take two gods. There is only One God. So be in awe of Me alone."

> 16:52 To Him belongs whatever is in the rest of the Universe and the Earth, and to Him alone is the everlasting devotion. Will you then fear any other than Allah?

Therefore, the Quran not only refers to the happenings on our planet but on another planet too! Note what Basel had pointed out about the themes of ET life being described in verse numbers associated with verses number 50!

Generally, those who are atheists do not like to acknowledge the destruction of civilizations (in any manner) as pertaining to calamities sent by God, but the Quran speaks of such destruction in the past after a rejection of the prophets in corrupt and severely unjust societies, in addition to the general decay brought about *gradually* by moral disintegration, wars etc., but this topic is for another book!

Chapter 5

'Religious' and Philosophical Implications of Life on other Planets

The Status of Extraterrestrial Intelligence

If there are other entities on far-flung planets, are there any with life as intelligent as we are, or at least do they have the potential to be intelligent in the way we are? Surprisingly, the Quran (17:70) does not state that we are the topmost species in the realm of the Universe in our overall attributes, intellectual and/or physical:

> And indeed We have honoured the children of Adam, and We carried them by land and sea. We have provided them with wholesome things, having specially favoured them above many of those whom We have created.

Yes, favoured "above many" but not all! Perhaps this verse is among the most overlooked in the Quran. It is here explicitly implied that there may be at least one, but likely many other species superior to us in these respects. In fact, the term *ashraf al-makhluqat*, as many Muslims erroneously apply to human beings (highest form of creation), by assuming it is the view of Islam, is a self-aggrandizing false concept—it is totally human-centric; it is like someone being Eurocentric, Asiacentric etc. It is frog-in-the-pond thinking, where the frog only knows of its pond in the garden, oblivious to the existence of other bodies of water on the vast Earth. Therefore, we can see from the Quran, that not only are there advanced forms of ETs, but many types would be superior to us in ways we do not know of at present; however, there would indeed be the 'free-will' class of species scattered across the Universe, we being one of them. In the Quran 13:15 categorically states that throughout the Universe there are those who either obey or deviate in matters of belief, which also then implies that they would likely have parallel developments on their respective planets, as on ours.

Chance or Intelligence[43]: Are there Alien Muslims?

Can ETs be Muslims. Indeed, what or who is a Muslim in the first place? Studying this subject is a great and perhaps the ultimate way for both Muslims and non-Muslims to understand "who is a Muslim"? In order to fully answer this question, we need to examine the Universe and Nature itself. This Universe, indeed, displays a remarkable vista of order and consistency. We can observe, for example, the great regularity with which the celestial bodies follow precise orbits, and marvel at the way in which water from the seas is brought to the land by wind-driven clouds, which are in turn formed by the evaporation of water: without this replenishment, life would be impossible. We are also amazed by the migration patterns of many species, including newborn eels, relentlessly trekking through thousands of miles of ocean, to nestle in their own local streams, and of bees, who use sunlight for navigation in their quest for nectar. We may ponder as to why all things exist, stabilize, join, split or procreate with functional parity manifested on various levels, and contemplate on the optimality of the processes which comprise the whole Universe. Even incredibly minute changes would disrupt the balances in nature: after all, had the Earth's orbit been slightly offset in either direction, water and the resulting forms of life would not have emerged. In fact, we can observe and are awed by the great unity in the laws of the cosmos; through the spectrum of life and non-life ranging from the microcosmic subatomic particles to the macrocosmic expanse of the Universe itself, integration is manifested on, and between, every level. Reflections may lead us to pertinent questions: Could such encompassing order have arisen purely by unintentioned accident? Or could there be an intelligent originator to this spectacular array of living and non-living form — a designer that may have developed or evolved them through processes which have yet to be fully determined? What conclusions are evidential? Is it probable that all the letters on this page unscrambled themselves by chance to form these meaningful and structured sentences? How then, could a human being— with ears, eyes and a mind— have been formed by chance? Is it credible that such a vast Uni-

---

43 Here I am incorporating one of my most well-known articles: *Chance or Intelligence?* It is the first published article I ever wrote, printed in 1989, for University of Toronto's ANALYS' (group's) distribution purposes, from where my 'writing ventures' began! Minor revisions were made over the decades; this article is now spread all over the internet. Its first version with a mathematical appendix was published by the OIC (Organization of Islamic Conference) in their Journal: *Islamic Thought and Scientific Creativity,* by COMSTECH, in 1990.

verse with an inestimable billions of galaxies could have evolved by accident? Does not the integration and complexity of a single cell far exceed that of a mere piece of paper with some intelligible writing on it, let alone this Universe and all that it contains? Especially since the Universe also contains this piece of paper! We know that we are not the cause of ourselves, for embryonic development is organized and directed in stages under natural laws. But directed by what and by whose laws? Chance or Intelligence?

What about a multiplicity of infinite beings? Could such have been responsible for this cosmological fabrication? Would not the resulting state of this Universe have then been disordered and chaotic due to the conflicting commands of these infinitely powerful entities, who would have been trying to accede to the throne of authority in rivalry? Indeed, in such a regime, we would expect to see inconsistency in the Universe as opposed to consistency. Instead of rain, we might conceivably have received a heavy downpour of elephants from the skies. Indeed, an umbrella would certainly not be terribly useful in such a Universe! Such a scenario would also give rise to the question: which of the infinite beings came first? And why? On the other hand, if such a multiplicity of infinite beings were in perfect agreement for all time, then there would not be any need for more than one — nor is there any evidence. If our response to the chance (unintentioned creation) and multiplicity (creation by two or more beings) hypotheses is negative, then our answer has to lie between zero and two. In other words, there can only be one unique governing intelligence — unique by the virtue of having no demigods, intermediaries, mystical incarnate beings, or any other human or nonhumans, as associates. This vast singular intelligence, then, must have created and developed all living and non-living things, as well as all particles/energy and time itself, and must therefore be independent of these. If this is our conclusion, then it means that the myriad forms of matter and energy as well as the physiological structure of the human being must be subject to the natural laws of this singular and independent governing intelligence. In addition to this involuntary physiological dependence of human beings to the prescribed natural laws, we are also endowed with a mind which has the capacity to voluntarily question and reason. A reasoning person would be naturally drawn to the logical conclusion of the existence of a unique originator, and therefore of a meaningful purpose to this existence. Such a person would live in full cognizance of this awareness, in peace with himself or herself and the rest of nature. Indeed, reasoning persons do indeed live, and have been living throughout the ages, in all parts of the world. They can be found dwelling in the midst of exuberant jungles or in our large, populous and crowded cities. They may even exist on earthlike planets, in the far reaches of our ever-expanding Universe. Such a people in any language would best be described, in a word or a sentence, as those who are in *voluntary peaceful submission* to this unique Intelligence, brought about by the proper use of the intellect, be that language, English, Japanese, Arabic, Swahili, Russian, a thousand other earth languages, or those used by possible sentient beings in the rest of the galaxy.

It must be realized that this system is universal and rational and in no way has tenets not based on evidence, the prime evidence of which is considered the Universe, the prime revelation. What would distinguish such individuals from the rest, be they Earthlings or Non-Earthlings, would be the employment of reason and evidence as the foundation for life. Such persons, in one Earth language, would be *Muslims* (i.e., those in voluntary peaceful submission). Consequently, if these extrasolar worlds do have or have had prophets, that is, Muslim exemplars, then they must have, or have had, revelation. To underscore the exposed evidence for extraterrestrials in Islam, here is a tafseer (commentary) on the Quranic Surah ayah 65:12 by one of the closest and most trusted companions of the Prophet Muhammad, Abdullah Ibn 'Abbas. When questioned about this verse:

> Ibn 'Abbas said: If I tell you its details, you would disbelieve, meaning you would reject it. (Then he said:) There are seven earths, and every Earth has a prophet like your prophet, Adam like Adam, Noah like Noah, Abraham like Abraham, and Jesus like Jesus. (Quoted by al-Suyuti in his al-Durr al-Manthur, 5:581-582).

Is there someone out there in the vast reaches of space, on a bluish-green or other shaded dot circling a lonely star or a binary star system, writing an article that refers to *us* as the extraterrestrials and discussing who is a Muslim? It is indeed something to ponder about!

In summation: Islam is universal and timeless—a person who believes in:

1. One God.

2. The hereafter (or is cognizant of accountability to God)

3. Does good deeds based on being conscious of #1 and #2

is a Muslim, that is, one in peaceful voluntary submission to a nonanthropomorphic God. This means that there could be an alien living in a forest on a planet circling the Trappist Star system who believes in all the above, who is a Muslim.

Note that Prophet Muhammad is only "**A** mercy for the worlds"— not "**THE** mercy for the worlds". If there are trillions upon trillions of other Earths, then there would be trillions upon trillions of 'Final Prophets', like Prophet Muhammad. Prophet Muhammad is only the Prophet for Earth—the final one. To realize this, one must broaden one's thinking. Any absolutely true system that is claimed to be revelatory and applicable to all advanced entities in the Universe as well must possess five properties which we discuss below:

Universality

Clearly, an ideology which is historically or graphically bound is not as good as that which applicable to all human beings, irrespective of the time and place of their origin. In principle the principles of such a belief system must be universal and applicable to any creature on any planet on any planet in any galaxy.

Timelessness

Since truth is timeless, those belief systems that espouse that one must believe in a Saviour who appeared on earth at a particular time, or else one will be cast into hell, by not being 'saved', have the problem of being time-bound belief systems that are unjust or redundant. They are unjust because they differentiate a person's salvation prospects by 'accident of birth'. If one were born prior to the Saviour's appearance, then how would one know the Saviour, in order for one to be saved? Indeed, we would have a perfectly valid excuse on the Day of Judgment for our ignorance. On the other hand, if it is not necessary to believe in such a Saviour, then such a Saviour becomes redundant, at least in this respect. Therefore, timelessness must be a property for any true belief system. This problem is literally an insurmountable ogre for Trinitarian Christianity if ET life is found. However, Islam's timeless nature is commensurate with the possibility of alien life.

Uniqueness

The truth must be unique and so must that belief system based upon it. From the example of timelessness, many belief systems espouse irrationality and ask one to 'believe' by adopting blind faith. As a result, they cannot give a reason for their beliefs, which they say are not based on reason, and if they do try to, they contradict themselves at the very outset, by giving reasons why one cannot use reason. All such belief systems therefore suffer from the timelessness problem, that leads to the uniqueness problem, which they all share or have in common. In other words, they are all non-unique in their irrationality The result of this is that they cannot attack other belief systems at their foundation because they will be undermining themselves, and therefore exposing the un-substantiability of their own belief systems.

Label-lessness

A truly universal belief system must also possess the property of **label-lessness.** In other words, it does not depend on labels, but seeks to go to the proper methodology as described above, by going to the essence of whether our belief encompasses the above criteria and indeed whether one is following these criteria in one's behaviour. This also goes for the label "Islam" or "Muslim"; merely using such a label does not mean that one is following the pristine rationality that these words imply, or following the peaceful and just behaviour that such a belief demands. ETs following the Creator's principles would be in voluntary peaceful submission to God, which is the meaning of the word *Muslim.*

Rationality (The Foundation)

We can see that the true belief system must possess **rationality** at its core as all these tests demand. However, one can only use rationality if one is sincerely seeking the truth and not bound by vested interests. One cannot be irrational and realize the true belief system if what one is adhering to is not: consistent, authentic, comprehensive, universal, timeless, unique, label-less and rational. And it is these attributes that lend Islam proper's credibility to being literally a universal belief system, that is literally cosmic in its extent, incorporating all planetary civilizations—the trillions of them, that exist in this Universe, at the same and various stages of development. The laws of cause and effect and *the mizan* (the balance) would be operative on any planet and therefore would have to be upheld.[44]

---

44 Haque, Nadeem; Masri, Al Hafiz B.A., and Banaei, Mehran. (2021). *Ecolibrium: The Sacred Balance in Islam*, Beacon Books, Manchester.

Major World Religions and Advanced ET

Hinduism, Daoism, Jainism and Buddhism do not come even close to explaining 'Earths' and life on these worlds, like the Quran, but they do not face such problems as Trinitarian Christianity, if such life is ever found. A Christian evangelist (Ken Ham) has said:

> The Bible, in sharp contrast to the secular worldview, teaches that earth was specially created, that it is unique and the focus of God's attention (Isaiah 66:1 and Psalm 115:16). Life did not evolve but was specially created by God, as Genesis clearly teaches. Christians certainly shouldn't expect alien life to be cropping up across the Universe.

But if any belief system believes that salvation lies in a person X, then the system becomes non-timeless and non-universal and therefore it cannot be true, as discussed in the previous section. A Christian priest and physicist (a personal friend of mine) has stated when confronted with the issue of extraterrestrial life with sentient 'free willed' ETs, that: "For an omnipotent, omnipresent and omniscient God Creator it would not be an issue to either provide redemption to extraterrestrials if necessary, or perhaps there might be no necessity for redemption because the extraterrestrials, unlike us terrestrials, never fell into sin." There are several major problems with this view that we cannot gloss over: If redemption is provided without Christ, then Christ is redundant in this matter. If ETs (have choice) and do not sin then they are infallible, which does not solve the problem; how come only on one planet out of perhaps trillions upon trillions are there entities that commit 'sin'? If they are infallible what was the point of creating them in this type of Universe (it would not be a test, as they would be unable to commit 'sin').

I call belief systems such as Trinitarian Christianity 'exclusive club' belief systems because they ask you to believe in a specific person or persons as God or gods (or god-men), born on Earth. They fail the test of universality and timelessness of belief because they ask you to believe in local and timebound entities. *New Scientist* quotes Arizona State University physicist/astrobiologist Paul Davies, who claims that finding life in space would cause problems for Christians:

> They believe that Jesus came down to earth to save humankind—not dolphins, Neanderthals or extraterrestrials. To make sense of this, either

you need multiple incarnations or a reason why this planet and this species was singled out for special attention.

In 2008, BBC World Service approached Paul Davies, the renowned cos-
mologist/physicist because they were preparing a program on the impact of the
potential discovery of advanced ET life in the cosmos. Davies suggested that
they contact me concerning the Islamic perspective on this subject. I was con-
tacted and the BBC producer told me at the outset that my interview would
not be aired but that they would include the discussion we would have on the
phone, on the subject, when presenting the Islamic perspective. Here is the
email initially sent:

> Dear Nadeem
>
> I'm working on a documentary about the search for life on other planets and
> what implications this would have for the world's main religions. Whilst doing
> research for this I came across your essay/ talk 'Extraterrestrials in Islam'. Would I
> be able to call you some time please to talk about the issues you discuss?
>
> And please can you tell me where you are based?
>
> With best wishes,
> Janet Ball, Producer, 'Heart and Soul', BBC World Service.
> Email sent to Nadeem Haque at 8/27/2008 at 1:47 PM

About two years earlier (Tue 2006-03-14 11:12 PM) the Physicist Paul Davies and I had corresponded with each other on this topic:

> Dear Nadeem,
>
> Your analysis of the status of extraterrestrial beings in Islam is a welcome
> addition to a much neglected topic. I regret that you were discouraged
> from delivering your paper in Islamabad, because I think it is clear that
> Christianity is indeed more vulnerable than Islam on this issue, and that
> makes the discussion all the more interesting and important. In fact, I
> was debating this very point last night at a meeting with the Bishop of
> Durham. Probably you are aware of my article "ET & God" in the Sep-
> tember 2003 issue of Atlantic Monthly. I was able to make only passing
> reference to Islam (and I used the quote from the Quran "And among
> His Signs is the creation of the heavens and the earth, and the living crea-

tures that He has scattered through them."), largely because of my igno-rance, so the information you have sent me is very welcome.

With regards,
Paul Davies
Australian Centre for Astrobiology
Macquarie University
New South Wales
Australia 2109

In the interview, I was asked if I would accept factual scientific findings over the Quran because Janet said that they had interviewed a Buddhist who puts science above religious belief. I replied that "Of course I would accept any scientific finding, even if it contradicted the Quran!" I then proceeded to inform them that not only is the Quran speaking of extraterrestrial life on other extrasolar planets, but that the Quran is ahead of science in many other areas, as for example in animal communication (both syntax and semantics). Sadly, before the program was to be aired, I got an email from the producer apologizing that they would not be able to speak on Islam and relay my views as they decided to focus on Christianity in the program. I listened to the broadcast later and they did indeed interview the Buddhist; there was no good excuse for not broadcasting my comments. Fortunately, Paul Davies saved the day to some extent because he stated that Christianity would have problems reconciling its belief system but there would be no problem with Islam!

A lot of other belief systems besides Christianity will be eroded by this discovery, but, in contrast, the Quran will be brought more to the forefront. It is only a matter of time. This discovery will also make us realize the affinity of all creation—not only on Earth but galaxy wide. Ironically, knowing ET will make us more human.

Further Implications

Both studying extrasolar planets and the possibility of life on them expands one's horizons and makes one think of God's creation—the plentitude of wonders. It leads to *taqwa* (God consciousness) and therefore proper mental attitude, behaviour and tranquility. It widens thinking—'racism' on Earth is meaningless when you can embrace even an entity that is sentient and not from your planet. It assists in helping us understand where we fit in nature: how special are we are, and what is the nature of the specialness: We realize that we are not at the centre of the Universe (anthropo-geocentric); and we are not chance products in a meaningless vast Universe (Copernican Principle). It leads to a theo-teleocentric view: meaning there are choice-based entities spread throughout the Universe, for whom it is a test to see who would be the most just and preserve the *mizan* (the Equigenic Principle) implying: Affinity and the Equigenic Flow[45]. It leads to an advancement of science and technology (concerning the 'sultan' (power)—towards peaceful ends, through discovery. It shows the universal and timeless nature of the Quran. It shows us how we will deal with ET life when we encounter it. The Quran provides the framework on this matter due to universality, timelessness and affinity. Also, if we do encounter ET, we will realize that their planets also have scripture like the Quran, holding the same precepts!

The Flawless Scientific Track Record of the Quran

It has been shown that the official pre-empting of the realization of extrasolar planets is around six years in terms of the conclusions published concerning their plentitude by my analysis. Why is it that we must take the Quran seriously and non-prejudicially look at the facts about the Quran without any distortions or cover-ups that are rampant, especially in the media and at universities? This next section will provide ample reasons for taking up such a stance, as we are introduced to the salient features of the correspondence between the Quran and scientifically discovered astonishing facts in other branches of knowledge.

One of the greatest philosophical conflicts in the dynamic vistas of human dialectical thought is that of the perceived incompatibility between science and religion. In the last few decades, a spate of books, articles and television documentaries have arisen, dealing with this issue as circumscribed by the Judeo-Christian tradition. Yet it appears strikingly odd and intriguingly compelling, that the general debate on such a universal theme has turned overwhelmingly into an exclusive debate between science and the Biblical account of the creation of the Universe and its multifarious processes. This has no doubt contributed to highlighting the existing variances between scientific facts and the Bible, in turn leading many people to dismiss religion in general, whilst concomitantly foster-

---

45 Haque, Nadeem; Masri, Al Hafiz B.A., and Banaei, Mehran. (2021). *Ecolibrium: The Sacred Balance in Islam*, Beacon Books, Manchester.

ing the growth of atheism and agnosticism. It seems even more odd, that such a discussion, by default, usually excludes all religions except the Judeo-Christian tradition. Yet, once this tradition is conclusively shown to be incommensurate with science46, all religions, including the initially excluded ones, are brought back into the fold of discussion and summarily tainted with the stain of scientific incompatibility.47 This is indeed a most bizarre state of affairs, especially when it emanates from those who advocate the scientific method of discovery— the very group that claims to value accuracy and objectivity.

One of these often-excluded worldviews is that of Islam, and its claimed revelatory foundation—the Quran. Muslims, however, claim that no dichotomy or chasm exists between science and the Quranic belief in monotheism. In fact, Muslims acknowledge that any book that claims to describe the creation of the Universe ought to accurately reflect the essence of the Universe in both principles and processes. It would therefore be most intriguing for the interested and contending parties to examine whether the Quranic model casts some light or indeed fresh new insights into this ongoing epistemological divide. Yet in the West, it is felt that Islam, far from being compatible with modern science, must be the underlying reason that has directly had something to do with fomenting retrogressiveness, intolerance and 'fundamentalism'. In fact, in this discourse on science and religion, Islam seems to have become unfairly excluded, since it has been misperceived to be an exclusive religion of the Arabs, emanating from a primitive and outmoded culture. However, it is not generally known that the word Islam is absolutely non-exclusive, universal and timeless, since, unlike most religions, it is not tied to a culture, nationality, race, region, personality or somebody's personal belief; rather, it is a description of a state of mind and action, linguistically denoting voluntary peaceful submission to the singular Creator, where one flows in concordance with the universal natural order of cosmic scheme (22:18). A Muslim is anyone, anywhere, at any time, who chooses to follow such ubiquitous natural laws in the realm of existence. Yet despite this misunderstanding, evolving incipiently, side by side with the resultant inordinate rejection of Islam, is an ever-growing realization among many Muslims, as well as some non-Muslim academics, that the Quran appears to be addressing

46 Bucaille, Maurice. *The Bible, The Quran and Science*, American Trust Publication, Indianapolis, 1979.
47 See the cover story written by Margaret Wertheim: "The Odd Couple: Can science and religion live together without driving each other crazy?" *The Sciences*, Vol. 39, No. 2 March/April 1999.

this age and the coming 21st Century and beyond, over and above the contents and approach found in many other scriptures.

Scientific Correlations

In the 20th Century, perhaps the greatest realization or discovery has been that the Universe has evolved from a 'singularity'—commonly referred to as the Big Bang. Indeed, it has been admitted by leading atheists, such as the late philosopher Antony Flew, prior to his embracing deism, that this point has become their nemesis.[48] This is because an origin implies that there was once 'no thing'—whatever that may mean—and that such a rude beginning borders on the now taboo or embarrassing question of 'God' or a Creator. This is not to say that many scientists have not tried to escape the dreaded 'beginning' by postulating an accidental Universe; however, their 'solutions' themselves have been highly problematic, unprovable or wildly speculative, such as: imaginary time, quantum fluctuation, multiple-Universes, infinitely cyclical Universes, etc. In fact, it appears that all the purported solutions to escape the singularity problem are haunted by the growing awareness that there appears to be intelligence embedded within the processes of the Universe. This line of thought, under the right conditions, would naturally lead to the logical question as to whether there is some connected *overall* purpose to the Universe and, concomitantly, a species such as the human being.

The verifiable fact about the Quran in this whole debate on origins, is that unlike other scriptures, in the Quran—during the depths of the Dark Ages, 1,400 years ago—it has been unequivocally recounted that the whole Universe and the Earth therein, were once, one piece and that the Creator suddenly ripped them apart and made every living thing from water (Quran: chapter 21, verse 30), that the Creator is continuously expanding the Universe (Arabic word used for expanding is musiuna, 51:47), and that the Universe has evolved to form celestial systems and the Earth, from the coalescence of dust and gas (41:11). These concepts were not realized until the 20th century, particularly after the discovery of galactic recession by red shift by Edwin Hubble in 1925.

---

48 Margenau, Henry and Varghese, Roy Abraham, *Cosmos, Bios, Theos: Scientists Reflect on Science, God and the Origins of Life and Homo Sapiens*, Open Court, La Salle, Illinois, 1992, p. 9.

Yet another branch of knowledge, among a myriad, where the Quran's correlation with science has been startling, is in the area of embryology. Although it was linguistically clear as to what was being said in the Quran, about human development before birth, by Arabic linguists, many of the verses on embryology were unconceptualizable to them, owing to a lack of specialized education in the subject. One of these intriguing verses which was queried, stated: "Read in the name of your Sustainer and Lord, who created the human from a thing which clings ('alaqa)" (96:1-2). The "clinging thing" 'alaqa is also the root word for the derivative meaning of 'alaqa which is "a leech-like structure". This is a pristinely accurate visual-cum-structural description of the embryo from day 7 to 24 when the zygote clings to the endometrium of the uterus much like a leech clinging to the skin. The University of Toronto embryologist, Professor Keith Moore, who was approached by linguists on these verses, explained, in the 1980's, that just as the leech sucks blood from its host, so too does the human embryo withdraw blood from the pregnant endometrium. By the 23rd to 24th day, the embryo has a strong physical and functional resemblance to a leech. The root meaning of the word for clinging is "alaqa", which, unfortunately, has been mistranslated into English incorrectly, as "blood clot", in many translations of Quran.

Yet another verse states that: There is a stage before birth when the human being is like a "chewed lump" (mudghah, verse: 23:14). The "chewed lump" verse was explained dramatically by Moore as follows: He made from special plasticine (imported from Japan) a shape resembling the 28-day-old embryo and then had it bitten into. When juxtaposed, the resemblance between the special plasticine model and the actual microscopically enlarged picture (on the overhead) of the 28 day old embryo, is strikingly similar, for one can observe that the structures on the embryo are the somites, which are the early stages of vertebrae; they do indeed resemble bead-like teeth marks imprinted on the plasticine model and hence the appropriate description of this stage as resembling that of a "chewed lump"—the mudghah.49 The staging of pre-natal human development was first described in 1941 by Streeter, and a more accurate system was proposed by O'Rahilly in 1972.

Another area that the Quran covers, most accurately, is geology. As geologist Z.R. El-Naggar points out concisely, "...the Quran consistently describes moun-

---

49 Moore, Keith L. *The Developing Human*, 3rd ed., Saunders Co., Philadelphia, 1992. This is the best edition, but this was before the publishing house started removing most of the discussion on Islam concerning the history of embryology, effectively censoring it, and Keith Moore did not fight back.

tains as stabilizers for the Earth, that hold its outer surface firmly lest it should shake with us, and as pickets (or pegs) which hold that surface downwardly as a means of fixation. So simply stated, the Quran describes the outward protrusion of mountains from the earth's surface, and emphasizes their downward extensions within the Earth's lithosphere, as well as their exact role as stabilizers and as a means of fixation for such a lithosphere".50 Some of the verses pertaining to these geological phenomena are: 78:6-7; 15:19; 16:15. The notion of mountains having roots was first hypothesized in the latter half of the nineteenth century, and their role in connection with providing stability to the dynamics of the lithosphere, through plate tectonics, has only begun to be comprehended since the late 1960s.

Nature of Belief in the Quran

Given these considerations, one might be led to question how these verses ended up appearing in the Quran. Historically, it must be pointed out that the undeveloped paganistic Arabic society in the 6th Century had no 20th Century notions of the Big Bang, the expanding Universe, plate tectonics and embryology, for the Quran was revealed to an illiterate Muhammad by God in the Dark Ages, and that the inductive aspect of the scientific method sprung up *after* the Quranic period. Several centuries prior to the advent of the Quran, superstitions, mysticism and a non-scientific way of explaining nature had gained a hold in most societies on earth. In this abysmal atmosphere, the Quran led untutored desert nomads and the people they came into contact with, to look into the nature of the Universe in order to fathom things, which led to a scientific revolution that helped foster the Renaissance and the Enlightenment periods in Europe. Indeed, the Muslims had learned and then further developed the thought heritages of the Ancients, and in so doing, evolved the conduction of science to new and novel heights. As medieval historian Thomas Goldstein has remarked in his book, *The Dawn of Modern Science: From the Arabs to Leonardo Da Vinci*: "Every single specialized science in the West owes its origins to the Islamic impulse—or at least its direction from that time onwards."[51]

---

50 El-Naggar, Z.R. (1991). "Sources of Scientific Knowledge: The Geological Concept of Mountains in the Quran", *International Institute of Islamic Thought*, Herndon, p. 47.
51 Goldstein, Thomas. (1980). *Dawn of Modern Science: From the Arabs to Leonardo da Vinci*, Houghton Mifflin Co., Boston, p. 99.

Methodologically and inspirationally, it was the Quran itself that led to the "Islamic impulse" that Goldstein refers to. To understand exactly why, we need to delve deeper into an analysis of the Quran itself. The Arabic word Quran literally means a book "to be read". It claims to be the complete and absolutely unaltered communication from the single intelligence that has originated and developed the entire Universe. The Muslims' claim is that if this assertion is true, then the Quran must be able to withstand, at least, the following tests: Firstly, there should be no internal inconsistencies and contradictions within its contents. Secondly, it should not contain statements that are contrary to known facts, regarding for example, the structure and function of the Universe. Thirdly, it must be linguistically clear, unambiguous, and precise. All these tests are necessary so that its contents can be objectively confirmed or refuted. Passing these tests, successfully, would indeed establish the credibility of the Quranic claim of its 'divine' origin. On the other hand, if inconsistencies and ambiguities do indeed exist, then the book in question is either entirely man-made, or might have originated from the Originator, but was subsequently corrupted by human beings. In a nutshell, this would mean that the book is not credible.

The analysis of any book, which claims to be a revelation, ought to include the most important resource accessible to us—the human intellect. It is only through the human intellect that we can confirm or negate the presence of contradictions and thereby substantiate or invalidate claims. Surprisingly, the Quran itself emphasizes that the reader subject its contents to rigorous analytical scrutiny with an objective and honest intent, in order to ascertain if there are indeed any internal or external inconsistencies (4:82). In this way, the Quran boldly and confidently challenges its readers not to take its claim of divine origin at face value, but to examine the book and always remain alert for any kind of inaccuracy, a challenge which is unequivocally open to all skeptics and those with a keen interest in scientific investigation, particularly in the area of the compatibility or incompatibility between science and religion. The claim of the challenge, even after 1,400 years, has still not been deposed, even by those who are no friends of the Muslims. More interestingly, from a scientific perspective, the Quranic proposition to find internal or external incongruity within its contents, as a way to dismiss its claim, is tantamount to a truly scientific method of falsifying invalid ideas and concepts.

In general, the aforementioned criteria may be used to test any claimed revelation. Contemporary Islamic thinkers point out that if the information contained in this book was unknown 1,400 years ago, one would perhaps be led to question its presence in so ancient a document. They ask: Does the Quran indeed withstand the tests of precision, consistency and non-contradiction? And if so, is the structurer of the Quran also the structurer of the Universe?

One certainly needs to question, where such 'scientific' verses came from? However, one thing is certain: If Muhammad did indeed write the Quran, expositing his own ideas and mindset, he would have had to have gained 21st Century knowledge regarding: embryology, cosmology, geology, ecology, archaeology, biology, sociology, anthropology, history, atmospheric sciences and cognitive sciences, whilst being deprived of libraries, laptop computers, telescopes, microscopes, universities, the internet and sophisticated databases. The Quran therefore points to the inescapable conclusion that it must be from a divine source that knows all the workings of the Universe and it is not a stretch of the imagination to conclude from this that when it states that there is life scattered throughout the cosmos, its claim must be considered seriously.

Track Record

With this track record of correspondence between newly discovered scientific facts and the Quran, will the Quran then turn out to be true concerning ET life? This is something which only time will tell, but the Quran's track record is impeccable and perfect so far, on all other such scientific and for that matter, historical matters. I leave this to the readers to ponder upon.

The Exploration of Space: A Quranic Imperative

Traveling to the Stars: The Quran views of Exploration

In the Quran, in numerous places it is exhorted that we ought to study the origins and processes in nature. In relation to space travel in the Quran, it is stated:

> O assembly of jinn and humans! If you are able to traverse the regions of the cosmic systems and the Earth then do so. You cannot do so unless you have the power (*sultan*) [i.e., root s/l/t—power, authority etc.; some form of adequate propulsion]. (55:33).

In this chapter we shall briefly examine some 'propulsion possibilities' for interstellar travel.

Rockets and Non-Rockets

Basically, rockets carrying propellants (chemical based)—action rection (Newton's Third Law). Several modes of space travel have been offered so far:

Rockets

Fusion: Still trying to obtain fusion—30 days to Mars instead on months.
- Intergenerational craft: Maybe nuclear powered, only a small fraction of light speed but much faster than current spacecraft.
- Matter/Antimatter: Not enough knowledge—storage problems for antimatter and energy; a huge amount of energy is required.
- Plasma: Ongoing research.

Non-Rockets

- Em-Drive: Based on microwaves. Yet to be proven; you need a net directional force and although claims have been made that this is produced, it is not very clear at this stage if this is accurate or that enough power can be summoned.

- ☐ Alcubierre: This is sheer fantasy! This deals with manipulating space, but as I showed with M. Muslim on physics unification, there is no such thing as curved space.[52]
- ☐ Solar sails: Pressure (using Newton's second law: F=ma) on the sails through lasers. This is a new initiative (breakthrough Starshot) to send very small probes with sails at 20% of light speed to the Alpha Centauri/Proxima Centauri system—take photos and other measurements on passby—would reach there in 20 years. Eventually, larger solar sail-based craft with human beings could be developed. The closest star to us, Proxima b, has a planet in its habitable zone. The challenge posed by the funder and initiator of this project, Yuri Milner, who was fifty-six years old at the start of this project, is to reach Proxima b within his lifetime. The Alpha Centauri system that comprises three stars, is 4.37 light years from Earth.
- ☐ Special craft based on new physics (the spacecraft material itself is the propulsion that can be activated/deactivated to move the craft)—in other words the construction of light-based structures—based on the true understanding of how light works and new concepts on the unity of physics: physical concepts need to be worked out through experiments—not achievable any time soon. The light-based composite structure would move at the speed of light in vacuum. This concept was introduced by M. Muslim (my co-author concerning the unification of physics, referenced earlier).

There are many problems associated with long duration space travel that must be overcome for human beings that would affect human physiology and psychology, either adversely or fatally. Firstly, there are issues concerning thrust—you can have either high thrust-short time, or low thrust-long time: but with much lower than light speed in vacuum, and unless you had intergenerational spacecraft, it would not enable us to reach even the nearest stars in tens of thousands of years. Intergenerational craft would pose their own insurmountable challenges of sustainability of energy, society, psychology etc., unless only a few generations were involved which means that the craft would have to be

---

52 Oppong, Nana; Haque, Nadeem. (2025), *Microbits: A New Unified Physics*, Optagon Publications Ltd.

travelling at a large percentage of the speed of light (c). However, the Quran encourages us to explore the regions as an assembly (that is, as teams of human beings) but states that there are physical barriers within space to overcome (Quran 55:35). This verse is akin to other passages in the numerous Quran that encourage us to explore and see the wonders of God's creation, the origin of things, and also the rise and fall of civilizations. As discussed in Chapter 4, the ETs of Sirius had a civilization that was destroyed. If we were to find the planet circling Sirius B that had ruins on it, that would be part of this exploration, and other Quranic verses beckoning us to see the demise of nations in history. How amazing that would be! It would be a new field of exo-archaeology. Unfortunately, a full appreciation of this will not be possible until we physically reach the stars and therefore instead of spending trillions of dollars destroying each other on Earth, like fools, a better way to live would be spending our resources on making such discoveries that bring us closer to God.

Here are some radical predictions or possibilities: the Apha and Proxima Centauri system has no habitable planets. The closest habitable planet almost exactly like us, with its ETs resembling us like twins, will take at least 1,000 years of technological development to reach, due to the vast distance involved. We predict that a planet, call it Planet Y exists just past our own solar system and at a farther distance than generally predicted for Planet X, that is, its distance may be from 700 billion to 900 billion km from the Earth, where Planet Y is orbiting the sun, even at that distance. Based on the recent shocking discovery, by the Voyager 2 spacecraft, of the 'Wall of Fire" outside the bubble of our Heliosphere that has temperatures ranging from 30,000 to 50,000 Kelvin at Heliopause, it is entirely possible that at the suitable distance (i.e. 700 to 900 billion km or 5,000 and 6,000 AU), respectively) there is life on Planet Y that is supported by heat from the Wall of Fire or Field of Fire (plasma) and protected from harmful particles by its own shield (like our Earth is). Planet Y would therefore be near the inner side of the Oort Cloud region, drawing energy from the Field of Fire where there is a balance between hot and cold and water can form, which carbon-based life needs. With the development of anti-gravity, using up to three rotary discs creating counter-fields canceling gravity, we may be able to reach Planet Y in 270 days at 10% of the speed of light. The craft should be able to go through water, if it is a water planet. In addition, we must embrace the idea of transition planets, as for example smaller bodies near Planet Y that can serve as acclimatization zones or stopping zones on our journey. If the hypothesized heat from plasma aided life on Planet Y is found, it will revolutionize our concept of 'habitable' zones. Intelligent life like ours with 'souls' would exist on Planet Y, but they would be very different in appearance to us. All this remains to be seen with the possibility of discovering Planet Y within the next 13 years with the development of new observational technologies! That there may be a large planet near or at the edge of the Oort Cloud is a possibility that is currently being considered.[53]

53 Raymond, S. N., Izidoro, A., Kaib, Nathan A. (June 2023). Oort cloud (exo)planets. https://arxiv.org/abs/2306.11109

Chapter 7

Uniformity of Laws in the Universe

In the Quran the origin of the Universe is described in the Big Bang. Furthermore, the second part of surah 65, verse 12 implies that once life on other planets is found it will be seen that a uniformity of laws applies, which in and of itself is not surprising, as one does not expect the laws of the Universe to be different in different places. Specifically, it states: "...the command descends between them so that you may come to know that God has control over all things, and that God's knowledge encompasses all things." In particular, I showed with M. Muslim, that there is only one type of particle (the microbit) out of which all creation has been created (see Part 4). It is the smallest particle and all particles, matter and energy originate, and everything develops from a re-configuration and recombination of microbits. Think about this: if someone asks your age then you may legitimately ask whether they want your physical cosmological age or your personhood age. Every part of you and the questioner is 13.8 billion years old reconfigured!

The word *amr*, or command is used—singular form, in the Quran. It is just one command with all contingencies and imagination stored in the intention of that one command coming from God that has evolved the physical Universe in absolute objectless space. I showed in a Part 1 that all life originated from clay[54] in the sense that clay was the vesicle that created the RNA and subsequently DNA due to the structure of clay. I therefore showed that intelligently directed macroevolution (through genetics but not through mutations, and so-called natural selection or randomness) has occurred for all species including man. *Likewise, if the same or equivalent conditions obtain, then we would end up with similar lifeforms on the countless life bearing planets strewn across the cosmos through the same clay based/water process!* All of these would be created from DNA, but they would be perfectly adapted to their niches just as all animals and humans are on Planet Earth. Shapes, sizes, features and colours may be the same or distinct, depending on the details of the Goldilock Zone, in a manner that

---

54 Haque, Nadeem. (2009). *From Microbits to Everything, Beyond Darwinism and Creationism, Volume 3: The Evolutionary Implications*, Optagon Publications Ltd., Toronto.

the animal communities on other planets would be configured to maintain the balance—*al-mizan*. What I mean by this is that you do not need a star exactly like the sun and a planet the same size and distance from that sun to produce life. Certainly, statistically there would be many which are the same or similar in these statistics, but others would be much different but not to the extent of not being based on water and carbon etc. For example, the Big Bang verse is not localized—it is not talking just about the Earth but all sentient life in the cosmos, with respect to entities made of water.

The other point being made by verse 65:12 is that God is not a Tinkerer and a God-of-the-gaps. He sets laws and they automatically take care of everything right from the get-go, through pathways based on pressure forces. In this case, the get-go is the Big Bang, so configured that everything developed because of the nature of the particles and the way they were made to split. The nature of the particles produced subatomic particles and then molecules, DNA etc. These facts will become all the more obvious once we find sentient life on other Earthlike planets. Not only that, but I predict that since you need a rocky planet plus water to get carbon-based life then the way the Earthlike planets would have evolved geophysically would be the same. To realize this, we must first realize that the Quran speaks of an expanding Earth, with water emanating and coming to the surface from deep inside it.

Expanding Earth: Ergo, Expanding Earthlike Exoplanets

The Quran actually directs us to the answer of the true geophysics of the Earth: in this case, geophysical evolution, through the word *dahaha*. Firstly, *dahaha*, contrary to popular understanding, does not mean egg-shaped but to expand—in this case, spherical expansion, because the Earth is not flat but a spheroid! Understanding the word *dahaha* requires deeper knowledge of an Arabic word and also about physical reality; in fact, the 'physical reality' aspect of it should change the course on our views on the geophysical evolution of the Earth. Let us first examine the word *dahaha* in its only occurrence in the Quran. In the Quran: Chapter 79, starting at verse 27, it states:

27. Are you more difficult to create than the entire Universe that He [God] has built?

28. He expanded its size, and proportioned it,

29. He darkened its night and brought out its brightness ([i.e., all Earth evolved and revolves creating day and night]),

30. And after [that], He spherically expanded [Arabic: *dahaha*] the Earth [the planet as a whole];

31. And brought forth from inside it (Arabic word: *min*, "from a thing"] its water and its pasture;

32. And the mountains He [God] has anchored firmly;

33. A provision and benefit for you and your livestock.

The reason for the confusion concerning this word is because *dahaha* comes from the Arabic words connected linguistically to *dahaha* which refer to what an ostrich does when it takes its eggs and buries them: It creates an expansive very shallow hemispherical spherical dug-out and places its eggs in that 'structure'. Therefore, the idea of sphericality and expansion is inherent in the word, but erroneously has gotten associated with ostrich eggs; in short, the word has inadvertently gotten lumped together with the eggs, rather than spherical expansion. Let us further investigate the actual dictionary definition of this word. The reader is advised to consult the word *daha* from Lane's Lexicon of English/Arabic. Note that in the lexicon it states that the word means, in its various forms, as noted: he spread, spread out, or forth, expanded or extended. Also: "The place of the laying of eggs...and the hatching thereof of the ostrich...in the sand...because that bird expands it, and makes it wide, with its foot, or leg; for the ostrich has no [nest]."[55] Therefore, *dahaha* = something pushed (pressure applied on one side) + expanding = spherical expansion (if it is a spherical object). Saying that it means that the Earth is an egg-shaped structure, is incorrect. There is indeed sphericality involved in this, but in terms of dynamical spherical expansion only, not the static egg shape. Misdirected discussions ensue on the internet about the shape of the Earth (pear shaped and oblate spheroid). Essentially, the Earth is almost perfectly spherical but bulges slightly at the equator and other minor variances. Another remarkable word in the Quran is: *tahaha*. The word *tahaha* means spreading, which in the context of the Earth's development in the following passage means the moving away of land masses from each other, because the word means to spread something around (i.e., continental drift, though this meaning changes when we speak of an expanding Earth): "And the Earth, and by (He) who spread it." (91:6). *Dahaha* means expand and *tahaha*

---

55 Lane, E. W. (1863). *Arabic-English Lexicon*, p. 857.

means spreading. Since the Earth expanded, the expansion, in turn, caused the spreading; so that is how the words are connected. The linguistic evidence exists in the triliteral root structure of the Arabic language. In the triliteral root system of the Arabic language, each root has the base meaning upon which derivative words have evolved. However, the initial word in the triliteral root structure, in turn, has the core meaning.[56]

The letter *dal* which forms the first letter of the word *dahaha* has to do with direction (i.e. expansion is a direction outwards) whereas *tahaha* has to do with surface (so surface spreading or dispersal), because the letter 't' (*ta*)—the first letter of this word—represents surface. So that is indeed how the words are connected and explain precisely what is happening. In fact, the 'ha' part of it, based on core meaning of this one word, that is, *ha* combined with *dal* and *ta* has the added significance of something which expands and spreads with life-sustaining features; the maintenance and evolution of life. This is because 'ha' has to do with life and sustenance (for example, the word *hayat* means life (note that it starts with '*ha*')). Here, not only do we witness an amazing evolutionary process of the Earth itself, but also the miraculous nature of the Quran in terms of the language, in turn pointing to the inimitable and greatness of Allah (the One God). We see an interfusion of linguistics and physics (dynamics). In the figure below, is a simple graphical representation of the concepts to make it even clearer, hopefully!

A small point and perhaps incidental but note that in the Arabic alphabet: *dal* comes before *toi* (or *ta*) and the fact is that *dahaha* causes *tahaha*! What of the origin of the oceans? As far as the mystery of the origin of water goes, the Quran tells us clearly that it is from inside the Earth. Here the Quran is speaking about oceans, because the context is the whole Earth's evolution. That water comes from inside the Earth is underscored by the recent discovery that several times the amount of the total volume of water, in all the oceans, is present inside the Earth mixed with rock in the form of "ringwoodite": A reservoir of water three times the volume of all the oceans has been discovered deep beneath the Earth's surface.

---

56 https://linguisticmiraclebook.wordpress.com/2012/09/08/chapter2/

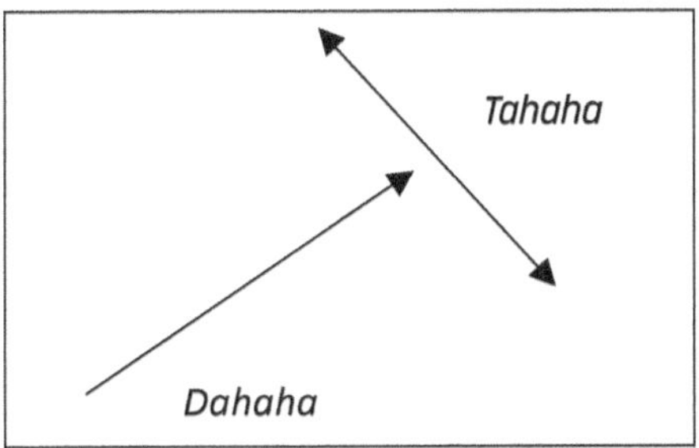

Tahaha = surficial spreading due to *dahaha*; i.e., *dahaha* = radial (directional) continental spreading Earth expansion 4.

The finding could help explain where Earth's seas came from. The water is hidden inside a blue rock called ringwoodite that lies 700 kilometres underground, in the mantle, the layer of hot rock between Earth's surface and its core. The huge size of the reservoir throws new light on the origin of Earth's water. Some geologists think that water arrived in comets as they struck the planet, but the new discovery supports an alternative idea that the oceans gradually oozed out of the interior of the Earth. "It's good evidence the Earth's water came from within," says Steven Jacobsen of Northwestern University in Evanston, Illinois. The hidden water could also act as a buffer for the oceans on the surface, explaining why they have stayed the same size for millions of years.[57]

Expanding Earth pioneer Alfred Lothar Wegener (1880—1930) was the person first known to have first hypothesized continental drift. The geologist, Samuel Warren Carey was one of the main pioneers of continental drift, but then realized the obvious truth of the expansion of the Earth, when he was reconstructing the land masses to depict/determine the details of tectonic shifts. He then converted to the expanding Earth idea. After studying this concept for many years, he wrote a book in which he summarizes his views:

> The Arctic paradox, the pleopole overshoot, the failure of the Pacific to compensate for the growth of the Arctic, Atlantic, Indian and Southern Oceans, the gross enlargement of the Pacific perimeter while its area should have been grossly shrinking, the anomalous "gape" artifact, the enigma of India's former neighbors, the thermal evidence that the conti-

---

57 Coghlan, A. (June 12, 2014). "Massive 'ocean' discovered towards Earth's core", *New Scientist*, https://www.newscientist.com/article/dn25723-massive-ocean-discovered-towards-Earths-core/.

nents have not moved over the underlying mantle [and many other problems cited by Carey]...all indicate Earth expansion.[58]

One of the reasons why the Expanding Earth model was not accepted was because the scientists assumed that an expanding Earth meant that the Earth's mass would have to increase if Earth is expanding, rather than as per Peter Woodhead's model, which in fact, is more plausible with the Quranic verse on water emanating from within the Earth; but it seemed impossible: how on Earth (literally and figuratively!) would that happen? So instead of relying on the actual fitting of all the plates at a lower diameter Earth in the past, as proved with the Expanding Earth evidence, a majority of the geologists threw the 'expanding Earth' concept out of the window! They had not considered that perhaps the mass does not change much, but only the internal configuration of the Earth changes, and more or less the same mass redistributed creates a centre of gravity locus not at the centre of the Earth, and Newton's Shell Theorem would then only be an idealization not suited to complex spheroids that have different layers of density (the mathematics/physics of this is currently under review by me), where the centre of gravity's locus is shifted outwards as in when we are dealing with complex internal layers of the Earth that have different densities.[59] Whatever the answer is, it cannot violate the obvious physical evidence of a smaller radius Earth and the Quran, which, when the language is understood, is so clear on this issue.

Hugh Owen, a geologist an Earth expansionist, states:

> The geological and geophysical implications of such Earth expansion are so profound that most geologists and geophysicists shy away from them. In order to fit with the reconstruction that seems to be required, the volume of the Earth was only 51 per cent of its present value, and the surface area 64 per cent of that of the present day, 200 million years ago. Established theory says that the Earth's interior is stable, an inner core of nickel iron surrounded by an outer layer that behaves like a fluid. Perhaps we are completely wrong and the inner core is in some state nobody has

---

58 Carey, S.W. (1988). *Theories of the Earth and Universe: A History of Dogma in the Earth Sciences*, Stanford University Press, Stanford, P. 172.

59 *Gas-Powered Planetary Expansion—Evidence And Calculations—Check The Evidence: Explaining the Expanding Earth—With Peter Woodhead Part 2*, https://www.checktheevidence.com/2015/04/14

yet imagined, a state that is undergoing a transition from a high-density state to a lower density state, and pushing out the Earth, as it expands.[60]

I would suggest, like researcher Peter Woodhead, that mass is not being increased substantially—that the Earth only is expanding. Indeed, the Quran refers it to be only expanding. Woodhead suggests a more or less constant mass and has postulated that gravity has increased over time. The frozen core heated up through radio-isotopes caused the Earth to expand: currently, this theory holds that the core is gaseous.[61] In a personal email communication with me in 2017, Peter Woodhead stated: "I have carried out weight measurements at various locations from close to the equator to Scotland, all of which confirm my hypothesis that the centre of 'mass' attraction lies at a depth of 1,800-2,000 km below Earth's surface. Further analysis on this is required."

All this boils down to the fact that the Quranic analysis and observation prove that the Earth is expanding. Analogously, this is like finding the expansion of the Universe using red shift; the implication is that once the Universe was a smaller size, even though we are not clear about the mechanics of gravity, etc. Similarly, concerning the Earth, the logical conclusion must be that the gravitational calculative aspects based on Peter Woodhead's hypothesis still need to be verified, even though we know for a fact from empirical evidence that Earth once was of an appreciably smaller radius. If all the continents (and more importantly their continental shelves) were brought together they fit almost perfectly (about a 99% fit) at a smaller volume size (radius) of the Earth, which means that the Earth has drastically expanded from to its present size over hundreds of millions of years. It is a plain fact that there are problems fitting the continents properly (there are wider gaps) if one tries to bring them together on the present sized Earth (for example, fitting Africa to South America) because we are fitting the fragmented land masses which were once one, at the wrong spherical curva-

---

60 Owen, H. 1984. "The Earth Is Expanding and We Don't Know Why", *New Scientist*, p. 27, November 22.

61 Woodhead, P. (2014). "A Mechanism for Earth Expansion", http://www.checktheevidence.co.uk/cms/index.php?option=com_content&task=view&id=394&Itemid
Woodhead, P. and Johnson, A. (2014). "Gas-Powered Planetary Expansion—Evidence and Calculations." http://www.checktheevidence.com/cms/index.php?option=com_content&task=view&id=409&Itemid

ture. Smaller Earth modelling and research has been done extensively by James Maxlow[62]: See also the late Neal Adam's brilliant animation.[63]

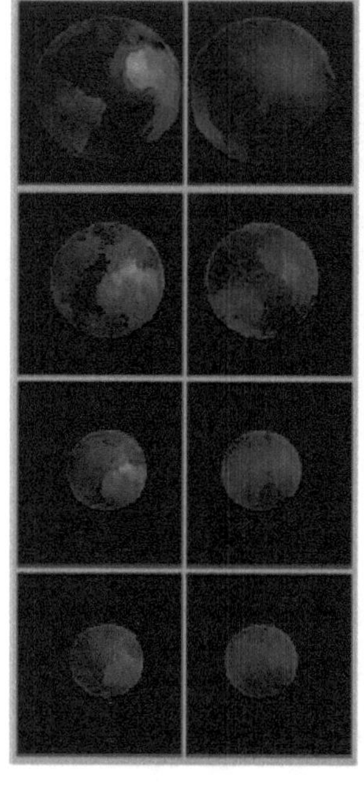

This figure depicts how all the landmasses on the earth were co-joined with no oceans at a smaller volumetric size of the Earth hundreds of millions of years ago. The form fitting is almost perfect and the probability for this to happen by chance is almost zero.[64]

Let us think logically about this concept of the Expanding Earth; indeed, we can know of the geophysical evolution's truth from logic and first principles alone, given a few empirical facts, as well as based on Peter Woodhead's concept:

1. If water did not come from outside (through comets), then it came from inside the Earth. But how?

2. Water accumulated gradually as the Earth was formed through the standard planetary process creation mechanism (gaseous and dust cloud collapsing etc.), but initially the gases that eventually formed water would have been in a frozen state. In other words, since space is 'cold' (temperature) the gases that contain hydrogen and oxygen would have been in a frozen state. Several years after this article on the Quran and expanding earth was published, a new discovery was made that goes in the direction that Woodhead postulated:

Earth's inner core (IC) is less dense than pure iron, indicating the existence of light elements within it.... Silicon, sulfur, carbon, **oxygen and hydrogen** have been suggested to be the candidates and the properties of iron-light-element alloys have been studied to constrain the IC composition. Light elements have a substantial influence on the seismic velocities, the melting temperatures and the thermal conductivities of iron alloys. However, the state of the light elements in the IC is rarely considered. Here, using ab initio molecular dynamics simulations, we find that

62 http://www.expansiontectonics.com/index1.html
63 https://www.youtube.com/watch?v=oJfBSc6e7QQ&t
64 (Artwork is by Michael Netzer)

hydrogen, oxygen and carbon in hexagonal close-packed iron **transform to a superionic state under the IC conditions, showing high diffusion coefficients like a liquid. This suggests that the IC can be in a superionic state** rather than a normal solid state. [Emphasis in bold is mine].[65]

The above quote is from the Abstract of the article and the original paper may be consulted for complete references cited in the abstract that have been excluded here.

3. The discovery cited in *Nature*, above lends credence to the following claim: Over eons, the frozen gases in the core heated up and the core then expanded through heat created by radiation (isotopes) creating outward pressure, that is, stream-like pressure.

4. This would have created an Expanding Earth.

5. The water was radially pushed upwards, by this steam-like pressure, and the interior would have become gaseous, through centrifugal forces.

6. Water then gradually 'seeped out' through cracks to form all the oceans over the eons.

7. Earth's mass has hardly changed, but since the density distribution of the Earth's layers has changed, then the 'g' (acceleration due to gravity) has changed.

8. Gravitation has, it is surmised, become 'stronger'.

There is a view that during the large dinosaur era, the Earth had less gravitation, able to support their bulk. It is hypothesized that this is why you see huge insects and large dinosaurs that would not have been able to move about properly, or at all, if the gravitational force of the Earth has remained constant; in other words, present day gravity would have made life impossible for the largest of these dinosaurs.[66]

It is obvious that the Earth has expanded because of modelling which shows it was one piece. As it expanded, continents were created. They fit from all sides,

---

65 He, Yu *et al.* (2022). "Superionic iron alloys and their seismic velocities in Earth's inner core", *Nature*, Volume 602, p. 258.
66 Hurrell, S.W. (2011). *Dinosaurs and the Expanding Earth: Solving the Mystery of the Dinosaurs Gigantic Size*, 3rd Edition, Oneoff Publishing.

whereas in plate tectonics we are led to believe that only the Atlantic sides and the Indian ocean sides grew apart and split lands into the continents we see. This is not logical. From both common sense, facts of the distribution of the land masses and the Quran, we know that the Earth is expanding and that a huge volume of water has been discovered under the Earth as a layer intermixed with rock as the source of water for all oceans; this further corroborates this Expanding Earth view. Earth's lesser gravitational field, as discussed in the previous section, would also help explain the large size of the dinosaurs and other creatures present at the time, their larger size being accommodate-able only if acceleration due to gravity was less. We can therefore see that plate tectonics is not correct from observational analysis, and natural deduction. It is not rocket science, but requires some study, observation and reflection and realizing that one cannot rely on authorities; 'authority' must be questioned. It is true that there needs to be further research to totally discount the redundancy of subduction zones, but the general idea of an expanding Earth, without (any or substantial) mass increase, which is highly implausible and has had a role in making the view less tenable, is true from logic and the Quran. Subduction zones are in fact like epicycles of the geocentric explanation of cosmology; wholly erroneous but concocted to explain discrepancies:

> All of these anomalies—the absence of subduction within Africa or Antarctica where it should be, the latitudinal extensional regime in the southern Andes when they should be under intense compression from the underthrusting Pacific slab, the nonsense of postulating the outcrop of a 7,000-km underthrust in the Peru-Chile trench...the total absence of any pre-Jurassic oceanic crust, and the stranding of the Zodiac fan in the open ocean without a sediment source—all arise by trying to compensate the observed ocean-floor spreading by subduction instead of by Earth expansion. Subduction is a myth![67]

According to the Quran then, water originated from inside the Earth, forming oceans through its expansion. I predict that all planets in the Universe that have carbon-based life on them, which need water and hence oceans, and there are trillions upon trillions of them in the Universe, undergo the same process of expansion. In other words, because of the universality of the laws, all other

---

67 Carey, S.W.(1988). *Theories of the Earth and Universe: A History of Dogma in the Earth Sciences*, Stanford University Press, Stanford, p. 187.

Earth-like planets would be expanding water planets like the Earth. According to the verse on water's origin, and the words *dahaha* and *tahaha,* all carbon based life needs water (and *dabbah* (creatures) scattered throughout the Universe are carbon-based)[68]; therefore, when such planets were formed, water came from inside them. The implication of this is that that the same (or equivalent) mechanism is applicable to all planets. This is a practical example of the Quranic passage in 65:12, which depicts that uniform laws are existent in the Universe, and the whole passage is implicative that in discovering such Earth-like planets, this fact of the "command" (*amr*) of God, will become as clear as daylight to everyone who is thinking at the time. The command descending down also implies the existence of conscious entities (based on verse...where command is associated with *ruh* (consciousness). Consciousness is a culmination of all the other processes creating life and this is what is being implied in 65:12.

Institutionalization in science gone astray

We must not be fooled by 'representations'. For example, Africa (area=30,370,000 sq. km), is around 14 times larger than Greenland (area=2,166,086 sq km), but if you ask most people they will not realize it because they are used to seeing Greenland represented on Mercator's projection where it is shown as being much larger. False visual perceptions create false conclusions, especially when they persist. Concerning plate-tectonics, why is only the Atlantic side being considered in the grand jig-saw puzzle fitting of continental drift? It's like the fallacy of Eurocentrism, where only Europe is considered as the cause of all true advancement in many fields (forgetting history). This is like Atlantic-centrism (forgetting the other side of the globe)! The other problem is the institutionalization of wrong ideas. Plate tectonics is obviously erroneous but it has now become entrenched in our 'educational system', where vested interests abound. We can see from here that confusion x confusion = multiple confusion and that knowledge of linguistics, context and physical reality is extremely important to determine the truth. If we ignore observation, basic reasoning and the Quran, we will not understand reality and will be led to the wrong conclusions. However, understanding the Quran, based logical contexual rules, will help lead to a furtherance of our understanding of this Uni-

---

68 Haque, N. and Shahbaz, Z. (Aug.-Sept 2015), "Extraterrestrials and Intraterrestrials in Islam", Nexus Magazine, Vol. 22, No. 5, pp. 55—61/82.

verse and our place in it. As humanity, we need to get our act together on these conceptual issues, non-prejudicially, for the sake of true human advancement, for truth is truth, wherever you find it, and whenever you find it!

Chapter 8

Non-carbon based sentient life forms on Earth and Elsewhere

For the sake of ontological completeness, we must bring to the attention of the readers the existence of non-carbon based entities that God has created and which are mentioned in the Quran. The Quran, considered to be a scripture of revelation, refers to other worlds and their life-forms including corporeal creatures and exotic energy beings. A new unified view of physics, informed by Quranic study, explains this diversity in terms of indivisible particles called "microbits" (see Part 4). According to the new unified view of physics postulated by M. Muslim and myself, there is no distinction between matter and energy, as all particles are groupings of microbits, e.g., quarks at a higher level; it is only the rate of motion and the composition of microbit groupings that lead to any distinction. Based on the realizations of the uniformity of laws, these entities would exist throughout the Universe and on other planets too. I call these entities Intraterrestrials (ITs). Such entities found on other planets could mind bogglingly be called Extra-Intraterrestrials (EITs).

According to the Quran then, throughout the Universe other beings exist that are not carbon or water based. Instead, they are comprised of forms of energy. Let us call this class of beings intraterrestrials, because they are present among us, unseen, according to the Quran. These intraterrestrials are of various kinds. There are the jinn, which the Quran states are made of "a smokeless flame" (*marijin*)[69], the word jinn coming from *janna* which means "he [or it] concealed"[70] (i.e., that which is hidden). There are also the angels. The word for "angels" in Arabic is *malaaikah*, and if the root word is taken as *malk* then this means "forces"—in this case, entities that act like forces but conscious forces cum-functionaries, i.e., those who follow God's commands 100 per cent[71] and with the same efficiency: they cannot make errors of any kind. Angels can move

---

69   Quran 15:27, 55:15; 7:12; 38:76.In the Quran, an entire chapter,Surah 72, is devoted to the nature of the *jinn* (the singular is *jinni*).

70   Asad, Muhammad, *The Message of the Quran*, Dar al-Andalus, Gibraltar,1980, appendix 3, p. 994.

71   Quran 66:6

around at great speeds[72] and they possess shape-shifting properties.[73] The Prophet Muhammad stated that angels are created from light (nur).[74] There are many classes of angel. Jibreel, or Gabriel, is described as a powerful entity[75] who brings revelation to humans, although in the Quran he is never mentioned as one of the angels explicitly but is singled out by the word al-Ruh, commonly translated as "the Spirit", and is accompanied by angels.[76] Angels do not have wings like those of birds—this is a remnant of mediaeval thinking—but the Quran does speak of what is usually thought of as wings (*ajniha*); however, the root meaning of this word is "sides", from the Arabic *janaha*, and the Quran speaks of them as having multiple sides.[77] In other words, this implies that angels are able to impart a directional force, using their "sides", in order to travel huge distances that can be equal to or surpass the speed of light in a vacuum.[78] They achieve this by using their will, just as we use our will to direct our limbs into walking.

On the other hand, the jinn, unlike angels, have "free will" like humans in that they can choose either to follow or to disobey the laws of God. In other words, like humans, some are obedient to God whereas others are rebellious. Iblees (the chief Shaytaan or Satan) is of the jinn[79] and became one of the rebellious ones[80] by refusing to prostrate to Adam, as commanded by God. Iblees still exists and God has given him leave to entice others onto the wrong path as a test, structuring a moral law which creates a situation where only those who believe and follow the laws of God will be secure and safe from harmful enticements.[81] In other words, it is indeed the evil among the jinn who try to seduce humans into going against the laws of God, but only those who adamantly pursue wrong temptations are led to this path.[82] Among the jinn, there are those who have the ability to move very quickly and transport objects very speedily.[83] They, like humans, have many powers and limitations and are not omniscient. For example,

72 Quran 70:4
73 Quran 15:61
74 Hadith of Sahih Muslim, vol. 4, no.7134, p. 1540.
75 Quran 66:4, 97:4, 78:38, 16:2
76 Quran 78:38
77 Quran 35:1
78 Quran 70:4
79 Quran 18:50
80 Quran 2:34, 7:12
81 Quran 38:79-85
82 Quran 72:6
83 Quran 27:39

the evil ones among them were bound by Prophet Solomon and made to work for him for a long period. In fact, they did not even realise that Solomon had died while literally sitting on his throne until a "lowly" creature on the ground ate the staff upon which he was leaning and he summarily fell to the ground.[84]

The Celestial Highest Chiefs (CHCs)

In addition to the jinn and the angels, other created entities also exist that have the capacity to choose but are neither jinn nor angels. The Quran alludes to them in two passages: "They cannot listen to the Highest Chiefs [almala-i al-aAAla] for they are pelted from every side"[85] and "I had no knowledge of the Highest Chiefs when they disputed".[86] Note that the disputation of the Celestial Highest Chiefs is an indication that they are not angels but are "free-willed" entities who have various views on issues. They are argumentatively discursive about the affairs of other entities in the Universe and God's plans, and in this way, they constructively engage each other about their individual views. This type of discursiveness is something which is absolutely not characteristic of angels, be they upper-echelon angels or not. In addition, these entities are among those referred to in 17:70, cited with respect to extraterrestrials. In other words, these are some of the beings more favoured than the Children of Adam in terms of the overall favours bestowed upon them. These entities are a type of powerful, "highly spiritual" being of the lighter microbitic particle kind who are close to God and glorify Him; they are probably engaged in serious tasks to which we are not privy. The Quran is silent about the details of these entities; in fact, most Muslims themselves are not even aware of the possibility of their existence. Not much more can be said about them other than that they converse on high matters directly with God, for, logically speaking, being the highest chiefs there is no barrier to such communication. In other words, the CHCs do not require the intermediation of archangels (such as Jibreel) for two-way conversations with God.

84 Quran 34:14
85 Quran 37:8
86 Quran 38:69

The Non-existence of Poltergeists?

It is surmised by Muslims that non-Muslims who experience poltergeists are actually being fooled by the evil and/or mischievous jinn, because according to the Quran, ghosts do not exist. When one dies, one cannot normally return due to the barzakh[87]—the barrier between the living and the dead, between this life and the afterlife.

Can a *New Unified Physics* Explain Intraterrestrials?

Can such intraterrestrial beings exist according to physics, and, if so, what would they be comprised of? Here is a very brief summary of an in depth investigation of these quranic claims, anecdotal interviews, analysis of the Quran and the Hadith (teachings and sayings of the Prophet Muhammad), and actual "field experimentation" by M. Muslim and this (Nadeem Haque). According to the new unified view of physics developed by us (refer to Part 4 of this book), there is only absolute space with particles out of which everything is comprised.[88] All particles, matter and energy are composed of the tiniest indivisible particle called the microbit. Everything is therefore a grouping and structuring of microbits, and all energy is thus defined as the effort required to move microbits. Since everything is comprised of microbits, everything in that sense is a form of energy, human beings being the slower spectrum of that energy (hence matter). In this view, particles such as quarks, electrons and photons are breakable and are comprised of smaller groupings of microbits; they are not elementary. The jinn and the angels are comprised of such smaller particles. The water/carbon-based body is cohesive due to a balance of forces and synchronisation due to photons and electrons in signaling, etcetera. The carbon-based body is also made of microbits, albeit larger and more dense groupings of them in the form of atoms, molecules, DNA, etcetera. Similarly, these intraterrestrials are also made of microbits, but are differently organised. The proof for this is from the Quran and Hadith in the following aspects: When the Prophet stated that angels were created from light (خلقت الملائكة من نور), in the *Hadith of Muslim*, in "Riyad as-Salih", 1846; Book 18, Hadith 39, what he meant was that they are made of subtle small particles, smaller than the photon. Whether the Prophet realized that light was particles and these were smaller is not known, but the statement turns out to

---

87 Quran 23:100

88 See also, Oppong, Nana, M.; Haque, Nadeem. (2025). *Microbits: A New Unified Physics*.

be interpretable this way, with accuracy. In this view, particles such as quarks, electrons and photons are breakable and are comprised of smaller groupings of microbits; they are not elementary. The jinn and the angels are comprised of such smaller particles because the word "from" (min in Arabic) can mean an extract of something (as, for example, in the case of embryology): "We created you from a *nutfatin amshajin*" (this is discussed in Part 1).[89] What is being referred to are the cells in the seminal fluid, i.e., an extract from something larger. In other words, what is extracted is part of a larger whole. As previously noted, the jinn are comprised of "a smokeless flame" according to the Quran.[90] We cannot generally see jinn and angels because our vision uses photons, and the image processing cannot occur due to the way the photons interact with the particles comprising these entities. They can increase their opacity by densifying the microbitic particles to form an exterior shell-like surface area, thus "manifesting themselves" as they did with Prophet Lot[91] and other non-prophets who were present, and then one can indeed see them in the particular form in which they choose to appear. It is because the jinn are comprised of less dense and smaller particles that the jinn see you but you do not see them.[92] Surah: ayah 24:45 of the Quran says that every *dabbah* is made from water. In other words, all the carbon-based creatures are indeed made from water. The parallel mention in 21:30, which states that all living things are made from water, refers only to those entities visible to the deniers of the truth of the Big Bang and God. That is, 21:30 refers to only carbon-based creatures as detailed in 24:45, though 21:30 would also include plants. Therefore, 21:30 excludes the intraterrestrials, since angels and jinn are not made from water but are nonetheless living beings. However, note that these intraterrestrials do not have internal organs like us, and angels do not eat food like we do.[93] Creating a manifestation for normal human vision would generate a temporary re-organisation of their structure with no internal human-like organs for processing food, etcetera. Angels are in charge of escorting the consciousness of human beings after earthly death[94], communi-

---

89 Quran 76 :2

90 It is hypothesized (by N. Haque), by analysing the words marjin, "a smokeless flame", in 55:15, and min nari l-samumi, "scorching fire [heat]", in 15:27, where it also states that the jinn['s] origin predates human beings, that the dynamic reactions occurring in intensely hot plasma produced the jinn.

91 Quran 11:77-81

92 Quran 7:27

93 Quran 11:69-70

94 Numerous sources, e.g. Quran 16 :28 and 16:32.

cating peace to the psyche of high-moral-calibre human beings[95] and even communicating in special circumstances with those who are not prophets, such as Mary (Maryum), mother of Jesus.[96] However, the door to scriptural revelation has been closed with Muhammad, the last Prophet for our Earth.[97]

Extra-intraterrestrials

Jinn can travel in space outside the Earth.[98] The angels, too, are reconnoitering all over the Universe[99] and they are therefore not limited to the Earth. In addition, according to the Quran, the destiny of carbon-based creatures is linked with intraterrestrials in the sense that the evil ones among them are prone to interact with humans by whispering evil suggestions to their minds, unbeknownst to the humans, or by direct, open communication if the humans have gained access to them. Considering the uniformity of the basic processes and plan of God, it would be safe to assume that these intraterrestrials would also be present on other Earthlike planets with the carbon-based extraterrestrials. They could, therefore, be termed, mind-bogglingly, extra-intraterrestrials!

We can clearly see from the quranic perspective that a much greater degree of diversity exists in life-forms than conventional, disunited physics and narrow modes of laboratory experiments have yielded or would have us accept. Over the last 50 years or so we have been looking for extraterrestrials outside the Earth, on distant stars, but we have become oblivious to the possibility that subtler life-forms might indeed be co-existing with us. We humans need to expand our peripheral vision and thinking to include these astounding spiritual-cum scientific possibilities if we are indeed to grow and thwart a very anthropocentric and stunted view of the domains of reality that has artificially dichotomised "scientific" and "religious" experiences.

95 Quran 41:30.
96 Quran 3:42 and 3:45.
97 Quran 33:40.
98 Quran 55:33.
99 Quran 16:49 and 53:26.

Epilogue

The possible future: With technological advancements concerning exoplanets there is bound to be a convergence between empirical evidence and the Quran, and as the Quran states, a gathering of humans and ET life at some point will indeed occur. I estimate that there is more than a 50% probability in less than 200 years, that we will encounter advanced ET life, in one way or another, and then humanity will gradually, though in an accelerative mode, change their worldview at that point: theologically, politically, ontologically and epistemologically. These will be the biggest changes other than us learning new technologies that these ETs would possess, through an exo-cultural exchange, as it were. With the transpiration of this momentous event and what will follow, the role of the Quran as part of the theological and epistemological realization will be accentuated. These things I conjecture will come to pass, but so far, the timing is known only to the Originator, and in this enthralling possibility we will have to remain. I extend peace to all sentient creation cast, as a puny Earthling, pondering on these ineluctable matters vast!

Bibliography

Asad, Muhammad. (1980). *The Message of the Quran*, Dar al-Andalus, Gibraltar,1980, appendix 3.

Banaei, Mehran and Haque, Nadeem. (1995). *From Facts to Values: Certainty, Order, Balance and their Universal Implications*, Optagon Publications Ltd., Toronto.

Brooke, John Hedley. (1991). *Science and Religion: Some Historical Perspectives*, Cambridge University Press, Cambridge.

Bucaille, Maurice. (1979). *The Bible, The Quran and Science*, American Trust Publication, Indianapolis.

Carey, S.W. (1988). *Theories of the Earth and Universe: A History of Dogma in the Earth Sciences*, Stanford University Press, Stanford, p. 187.

Coghlan, A. (June 12, 2014). "Massive 'ocean' discovered towards Earth's core", *New Scientist*, https://www.newscientist.com/article/dn25723-massive-ocean-discovered-towards-Earths-core/.

Davies, P.C.W.(1982). The Accidental Universe, Cambridge University Press, Cambridge.

Denton, Michael, film: "Privileged Species: How the Cosmos is Designed for Human Life." https://privilegedspecies.com

Denton, Michael J. (1998). *Nature's Destiny: How the Laws of Biology Reveal Purpose in the Universe*, The Free Press, London.

ESA Science & Technology - Exoplanet detection methods", *Exoplanets, ESA*, https://sci.esa.int/web/exoplanets/-/60655-detection-methods

El-Naggar, Z.R. (1991). *Sources of Scientific Knowledge: The Geological Concept of Mountains in the Quran*, International Institute of Islamic Thought, Herndon.

Goldstein, Thomas. (1980). *Dawn of Modern Science: From the Arabs to Leonardo da Vinci*, Houghton Mifflin Co., Boston.

Haque, Nadeem Masri, Al-Hafiz B.A., and Banaei, Mehran. (2021). *Ecolibrium: The Sacred Balance in Islam*, Beacon Books, Manchester.

Haque, N. and Shahbaz, Z. (Aug.-Sept 2015). "Extraterrestrials and Intraterrestrials in Islam", Nexus Magazine, Vol. 22, No. 5.

Lane, E. W. (1863). *Arabic-English Lexicon*, London: Williams & Norgate.

Loeb, Avi. (2021). *Extraterrestrial: The First Sign of Intelligent Life Beyond Earth*, Houghton Mifflin, Boston.

Margenau, Henry and Varghese, Roy Abraham. (1992). *Cosmos, Bios, Theos: Scientists Reflect on Science, God and the Origins of Life and Homo Sapiens*, Open Court, La Salle, Illinois.

Moore, Keith L. (1992). *The Developing Human*, 3rd ed., Saunders Co., Philadelphia.

Oppong, Nana, Haque, Nadeem. (2025). *Microbits: A New Unified Physics*, Optagon Publications Ltd, Toronto.

Rahim, Ata-ur. Jesus. (1990). *Prophet of Islam*, Tahrike Tarsile Quran, Inc., New York.

Woodhead, P. (2014). "A Mechanism for Earth Expansion", http://www.checktheevidence.co.uk/cms/index.php?option=com_content&task=view&id=394&Itemid

Woodhead, P. and Johnson, A. (2014). "Gas-Powered Planetary Expansion—Evidence and Calculations."

http://www.checktheevidence.com/cms/index.php?option=com_content&task=view&id=409&Itemid

Universe Today: Space and Astronomy News, "22% of Sun-like Stars have Earth-sized Planets in the Habitable Zone - Universe Today" https://www.Universetoday.com/106121/22-of-sun-like-stars-have-earth-sized-planets-in-the-habitable-zone. See also: "Nearly All Sun-Like Stars Have Planetary Systems - Universe Today", https://www.Universetoday.com/99309/nearly-all-sun-like-stars-have-planetary-systems

Wertheim, Margaret. (1999). "The Odd Couple: Can science and religion live together without driving each other crazy?" *The Sciences*, Vol. 39, No. 2 March/April.

Part 4

Physics United

Introduction

In Parts 1 and 2 we have shown how integrated the realms of biology and consciousness are to what has been eluded to as microbits. We shall be exploring a new approach to the unification of physics, a united physics or alternatively speaking 'Physics United'. 'Physics United'—this sounds like a nerd's version of the football club, Manchester United, but it also sounds like an unachievable dream! The tragic fact is that for over 100 years the scientific community has 'backed the wrong horse' and developed a disunited and incommensurate physics of the micro and macro domains, that is, Special/General Relativity and Quantum Mechanics. The inconsistencies and illogicalities in these approaches have been apparent from the outset, by many astute physicists not caught up in the hype and propaganda, and fallacies of "appeal to authority", but sadly, Einsteinian Relativity has become entrenched and institutionalized with vested interests over the multi-decades. Indeed, the popular superficial treatment of this serious and deep topic has sanctified a kind of a new holy trinity, of special, general relativity and quantum mechanics, by a new priesthood of scientists. Part of the reason is also because of the fact that, to realize that the fundamentals of these approaches are not correct one must be attuned with enough knowledge to critically engage in a meta-analysis on scientific theories. Our educational system at even the leading universities like Cambridge, Oxford, Harvard and MIT are not producing critical thinkers in this field. Ibn al-Haytham and the earlier Muslim scientific geniuses who were founders of experimentalism and inductive knowledge which spread to Europe through, for example, the Sicilian and Andalusian Universities and libraries, and were among those giants upon which the intellectual giant of the secretive Unitarian, Newton, himself stood, had a different approach. Their approach was based on the principles of the Quran, which is claimed by Muslims to be the creation of the Creator, just as is the Universe. It is argued in this final part of the book, that this sound and logical, non-contradictory approach has gone missing in modern physics, let alone other branches of knowledge, and needs urgently to be reinstated with all the advanced mathematical and computational tools at our disposal. Yet the nominal Muslim world, which continues to follow these concepts uncritically and blindly, has gone against the Quranic view of space and time which coincides with the clear thinking that unifies physics. At Western non-Muslim universities, on the other hand, the Quranic phenomenon, which was the cause of the inductive revolution as a direct causative factor, and the current Quran-Science correlations are kept hidden, shielded and misrepresented, with the result that those trying to fathom correlations between science and so-called religion remain blissfully ignorant about the truth of the situation. But for how much longer will this abysmal situation prevail? In this part of the book, the Quranic concept of space, time and the unity of reality will be delved into. Subsequently, *From Microbits to Everything* has been updated and expanded and has been published as *Microbits: A New Unified Physics*.

As a result of following the methodology of Newton, who was influenced by the methods, knowledge and discoveries of Ibn Al-Haytham, who in turn was influenced by the Quran, it is held that this new view/model for unification presented here as a summary of the book that propounds the new model (*From Microbits to Everything* v.1 and the recently published *Microbits: A New Unified Physics*), is the direct and logical consequence of the research project advanced by Newton, his predecessors and others who came after him, which has tragically become deflected for over one hundred le

years. The implications of the microbits' view in the philosophical domain with respect to the clear existence and nature of God via dispelling of the fog of confusion, due to incorrect notions of space and time, is also introduced briefly and is shown to correspond with the Quran, as an integral corollary of the new unified physics. Part 4 links therefore to Part 2 on Consciousness.

It tragically appears that the current and oldergeneration, due to institutionalization, corporatization and media-ization, has become mired in this situation of an irrational and unrealistic physics at its very foundation. This blockades the true understanding of reality, that is, the wider issues of God and the reasonand purpose of existence. Part 4 has been presented with a view to make future generations think about this issue more deeply and to be directed towards a foundationally logical path of a sounder paradigm, that corresponds with reality. The full technical details of the new concepts in physics are explained in the latest book: *Microbits: A New Unified Physics* and, where relevant, I have provided the reference to where this information can be found in this book and the earlier version.

Chapter 1

History of the Problem

For the better part of over 100 years, physicists and philosophers had been trying to understand and fathom the secrets of nature with ever greater scrutiny. As they started probing deeper, electrons were discovered and a plethora of subatomic particles emerged. With the discovery of subatomic particles, their existence and motions became part of what is known as quantum mechanics. At the same time, after the introduction of 'Newton's three laws' in Europe and the law of universal gravitation which was Newton's crowning achievement, the perplexing questions of action at a distance remained. When an object falls to the ground or is held stable in an orbit, what exactly is making it fall to the ground or revolve in an orbit? To Newton, although he mathematically obtained the universal law of gravitation, it appeared like magic and he did not have a satisfactory answer in terms of the actual mechanism or the 'nuts and bolts'; consequentially, he regarded his gravitational equation as provisional.

When Einstein claimed to have resolved the action at a distance problem, in what became known as General Relativity, there was a paradigm shift. For this, the idea of space had to take on a new meaning, just as time had taken on a new meaning with Special Relativity, earlier on. For Einstein space was bendable—bendable by masses (or more popularly called "curved space") and so the purported curving of space produced the elliptical motions in the heavens. This claimed to have solved the action at a distance problem. How and why mass in space causes its curving, even if true, was never explained and never has been. This geometrical fiction has been accepted blindly much as superstitious or mystical religion asks you to believe or buy their ideas with blind faith. So we have the astounding situation that one of the main theories in vogue is based on a kind of a blind faith religion. The late physicist Thomas Phipps was very correct when he criticized this state of affairs and characterized modern day foundational non-Newtonian physics as a religious cult, in a personal communication to me. Similarly, in order to explain the symmetrical effects of electromagnetism yet asymmetrical equations of James Clerk Maxwell in the form developed by the amazing self-taught applied mathematician, Unitarian Oliver Heaviside, in order to maintain Galilean relativity, space and time were fused into one by 'symmetrizing' the equations; in other words the equation had to be made what is known in mathematical jargon as 'co-variant'. This was achieved using the speed of light as a constant in any frame to preserve Galilean Relativity. To keep c constant, a mathematical equation known as the Lorentz transformation, formulated by Lorentz, was used by Einstein, the result of which was a constant c for the speed of light in any frame of reference, but which permitted the varying of length and time due to motion; in other words, the formulation allowed a slowdown/speed-up or lengthening/contraction whilst leaving the speed of light unchanged in any frame of reference. The implication of this is that no matter how fast you are travelling you cannot catch up to its speed; even if you were an electron travelling at 99% of c, you as the electron would still perceive light travelling at c, relative to yourself!

In quantum mechanics, on the other hand, measuring one or another variable disturbed the particle and hence it was held by the Bohr's school of thought that these subatomic entities do not have a definite position or momentum unless measured, when the 'wave function' would collapse. This implied that things do not have a specific location, ontologically, until collapsed by the act of observation! As time elapsed, from the 1920s, the 1950s to the 1960s, on the surface at least, scientists claimed in experiment after experiment to have corroborated special and general relativity and from a limited calculational perspective, quantum mechanics proved successful. However, these two, General Relativity and Quantum Mechanics were not commensurate with each other. Something was and is amiss—something major. We know deep inside each of us and observationally that this Universe is integrated and united and yet we had, or do have, two schemes for trying to explaining it, which were, and are, not completely compatible with each other. In addition, Einstein's explanations were not the only ones that explained time dilation etc. The problem that had occurred was that the generation of physicists brought up at the turn of the 20th Century were viewing space and time in a way that did not involve the Lorentzian transformation. Yet despite strong misgivings they were reluctant to challenge the newer generation of physicists, that is, those whose physics was dominated by mathematics rather than physical evidence. Furthermore, the younger groups' physical evidence was interpreted to match the mathematics, rather than the other way around.

As these notions of General Relativity and Quantum got implanted in Universities around the world, they became institutionalized and as the Muslim world collapsed due to mysticism, ritualism, colonial rule and a lack of the usage of reason that the Quran commands, the universities in the so-called Muslim world based their engineering and physics curriculums on the interpretations of a disunited physics of quantum mechanics and general relativity, buying into all this blatant falsehood—a burial of their erstwhile intellectual legacy.

The problems in the unification of these two areas of General Relativity and Quantum Mechanics rests on the problematic interpretation of space and time; once these are understood properly (as the reader will be shown) a unification is easy to behold and promises a revolution in all fields of human understanding, tantamount to being the next major revolution in all fields of knowledge. Instead of being leaders in science, the experimental method which Quran gave birth to and for which it was the direct cause of the Renaissance in Europe, the Muslims and the Muslim world became, in a sense, enslaved to a weird combination of correct and incorrect and partially illogical concepts that emanated from the Western World as it evolved only aspects of the total Quranic paradigm. The current Muslim psyche is the outcome of an inferiority complex that has depressed the nominal Muslim world for so long. In reality, as one 'human race', evolved from common origin, on a probably quite mediocre planet floating in the outskirts of the Milky Way, one ought not to have either a superiority or inferiority complex. There is the reality that lies before us, and we must, as stumbling and imperfect human beings seek to know things the way they are, the best we can, without hidden agendas or for selfish motives. We must be, as Newton said of himself, like a curious child on a seashore, examining the washed up natural objects on the beach, with awe. The beginnings of this process of realizing the entrenched illogicalities and disunification in physics is well under way, though still an undercurrent and will indubitably lead to a culmination of the ideas in the Quran concerning 'space' and 'time', which it is attempted to highlight here. We will then have come full circle in our quest.

Chapter 2

A New Solution: Enter the Microbits

In 2001, a book was published by this writer with colleague, M. Muslim aka "The Bridge", on the unification of physics that has laid the foundation of a totally new way to look at the Universe[100]. The book dealt purely with logic and physics and the Quran was not referenced at all. In this book, however, an attempt is being made to introduce the new ideas in an overview, justify them according to not only logic and evidence, but the Quran itself, and lastly it is hoped to connect to work done subsequent to our work by one of the world's leading dissident physicists, Harvard's Thomas Phipps, which is totally complementary and dovetails with microbit's methodology and most of the conclusions about how nature works, derived thereof. In fact, Phipps in a personal communication to this writer (Nadeem Haque), states:

> Some years ago the Russians, under the influence of their political system, boasted that they were going to recheck everything about Western science, do all the basic experiments over, etc., and take a fresh look at the whole business. That gave me some hope ... but they never did it. It was all just talk.

> It would be good if the Muslim world should rethink Einstein's work. When I went about that myself, I found it was all based on Maxwell's equations, and those were readily capable of being improved. When one made them invariant, it turned out to be a new ballgame. Kinematics had to be reconsidered from the ground up, there was no spacetime symmetry, and very little of Einstein's work survived. But I do not expect any "real" (academic) scientists to accept that. Anyway, they don't, regardless of my expectations.

Some eighty years ago the Muslim Philosopher-Poet Muhammad Iqbal astutely remarked that:

---

100   Muslim, M. and Haque, Nadeem. (2001). *From Microbits to Everything: A New Unified View of Physics and Cosmology, Volume 1: The Cosmological Implications.*

> Indeed, more recent developments in European mathematics tend rather to deprive time of its living historical character, and to reduce it to a mere representation of space. That is why Whitehead's view of Relativity is likelyto appeal to Muslim students more than that of Einstein in whose theory timeloses its character of passage and mysteriously translates itself into utter space.[101]

While issue can be taken with his remark concerning the philosopher Whitehead, Iqbal is generally correct. Unfortunately, in the quasi-Muslim world, up until 2001, no one since had taken the gauntlet to determine what the basis and details of that unification should be,other than in FME (*From Microbits to Everything*, Volume 1). In part, this outcome is symptomatic of the state of the nominal Muslim world. Indeed, once they had led the world in science but are now relegated to only unquestioning pedantic followers of "authorities",not heeding the warning of the Quran itself of not blindly following one's forefathers. This is mentioned so many times in the Quran that it is not even worth referencing.

In 1996, when M. Muslim discussed Einstein's theories, he saw many logical problems with both Special and General Relativity as many others had, including this writer. Muslim then expostulated his idea for unifying physics. His proposed solution was very simple, yet at the same time most profound. Everything he said is made of one type of particle, which he termed the microbit; that means that all forces and structures, all matter and so-called energy is just a grouping of these microbits in absolute space. He also explained the unique nature of the photon. However, all of these needed an overall formulation in terms of how all the forces were to be explained by microbits. My role in all this re-evaluation of the origins and structure of the Universe, was to technically explain how all the forces are united based on this concept of the microbit in absolute space, primary of which was gravity, the great stumbling block for unification, and for which a coherent explanation has been postulated that explains action at a distance and which also unifies with the rest of the 'forces'. And thus it was that after a number of years of intense research and thinking, From Microbits to Everything: A New Unified View of Physics and Cosmology, Volume 1: The Cosmological Implications, was published. In Part 4, this book will be referred to

---

101 Iqbal, Mohammad. (1930). *The Reconstruction of Religious Thought in Islam.*Now available on many internet sites.
Website: http://www.allamaiqbal.com/works/prose/english/reconstruction/

as FME v.1. Following this book, in 2025, 24 years later, another was published called: Microbits: *A New Unified Physics,* updated and expanded.

By way of introduction, to give the reader a flavour of the problems at hand, consider gravity: The problems with current explanations of gravity are concisely summarized by maverick physics researcher Miles Mathis:

> Gravity has long been the greatest mystery in physics, and it still is. For Newton, gravity was a force at a distance. This was inherently mysterious, as he admitted, since there was no causal mechanism. Einstein provided gravity with a new mathematics, but he also failed to provide a mechanism. Einstein denied that gravity was a force at all; for him it was simply a new geometry—curved space. This was novel, except that it failed to explain how mass curved space. The mechanism was still missing, force or no force. Some contemporary physicists believe that gravitons may be the force-carrying particles, but they have no theory to explain the force at a quantum level. Not only have they been unable to find a quantum mathematics that includes gravity, but they have utterly failed to explain (or even to attempt to explain) how trading particles can mechanistically cause an attractive force. A repulsion can easily be explained by bombardment, for instance; but attraction is impossible to explain in any analogous way. As an example, if you throw nerfballs at a balloon it will move away. But try getting the balloon to move toward you by doing anything with a nerfball. The balloon and you can absorb or eject nerfballs in a billion different ways, but none of them will make the balloon come to you.102

The microbits' explanation of gravity overcomes all these problems and we shall be discussing this in due course in this part of the book. But first a brief introduction to the basis of 'microbits'.

The Basic Concept of Microbits

In 'conventional particle physics', the hydrogen atom consists of a proton; this is in turn comprised of 'quarks'. Three quarks make up each proton. The quarks, are, in turn, held together by 'gluons'. The Microbit Model, however, goes further and proposes that the quarks are in turn comprised of smaller particles; and

---

102 *The Third Wave: A Redefinition of Gravity* by Miles Mathis. Website: http://milesmathis.com/third. html

those smaller particles in turn are comprised of yet smaller particles and so on and so forth. But this does not go on forever—it comes to an end. You need a base for starting out, otherwise the cause and effect of the existence of particles would go on forever and the Universe would not have 'started'. As stated in FME v.1 and the latest book on this subject of microbits: The microbit model is based purely on two primary notions:

1. The existence of absolute so-called (flat) space.
2. The motion, shape and distribution of the sub-submicroscopic structures in absolute space which we term microbits, or the origin particles (O-particles). One could say that the microbits are the 'atoms' or unit building blocks of the sub-atomic particles and all the known 'forces'.

They are the smallest inanimate entities next to absolute nothingness.[103]

The Big Bang is no longer a theory but a fact; but these microbits were the first particles to emerge when the Big Bang 'lump' exploded. So in FME v. 1 we (M. Muslim and I) explain how all the forces arose from the logically simplest possible beginnings: only one type of particle and flat space; that is all. There are three forces: the gravitational, the strong and the electro-weak. We explain these using microbits, in the sense that after the Big Bang, these microbits started to stick together by their paths, crossing each other in a precisely contrived and designed initial explosion. Why contrived and designed will become evident by the end of Part 4! The various zoo of particles is nothing but a grouping of these particles, which formed as the Universe 'cooled down'. A detailed explanation of each of these forces is given in FME v. 1 and the new book *Microbits: A New Unified Physics*, and it is not intended to reproduce all the arguments here; suffice it to say that from a conceptual point of view, physicists and cosmologists have been focusing on the red herring of uniting abstract mathematical forces, rather than determining what the 'physical matter' out there is.

Once it was realized that everything is just a grouping of microbits, both the micro and the macro aspects of the Universe were, in one grand stroke, united then really all that remained to be explained, though indeed most challenging to say the least, was how the various particles moved or combined, collided etc., to produce all structures and forces. The distinction between matter and energy disappeared in a natural way because matter is energy and energy is matter—it

---

103   Muslim, M. and Haque, Nadeem. (2001). *From Microbits to Everything: A New of Physics, Volume 1: The Cosmological Implications*, pp.32-33.

just depends on the grouping and motion of microbits in absolute space. Attraction or repulsion of particles/matter is based on the pressure forces of gravity particles (they are not being termed gravitons, as these have other connotations) colliding and retracting from any object in the g-particle field. It was shown in *From Microbits to Everything* and *Microbits: A New Unified Physics* why that force would be 'downwards' and accelerative on a planetary body and why acceleration to the ground would be the same for any object.[104]

Some alternatives to the Einsteinian theories have been proposed that do not involve 'curved space'. However, they all beg the question and fall far short of explaining many aspects about gravity, but are valiant attempts, nonetheless. It is indeed not adequate to explain gravity as some type of emergent force emanating from electromagnetic fields as some of the opponents of GeneralRelativity have postulated, because it leaves many questions begging, such as what those fields are comprised of, how to explain its universality, the directionality of gravity, its weakness compared to the electromagnetic force, and lastly, how did those fields arise in the first place?! The Microbits concept explains all of this. However, the famous Russian physicist, Andrei Sakharov was on a path that could have culminated in microbit concepts for gravity, as he was thinking about how submicroscopic particles may induce gravity. He came close, but no cigar, as they say!

In the microbit model, the answer is straightforward: The basic reason for acceleration due to gravity is that when one is comparing two objects in space, the differential forces from the g-particles on both objects would be the same, and they would therefore both experience the acceleration due to gravity, but the pressure of the g-particles felt on denser objects would be greater because the denser particles are comprised of more particles in a given space and hence they would be heavier, where the 'heaviness' is the pressure felt by the object as the ambient g-particles interact with the objects comprised of an arrangement of microbits (as are all things arranged of microbits).

Mass therefore is a relational property though it also depends on the amount of 'stuff' the object has. The dual nature of light was also explained, by showing that the photons collide with each other and are essentially passive unless disturbed; it is a disturbance that causes the pulse to travel along a chain of photons lined up that gives the illusion of photon travelling from a spot A to spot B. No photon travels huge distances—only the pulse. This motion also explains

---

104   Ibid. p. 49-55. On the 2010 internet version pp. 45-52.

the wave nature of light in one stroke. Experiments done in the 20th Century that show that simultaneously the wave and particle nature of light which can only be explained by the microbit based model of light and no other way.105

The most fundamental concept to understand, however, was that time was seen as nothing but the measure of movement, using constant movement and not some abstraction which one fused with space. In fact, at the outset of the book, FME v. 1 its co-author, M. Muslim states:

> My thesis is that Einstein's theory of general relativity is incorrect. Specifically, I demonstrate that it is not space and time that are relative, but only motions. Space is constant, it does not contract, simultaneity is not relative, and time does not dilate. I also establish that the speed of light is not the maximum and that there are particles which travel unimaginably faster than light. In sum, I call for a paradigm shift in our concept of space, time and matter.106

Using these concepts it was easy to show how and why Einstein was incorrect and simultaneity is being confused with the reception of signals[107]. It is totally absurd and illogical to state that there can be no simultaneity. In fact, prior to a discussion of Einstein's General Relativity, in Chapter 1, M. Muslim debunked both Special Relativity by showing that only the motions are relative.

---

105   Ibid. pp. 49-55. On the internet version pp. 45-52.
106   Ibid. p. 1. On the internet version p. 1
107   Ibid. pp. 11-13. On the internet version pp. 11-13.

Chapter 3

Mainstream Physics Gone Haywire

A Multidimensional Error

Prior to the 19th century, space was seen as three dimensional in which objects existed. The whole abstract notion of multiple spaces, curved space etc. developed in the 19th century after Nikolai Ivanovich Lobachevsky (1792–1856) who developed the mathematics of non-Euclidean Geometry. János Bolyai, known for his work in non- Euclidean geometry and Lobachevsky, also were precursors to Georg Friedrich Bernhard Riemann (September 17, 1826–July 20, 1866). Riemann was a Student of Johann Carl Friedrich Gauss (30 April 1777–23 February 1855) who had pioneered but not published his work on non-Euclidean geometry first. William Kingdon Clifford (4 May 1845–3 March 1879) of Clifford Algebra fame, now the leading superior mathematical technique to supplant traditional Vector Algebra, and used extensively in graphics to produce video games, was the first person known to have postulated the curvature of space as a hypothesis for gravity. Riemann further developed these ideas. Einstein used non-Euclidean geometry. The concept of the curvature of space, in turn led to the positing multiple dimensions, as the physicists tried to tackle the problematic nature of the gravitational force based on mathematical equations by treating space as a "fabric". This material, it was thought, could have many dimensions. Indeed, it started to be assumed over the course of the 20th century that many dimensions were needed to unify the forces; these dimensions were described by analogies. Theodor Franz Eduard Kaluza (9 November 1885—19 January 1954) and Christian Felix Klein (25 April 1849—22 June 1925) tried to expand the dimensions of space in order to solve Einstein's field equations to unify all of the forces. However, there was no evidence of a fifth dimension! These theories were subsequently dropped but resuscitated later on with string theory. So far no one has seen any other dimensions or proven their existence. Even if they did exist, by definition they would not be part of our Universe and hence unprovable. The whole notion of other dimensions is wrongheaded and is a way to escape from some fundamental problems. As such, the whole venture is turning out to be ridiculous from a logical perspective and it is predictable that this whole deck of cards will eventually come crashing down like Humpty-Dumpty who sat on a relativistic wall! Professor Richard Ellis states in a candid article for Scientific American that:

> All in all, the case for the multiverse is inconclusive. The basic reason is the extreme flexibility of the proposal: it is more a concept than a well-defined theory. Most proposals involve a patchwork of different ideas rather than a coherent whole. The basic mechanism for eternal inflation does not itself cause physics to be different in each domain in a multiverse; for that it needs to be coupled with another speculative theory. Although they can be fitted together, there is nothing inevitable about it.... Nothing is wrong with scientifically based philosophical speculation, which is what multiverse proposals are. But we should name it for it is. [108]

There is, in addition, often a confusion between multiple dimensions in terms of variables and actual hypothesized multiple dimensions. The former relates to the number of unknowns in the physical sciences, whereas the latter specifically refers to existential spaces. The two must never be confused. What this means is that the former is a fact of life, but the latter does not exist!

The Demise of the Concept of the Expansion of *Space*

The concept of curved space also influenced trying to explain the expansion of the Universe as the expansion of space itself. However, you cannot have your cosmic cake and eat it as well, but most Einsteinians would have you engage in such gluttony on a very foundational matter in cosmology. They themselves have debunked the expansion of space with matter without debunking the concept, in another article, again in Scientific American. This sounds paradoxical but the reader should read on to realize what is meant. In the article, the whole notion of space as a 'fabric' that is expanding, with matter from the Big Bang is shown to be impossible, because it violates the conservation of matter and energy. This fact was not highlighted in mainstream publications and journals because certain notions that reify space as stretching etc. are being clung on to dogmatically in conventional institutionalized fundamental physics. The editors of Scientific American summarize the situation:

108   Ellis, George E.R. (August 2011), @Does the Multiverse Really Exist?@ *Scientific American*, Vol. 305, No. 2, pp. 38-43.

The Universe appears to be expanding, as if space itself were getting stretched out. In consequence, the electromagnetic waves that compose light get stretched as well, shifting, in the case of visible light, toward the red part of the spectrum (below). Photons of longer wavelength have lower energy, so logic dictates that each photon must become less energetic as it travels toward us. But does the Universe as a whole lose energy? The total energy of the photons in the Universe cannot be calculated, but one can in principle calculate the energy contained within an imaginary membrane that expands in concert with the Universe (at right, the region inside a membrane is represented as two-dimensional). Photons can enter or exit through the membrane, but the uniform density of space tells us that the number of photons in the enclosed region will roughly stay constant. Because each photon in the region becomes less energetic as space expands, this calculation suggests that the total amount of photon energy in the region and, by implication, in the rest of the Universe must be going down.[109]

The fact explained above is the case because if the conventional FRW model is used, in which space is supposed to expand with matter, then the question that arises is that as space expands, the photon's energy is lost. But then the question arises as to where this energy goes. In other words, if space itself is expanding we see a loss in the energy of a photon—it simply vanishes. This violates the conservation of matter and energy. The author then takes the unusual step to advance the correct idea that it must not be the case that space expands, but that expansion takes place *in* space which resolves the problem. The dispersion of photons from the Big Bang, therefore, occurs *in* space, analogous to sound waves in the Doppler effect of a police siren, for example. However, the implications of this are far greater than what is mentioned in the *Scientific American* article and stares at us blatantly like an elephant in a China Shop, with no one looking at the elephant but still busily engaged in shopping. It shows that the current conventional cosmological model is incorrect and that the Big Bang occurred in space as has been endeavored to be proved by the work of M. Muslim and myself, which is in agreement with the Quranic view. Note that the current Friedmannian model is only one of several options that could have been chosen, not that there is proof of space expanding with matter. Unfortunately, the physicists,

---

109   Davis, Tamara. (July 2010). *Scientific American,* "Is the Universe Leaking Energy?" p. 34.

decades ago, chose the wrong option; as has been said by one recent Muslim thinker before: "If you catch the wrong train, every station you get off will be the wrong one"[110]. How many wrong train stations will be passed by, before the 'scientific community' gets off the train which is headed toward a steep cliff to fall into the cauldron of ignominy? Faced with the problem of the false concept of the 'expansion of space' the author says:

> The point is that our metaphor of the expanding rubber balloon, though useful to visualize the expansion, should be taken with a grain of salt: empty space does not have a physical reality. As galaxies recede from one another, we are free to consider this relative motion as "expansion of space" or "movement through space"; the difference is mostly semantics. The amount of redshift seen in the galaxy turns out to be identical to the Doppler shift the observer would see in a car that is receding at the same relative velocity [see box above]. This happens because in small enough regions the Universe makes a pretty good approximation of "at spacetime". But in "at spacetime" there is no gravity and no stretching of waves, and any red-shift must just be a Doppler effect. So we can think of the light as making many tiny little Doppler shifts along its trajectory. And just as in the case of the police car—where it would not even occur to us to think that photons are gaining or losing energy—here, too, the relative motion of the emitter and observer means that they see photons from different perspectives and not that the photons have lost energy along the way.[111]

The above explanation makes sense but goes against the prevailing (incorrect) view of the expansion of space itself. So, one cannot prevaricate and equivocate and hold two opposing viewpoints which are mutually exclusive: which one is going to go into the proverbial trashcan of ideas? Are we still going to claim the expansion of space when there is such a contradiction of a basic law of physics? Or did particles from the Big Bang explode in pre-existing space which creates no problems and is akin to the Doppler effect, Does space expand with matter after the Big Bang, where we have this fundamental problem? Do we calculate using the no stretching of space and still maintain that space is expanding or do we, being honest with ourselves and as logic and evidence would demand, drop

110   My friend and colleague, the mathematician and Islamic lecturer, extant in the 1980s, currently back in Canada: Dr. Gary Miller, aka, Abdul Ahad Omar.
111   Ibid., *Scientific American*, "Is the Universe Leaking Energy", p. 38-39

the idea of the expansion of space? Here it appears that one is desirous of having one's cosmic cake and eating it as well, and perhaps, in pursuing such a culinary path, one might be beset, in time, with indigestion of cosmic proportions!

In the Microbits' view, only particles are ripped/split apart from the Big Bang and not space and there is a centre to the expansion. Space is infinite in all directions and had no particles, for it is an eternally pre-existing particleless space. The Friedmann–Robertson–Walker (FRW) model is sometimes called the Standard Model of modern cosmology. It was developed independently by the named authors in the 1920s and 1930s. This is only an optional model which provides solutions to Einstein's equations based on the assumption that space is tied to matter etc. However, the fact is that the Universe can be perfectly explained with models that have a centre of the Universe. These solutions, now known as Lemaître-Tolman-Bondi (LTB) models, provide solutions to Einstein's equations as well. This is not to agree with general relativity but only to show that the wrong model itself can be modelled, in part, differently!

The falsehood of two examples purported to prove relativity

Let us briefly examine some claims of relativity: starlight bending around the sun was known long before Einstein as a kind of a refraction albeit with gravity (first hypothesized by Newton and then by Soldner, before Einstein). It does not have anything to do with curved space because curved space is a fiction—space is not an object to be curved as Muslim points out in *From Microbits to Everything: Volume 1* and in *Microbits: A New Unified Physics*. However, gravitational particles that we call g-particles in the microbits' view, will affect the particles of light as it moves through a field that has a dense concentration of these particles as described by the microbits solution to what exactly gravity is. The question of Mercury likewise is a tautological use of mathematics to explain the motion of Mercury around the sun a posteriori. It does not explain the causative mechanical reason why this is happening; remarkably, in the probably most underestimated peer reviewed physics journal paper in the world, Ives derived the perihelion formula from Newtonian Mechanics and showed that there is an extra force that acts to cause the required advance of the perihelion51112. This

---

112 Turner, Dean and Hazelett, Richard, (Editors). (1979). *The Einstein Myth and the Ives Papers: A Counter- Revolution in Physics*, "The Behavior of an Interferometer in a Gravitational Field. II. Application to a Planetary Orbit", pp. 132—135.

derivation is from accepted Newtonian mechanics, step by step and not an arbitrary interpolation. We need a physical force (which is not based on action at a distance, and which the microbit concept of gravity establishes) based on actual motions in absolute space to explain the perihelion, not geometric explanations and confabulations that merely describe the motion, once it is known. Whether the parameters that Einstein used to come up with his equation to explain the motion of Mercury were arbitrary/free or not as has been argued by some physicists is a moot point once we realize the tautological and hence fallacious nature of the proof. In *Microbits: A New Unified Physics*, I have highlighted Paul Marmet's solution again based on purely Newtonian mechanics and the conservation of energy. In having looked at this example, it becomes apparent that perhaps a course on philosophy and logical fallacies should be made mandatory for all physics students at university. But then perhaps the physics department will be producing astute and questioning students rather than blind followers, thereby undermining the very basis of their own foundational beliefs!

Dirac's Equation: The Good, the Bad and the Ugly

Dirac's equation has utilized both quantum mechanics and relativity to tell us about the Universe. Due to the fact that, as we have shown in *From Microbits to Everything, Volume 1*, the relativity of curved space is fictional, but in a way can be a useful tool in depicting motions and trajectories using geometry and secondly, due to the problems with the Copenhageninterpretation of Quantum Mechanics, it is not possible to come up with an equation that explains an aspect of reality the way it is because confusion times confusion is nothing but multiple confusion, to quote one of my colleagues. Such is the problem with Dirac's equation. In terms of the discovery of the positron and its properties, it has been successful, which can be deemed 'the good'; it yields infinities which Dirac himself was never satisfied with and thought to be highly problematic to the end of his life, which is the "the bad", and the "ugly" part of it has to do with his equation predicting innumerable sea of particles in space, and in that sense lacking in specificity. However, it is noteworthy that it does predict other particles that now are known to be 'out there' though the interpretation of how they arise and exist is at odds with microbit concepts in the sense that microbit concepts also hold that innumerable particles exist out there which we can tap into for energy, but they are actual particles and not virtual and, furthermore, are not arising from nothing; they are composites of microbits.

Indeed, we have particles even smaller than the so-called fundamental particles with the microbits' model. Lastly, it must be understood that Dirac's equation does not resolve the issue of gravity let alone the above problems (calculational infinites). Dirac's equation of course is not the originator of these infinities but the basic understanding of particles in mainstream physics and the mathematical modeling of them has led to these infinities and the equation is just a natural child of these largely erroneous concepts. The equation is, as such, not true unifier of physics but combines aspects of relativity and quantum mechanics to give us partially correct glimpse of 'what is out there' and helps us calculate some effects. Although Dirac used mathematics and had an obsession with 'beauty' in it, he would always take, as his lead, experimental results with which to toy with abstract ideas that led to mathematical expressions. As a partial calculative 'device' it is an achievement to be heralded as a piece of mathematical brilliance. Dirac was, however, careful in seeing if his concepts matched cause and effect exhibited in experiments. Though it is unfortunate that he did not challenge relativity and the interpretation of quantum mechanics, his approach was more rational than that of Einstein, who bent reality to suit his equations.

Exposing Establishmentarianism: The Case of Io

In FME v.1, it was shown extensively that light speed would vary depending on the motion of the observer. A few excellent articles have been written since 2001 describing some astronomical and physical data that prove beyond a shadow of a doubt that this is the case by Stephan Gift. One of them concerns Jupiter's moon Io, where it is shown that the speed of light that reaches us from Io varies depending on where we are in orbit in relation to Jupiter, as the velocity is either additive or subtractive[113]. This is another nail in the coffin of relativity that even a good high school student taking grade 11 or 12 physics can understand, and these papers are certainly worth reading. These facts completely invalidate Special Relativity and ought to be known widely by a consumeristic public generally illiterate about deeper scientific knowledge and critical thinking. Stephan

---

113 Gift, Stephan. (January 2004, Preprint)). "Successful Detection of Ether Drift Using Eclipses of Jupiter's Moon Io." https://www.researchgate.net/publication/351871789_Successful_Detection_of_Ether_Drift_Using_Eclipses_of_Jupiter%27s_Moon_Io

Gift has also written a paper invalidating General Relativity via debunking the principle of equivalence, whereas in FME v.1, we had proven this using a different method and also discussed Burniston Brown's argument debunking the principle. The question that arises is how come these faulty, and on the face of it, inconsistent and then shown to be physicallywrong ideas, can be held and supported for about 100 years by the 'scientific' community? We also discussed this seemingly strange phenomenon in FME v.1, but a few more points must be mentioned. We need to be honest if we are to truly move ahead.

Once ideas get established for socio-political, or psychological reasons they often becomeinstitutionalized. Once they become institutionalized, they become an industry or quasi-religious sanctum that is difficult to topple. Many vested interests get involved; in maintaining such falsehoods many people who know that there is a problem or suspect a problem with a particular theory/paradigm no longer remain honest and society at large suffers for it. Furthermore, an alternative view that is pointing to the truth has ramificationsin many other areas that harm vested interests of those are bent on keeping the status quo.A typical example is the theory of natural selection which is in crisis but is, like relativity, being propped up like a house of cards. Any dissent by professors who still believe in creative evolution but not in the necessarily in the ridiculous seven-day creationism, is met with harsh retribution in many, if not most cases.

People also win prizes for such false ideas. This, in a way, legitimizes ideas. The media, controlled by lobby groups, propagates only certain views, whilst the illusion of objectivity is maintained. Granted that some areas are complex and the lay public may find such involved concepts difficult to understand and in this fast paced life, one is just trying to survive and may only superficially read superficial accounts in the popular press of theories or claimed discoveries that require more critical study. Therefore, in this consumer and survival mode society that has developed (except for the very rich and financial elite), few people want to get to the root and determine the truth or have the time. After all, why would anyone want to get castigated and excommunicated for speaking up! The problem gets compounded when the false concepts propagated are partially correct and therefore it appears that the whole is correct, particularly by the special pleading and mass propaganda heaped upon the masses through various forms of media. Special and General Relativity/Einstein are prime examples of this. Supposed authorities and experts are interviewed ad nauseum to regurgitate sheer illogicality and publish books supporting such ideas. In this abysmal climate, the few people who disagree in these positions of education hold dissenting views privately until it becomes unbearable or until it 'slips out' in a letter or article written by them. Then the axe falls on their careers. This is not how science, which is supposed to be the search for the truth, is supposed to operate. The result is a misdirection, retrogression, stagnation or slowing down in particular areas of science and toward a broader understanding of the basis of reality, which if it will be understood, should help us solve problems in many areas because all knowledge is interrelated. The saving grace these days perhaps is that for such a topic, dissenters are not burned at the stake; however, if they lose their job they will not be able to enjoy steaks!

Would not it be simply marvelous to describe the workings and complexity of the evolution of the whole Universe with just a few simple rules at its core, or absolute basis? Well we can do so! The Universe is made up of only microbits in absolute space, organized to give us all matter and energy. The microbit itself has maximal properties that this writer calls the "Three **S**'s": it has the potential to spin (**S**pinability); to deform upon collision with another microbit (**S**quash-ability)', and it has **S**tickability (temporary conjoining with zero distance: what one anonymous peer reviewer of this work, when it was an 'article' submitted for publication in another journal, called the "fusing of microbits"). Using these properties of one type of original particle in absolute (flat) space, we have a Uni-verse with maximal complementary diversity that we see. One can use a sticky squash ball, for example, for visualization but it must be remembered that this would only serve as an analogy and these three S's must not be perceived in a simple-minded fashion (and besides, squash balls are comprised of many par-ticles but the microbit is a unit and indivisible particle; the atom's atom, as it were!). For example, stickability does not mean there is glue on the surface of the microbit but that when two microbits collide there is no gap between them whatsoever and they temporarily become conjoined as one! It is at the micro-bit level at which contact actually occurs, through a cascading chain-like effect, thereby resolving the action at a distance problem, which has never really been solved but swept under the rug. It is as if somethingnoxious was swept under the rug and then people forgot about it but those who were not completely desen-sitized could still smell the foul odor, one of these being the 'infinities problem', as a real problem. If one recalls historically, in Newtonian physics the action at distance problem was at the forefront. Newton could not resolve it, but being the true genius that he was, saw this as the central problem:

> It is inconceivable that inanimate Matter should, without the Mediation of something else, which is not material, operate upon, and affect other matter without mutual Contact...That Gravity should be innate, inherent and essential to Matter, so that one body may act upon another at a distance thro' a Vacuum, without the Mediation of anything else, by and through which their Action and Force may be conveyed from one to another, is to me so great an Absurdity that I believe no Man who has in philosophical Matters a competent Faculty of thinking can ever fall into it. Gravity must be caused by an Agent acting constantly according to certain laws; but whether this Agent be material or immaterial, I have left to the Consideration of my readers. (Isaac Newton, Letters to Bentley, 1692/3)

In Einstein's General Relativity, since space curvature is a fiction and therefore does not really solve this problem and quantum mechanics, where we talk of 'fields' and point particles and exchange of particles using equations, there is no actual contact (zerodistance), and the problem again remains unresolved. However, without zero distance at some level, the whole scenario is magic and not physics. You need the ultimate explanation that does not beg the question of 'contact' and the microbit is logically it.

Why and How Modern Physics has taken the Wrong Turn

Usually in horror movies, we have the young heroine driving along a lonely road—she takes a wrong turn and is met with unsavory characters bent on doing her harm. Such it is with what we have come to call 'physics'. However, the unsavory characters in this case are not 'bad men', but the omnipresent facts from reality that keep creeping up on theoverall erroneous concepts of the body of Einsteinian physics. With relativity, consistency and empirical testing was dispensed with, by relying on vacuous, false and subjective notions such as 'beauty in mathematics' and the subversion of mathematics as a tool to understand relations of objects in absolute space. The reality is that we may have an ugly looking equation which reflects reality but a so-called beautiful equation that is sheer nonsense. Beauty in mathematics has nothing to do with the truth and this is one of the delusions the Einsteinians are fraught with. This was one of the first wrong turns.Concerning the misuse of Maxwellian equations using the Lorentz transformation, there were indeed three options to choose from; unfortunately, Einstein made the wrong choice,and his being backed by both covert and sensationalistic wrongheaded media at the time, the institutionalization of physics as dogma, rather than as a way to understand and seek the truth without violating basic laws of thought—i.e. the law of non-contradiction, which trumps, or ought to trump everything—had the odious effect of fracturing an understanding of reality for over 100 years. For in FME v.1, it had been stated that:

> There was and is nothing sacred about Galilean Relativity that must be preserved in the case of electromagnetism by altering perceptions of reality—of space and 'time'—the way Einstein did, especially if other choices were available for preserving Galilean Relativity in absolute space.[114]

How exactly did we end up in this relativistic conundrum? At this point, once again bringing cinema as analogy, one is justified in proclaiming, like Oliver Hardy to Stan Laurel: "This is a fine mess you've gotten me into!" But how did we get into this mess, in the first place, in the sense of how did it start? In FME v.1 it was explained that:

> Einstein tried to reconcile Maxwell's equations to satisfy the two postulates of relativity including the constancy of light. Einstein's ultimate aim was to reconcile kinematics with electromagnetism, andhis method of approach differed from that chosen almost automatically by others in that it proposed a modification of kinematics rather than of electromagnetism for this end. Dingle elaborates that electromagnetic experiments to test special relativity cannot work because the theory has to be tested on kinematics upon which it is based.[115]

All that its success in electromagnetism, however extensive and various, can show that, if the proposed kinematics is tenable, then it has achieved its object; it can do nothing at all to show whether the theory is right or wrong.[116] As the late renowned physicist, David Bohm explains, with regards to electromagnetism,

---

114 Ibid., From Microbits to Everything, Vol. 1, p. 108. On the internet version p. 103.

115 Ibid., *From Microbits to Everything*, Vol. 1, p. 105. On the internet version, pp. 99-100.
The two postulates of Special Relativity are:
The laws of physics are the same in all inertial systems. No preferred inertial system exists (the principle of relativity).
The speed of light in free space has the same value c in all inertial systems (the principle of the constancy of the speed of light).

116 Footnote 69, *From Microbits to Everything*, Vol. 1, p. 105: Dingle, Herbert. (1972), *Science at the Crossroads*, p. 149.

which was the main factor that inspired Einstein towards his Special Theory of Relativity:

> In one case the magnet is considered to move past the conductor, a loop of wire is connected to an electrical meter. Through the electricalfield associated with the moving magnet, a current is induced in the wire— the net result is a deflection of the meter. In the second explanation, the electrical conductor is moved past the magnet, which is now at rest. No electrical field is produced in this case; rather the magnetic force on the charged particles (electrons) in the wire cause a current to flow and a deflection of the meter. Two quite different and apparently incompatible explanations are therefore produced for one and the same phenomenon: the flow of an electrical current when a magnet and a wire move relative to each other.[117]

For this, Einstein introduced the Lorentz contraction. David Bohm goes on to state that:

> Through his [Einstein's] perception that relative motion was the essential point, Einstein was led to see electrical and magnetic effects not as absolute and independent but rather as relative to the state of motion. ...To achieve the new unity between electricity and magnetism, Einstein had to suppose that time, measured in the frame that moves relative to the laboratory (say, the magnet), is different from time measured in the stationary laboratory frame (say the fixed wire).[118]

Philosopher Paul Thagard also elaborates on this:

> [Einstein's] initial paper, "On the Electrodynamics of Moving Bodies," begins by discussing the asymmetries in the applications of Maxwell's equations to the reciprocal action of a magnet and a conductor. [According to the equations if] the magnet is in motion and the conductor is at rest, then an electric field arises, but not if the magnet is at rest and the conductor is in motion.[119]

---

117 Footnote 70, *From Microbits to Everything*, Vol. 1, p. 106: Bohm, David and Peat, F. David. (1987), *Science,Order, and Creativity*, p. 74.

118 Footnote 71 in *From Microbits to Everything*, Vol. 1, p. 106.

119 Footnote 72 in *From Microbits to Everything*, Vol. 1, p. 107, Thagard, Paul, (1992), *Conceptual Revolutions*, p.207.

In that paper, Einstein wrote that "...the same laws of electrodynamics and optics willbe valid for all frames of reference for which the equations of mechanics hold good."[120] He then postulated the Principle of Relativity. This refers to the exact correspondence between the compared expressions of physical laws between a stationary scientist and a moving one, each observing each other's experiments from their own frames of reference.

Now we shall examine the recent work of Physicist Thomas Phipps who has, instead of revising Maxwell's equations decided to use Hertz's equations which help us understand the proper concepts of space and time and which 'dovetails' with the microbits model of physical reality. Thomas E. Phipps used to be a follower of Special and General Relativity as are most physicists, but after he saw some inconsistencies he started to question the whole edifice. At the beginning of his book he states:

> Virtually the whole of "established" modern fundamental theoretical physics (quantum mechanics aside) is based upon two sacred cows, Einstein's special relativity theory (SRT) and Maxwell's equations ofelectromagnetism, the latter being postulationally supplemented by a Lorentz force law.[121]

He further states that the shortcomings of Maxwell's equations lead to "pressing problems with field theory." In his own words he states that:

> The most prominent deficiency to be noted about the above specific field equations is that they are not invariant under first order (Galilean) inertial transformations. This is an extremely serious matter. It implies that in electromagnetism there exists an order of description....at which the relativity principle does not hold. [Due to this reason, if an] inertial system moves with respect to a "fundamental" system the operator $\partial/\partial t$... is non-invariant under the Galilean transformation.[122]

In *From Microbits to Everything* and *Microbits: A New Unified Physics* we explained that this non-invariance was the reason that led to the creation of Special Relativity.

---

120 Footnote 73 in *From Microbits to Everything*, Vol. 1, p. 107, Einstein A., (1952), *The Principle of Relativity*, NewYork, Dover, p. 37f.
121 Phipps, Jr., Thomas E. (2006). *Old Physics for New—a worldview alternative to Einstein's relativity theory*, Apeiron, Montreal, p. 1. (See also 2nd Edition, published in 2012).
122 Ibid., p. 4.

Phipps further elaborates on the historical development of electromagnetism:

> In the nineteenth century this feature of non-invariance was taken seriously. Maxwell's predicted fringe shifts were looked forexperimentally but not found. Relativity at first order was thus discovered (by Mascart and others) to be an empirical fact. That forced the conclusion that Maxwell's equations were wrong, or that something else was wrong. A "solution" was offered by Lorentz and subsequently reinforced by Einstein (in 1905). This was that "inertial" motions are to be described not by the Galilean transformation. ..[but by Lorentz transformations].[123]

The primary reason why the Maxwellian equations are problematic stems from a very basic fact that was overlooked in their formulation. As Phipps states:

> A directly related difficulty evidenced by the Maxwell magnetic induction equation... is that it misrepresents the Faraday observations on which it is allegedly based.[124]

This is because, as Phipps continues to explain elaborately, in Faraday's observations of the reality of magnetic induction there is a time derivative (d/dt) involved. This is most significant because using d/dt allows for the determination of the electromotive force, represented by the line integral and a partial derivative cannot be used to take care of accelerated relative motions of circuit parts when there is a shape change. Phipps states:

> Among those changed by Faraday was the shape of his circuit. That is, he moved part of the circuit in the magnetic field and observed that this produced an emf in the circuit as a whole. It is the shape-changing aspect that necessitates using a total time derivative d/dt native to traditional field theory... There is no escape from d/dt, because a shape change cannot occur without accelerated relative motions of various circuit parts. Such different motions in different places require for their local (differential) description different values of a local velocity parameter v_d (t), of the sort that is present in d/dt but not in $\partial/\partial t$.[125]

---

123 Ibid., p. 5.
124 Ibid., p. 9. 2nd Edition.
125 Ibid., p. 10. 2nd Edition.

The mixing of local accelerations and non-accelerations which cannot be dealt with by Special Relativity, should be handle-able by General Relativity but this has never been done so far and besides the fallacious nature of General Relativity, a simple line integral will do the job. Phipps then goes on to recount how ineptly and fallaciously relativists, who see the obvious problem, try to overcome this problem by other technical means. Phipps technically derives the correct formulation and states the crux of the matter:

> The introduction of the d/dt operator completely spoils the formal symmetry of space and time differentiations and thus destroys the basis in electromagnetism for SRT and for all modern physics built upon space-time symmetry. And it leaves no justification for "universal covariance", the mathematical expression of spacetime symmetry that is the touchstone or shibboleth of our scientific age. [126]

What symmetry is violated? Phipps states that: "The reputation of every physicist of the modern era, dead or alive, depends on that little $\partial/\partial t$. Empiricism calls for the field equation...to be replaced by the Herztian invariant form...but that would destroy spacetime symmetry..."[127] whereas the total time derivative upsets the perceived balance of space and time of those physicists who are not looking at the reality of events in space but have notions of mathematics such as beauty, symmetry etc., which cannot be the foundation of realty. In his book, Phipps goes on to expand the Hertzian equation to different orders. He states that the phenomena of stellar aberration was given an incorrect explanation from Special Relativity and the Hertzian third order equation would accurately measure this phenomenon which we can now adequately test using Very Long Baseline Interferometry.[44][128] This is easily testable now and can decide as to which is the correct theory: Special Relativity or Neo-Hertzian. This is another nail in Einsteinian Relativity's coffin: Stellar aberration refers to the angle at which starlight is seen through the telescope—the aberration effect being caused because the telescope is aimed from an object which is moving (the Earth) and this motion causes the aberration. There is an error on the part of Einstein in his analysis of stellar aberration and is not addressed by modern day physicists, but rather, is swept under the rug. The error hasbeen made because Einstein, due to

126 Ibid., p. 15. 2ⁿᵈ Edition.
127 Ibid., p. 13.
128 Ibid., pp. 76-77.

his notions of relative velocities, based the velocities on source/sink and also to preserve spacetime symmetries. Phipps succinctly and concisely summarizes the situation:

> But of course that wasn't empirically correct. The stellar light sources we seeare known to be in all sorts of motion, implying all sorts of values of source-sink relative velocity...yet in fact all stars show the same SA [Stellar Abberration], the same α-value. The great distance of the stars makes no difference because relative velocity is unaffected by distance. The "fixed stars" are a fiction and of no interest to physics.[129]

The astute and valiant late Canadian physicist Paul Marmet (who was largely ignored by the Einsteinians) explained very clearly in his paper on this subject as to why relativity asapplied by Einstein is incorrect[130]; it is because we have to consider the direction of the photons emanating from the star in relation to the Earth rather than the motion of the source(i.e. the moving star) and once we do this the situation is not symmetrical as per relativity as conceived by Einstein (by symmetry we mean that if A moves it causes an effect X on B which is not moving; and if B moves but A is still, then the same effect X would occur on B): in other words, contrary to relativity, the movement of the star in relation to the Earth will not cause the type of aberration as is to be expected with Einsteinian relativity because photon directionality, the source's motion and the motion of the Earth keep adjusting and compensating so that aberration for all stars is the same (irrespective of which model of photons one uses: the particle, wave or microbit model of the photon). Phipps also discusses the irrelevancy of the source's motion:

> Given that the Hertzian or neo-Hertzian description of SA [Stellar Aberration] depends only upon detector motion, it is worthwhile...to mention a simple physical explanation that makes it clear why source motion is not relevant to the phenomenon....Visible stellar objects, by their nature, are omnidirectional radiators.[131]

---

129 Ibid., p. 85
130 http://www.newtonphysics.on.ca/aberration/
131 Ibid., pp. 93-94. 2nd Edition.

He goes on to use the analogy of "spokes on a wheel" such that the "turn [of the wheel] is such as to cancel the effect upon aberration of any transverse motion of the star; since the centre of the wheel [i.e. the star/source] stays put."[132]

Concerning stellar aberration then, the fact is that one is forced to use the orbital velocity of the Earth and because the first order equation used by Einstein agreed with the physical results, few physicists looked at the incorrect thinking behind the first order formula.[133] There is, as such, no symmetry as Phipps argues correctly and that is what was "born out of a parametric deficiency of Maxwell's equations, and fails the first test (SA) [Stellar Aberration] of ability to describe one-way light propagation..."

Which relativist is bold enough to now put his/her money where his/her mouth is? To quote Phipps on the challenge:

> The absence of a second-order term in the neo-Hertzian result...and the presence of such in the SRT result, ...is especially to be noted. It marks a significant difference, and thus provides the basis for a crucial test to decide between the two theories as to which is physics.[134]

Phipps also views time dilation as a physical phenomenon because he does not objectify time irrationally; time is simply a measure of motion and in their trajectory particles can be affected by other particles slowing them down, slowing their decay etc. This had been discussed at length in FME v.1. However, the question of length contraction had been leftopen in FME, in the sense that either it is a physical phenomenon as Herbert Ives was inclined to believe, from some experiments that were indicating this, or it is not, as Phippscontends. Phipps covers these topics in great detail from Chapters 6 to 8 in his book. However, these are matters of detail and can be resolved on the basis of a secure physics that does not violate common sense and is deterministic and is really a continuation and expansion of Islamic methodology of testing and formulating mathematical equations thatthe Unitarian Newton and others followed from his predecessor Islamic scientists (Ibn Al-Haytham, etc.). This is a physics that does not confuse metaphors with reality and plunge into the various fallacies as highlighted by Dingle. It is okay for a three-year old to mix fantasy with reality but it is inexcusable for adults!

---

132 Ibid., pp. 93-94. 2nd Edition.
133 Ibid., p. 85.
134 Ibid., p. 88.2nd Edition.

Chapter 4

Subquarks: On the Road to the Inevitable Microbit

Eventual Discovery of Subquarks and Beyond

Even though we cannot say, for sure, how many levels of groupings of microbits exist, we can, nonetheless, derive an approximate mathematical model using the most recent advances in mathematics. For reasons which I will not delve into in this article, I believe thatthere are three levels below the quark level before we get to the microbit itself, that is quarks(subquarks(sub-subquarks(microbits, where I make the notation '('means 'are comprised of a grouping of"; this reason will be covered in another planned article. Severalmajor particle physicists who accept and work on the Standard Model of particle physics have written papers over the last few decades where they have hypothesized, strongly, subquarks. Chief theoretical physicists who opted to investigate the possibility of subquarks were: Abdus Salaam (the Physics Nobel Prize Winner of 1979) his collaborator Jogesh Pati and the Japanese physicist Hidezumi Terazawa. Indeed, the distinguished Terazawa, still going strong, stated in one of his most recent papers that:

> In January 1996, the CDF Collaboration at the Fermilab Tevatron collider [9] released their data on the inclusive jet differential cross section for jet transverse energies...which may indicate the presence of quark substructureat the compositeness energy scale, ΛC, of the order of 1.6 TeV. It can be taken as an exciting and already intriguing historical discovery of the substructure of quarks (and leptons), which has been long predicted, or as the first evidence for the composite model of quarks (and leptons), which has been long proposed since the middle of 1970's [3, 4, 5, 6, 7]. It may dramatically change not only the so-called "common sense" in physics or science but also that in philosophy, which often states that quarks (and leptons) are the smallest and most fundamental forms (or particles) of matter in the "mother nature". Note that such relatively low energy scale for ΛC ofthe order of 1 TeV has recently been anticipated rather theoretically [10] or by precise comparison between currently

available experimental data and calculations in the composite model of quarks (and leptons) [11]. However, the experimental indication would certainly encourage us, "composite modelists", to continue to study the composite model of quarks (and leptons) extensively and to make more predictions for future experimental tests of the model.[135]

Hidezumi, in fact, went beyond this in his earlier paper and speculated that subquarks may have formed in the early Universe after the Big Bang. In his paper "Possible Effects of Non-Vanishing Particle Sizes in the Early Universe", he states that:

> Possible effects of the non-vanishing sizes of particles (atoms, nuclei, nucleons, quarks, and leptons) in the early Universe (the temperature T)... are discussed in an extended Friedmann model of the Universe... Especially pointed out are the following possibilities: (4) for T 103TeV, the Universe was filled not with quark-gluon plasma but with "subquark plasma".[136]

> ...However, it seems difficult to extend ...the Einstein-Friedmann field equations, so that the non-vanishing sizes of matter particles may be accommodated. The reason for this is simple: Neither Einstein's picture of gravitation in general relativity nor Friedmann's picture of the Universe is consistent with particle physicist's picture of particles with non-vanishing sizes. Probably, either completely particle-theoretical description of theUniverse in the continuous space-time or drastic modification of the space- time metric into a discontinuous one seems to be necessary. Which way to proceed is a subject for future investigations.[137]

In a recent *Scientific American* article it is stated that there may be indications that quarks and leptons themselves are comprised smaller particles:

> The Standard Model views quarks and leptons as indivisible. Astoundingly,though, various clues imply that they are instead built of still smaller components. If quarks and leptons are not fundamental at all, and

---

135 Terazawa, Hidezumi. (2011). *High Energy Physics in the 21-st Century*, "Unified Supersymmetric CompositeModel of All Fundamental Particles and Forces", p. 3.
136 Terazawa, Hidezumi. (1997). INS Report: *Possible Effects of Non-vanishing Particle Sizes in the Early Universe*,CERN, Institute for Nuclear Study, University of Tokyo, Tokyo, p. 1. This article was also published later on in: *Modern Physics Letters A*, Volume 12, Issue 38, pp. 2927-2931 (1997).
137 Ibid., p. 6.

smaller bits do in fact exist, their presence will force extensive revisions of our theories.Just as nuclear power was inconceivable before Earnest Rutherford discovered the structure of the atom in 1911, unveiling another sub-atomic onion will certainly reveal phenomena we cannot yet imagine. [Yes it will indeed and the endpoint will be the microbit!].[138]

The Fermilab physicist, Don Lincoln, goes on to say:

The Standard Model treats the quarks and leptons as pointlike particles without any internal structure. But the patterns within the table, as within chemistry's periodic table, raise the possibility that the differences in generations stem from the configuration of even smaller building blocks of matter within quarks and leptons.[139]

It goes without saying, but must be mentioned nonetheless, that any particle has a finite size; just because we cannot measure it does not mean it does not. Or just because our concocted mathematical formulations may have problems dealing with this basic logic does not mean that it has no structure. They are not 'points' but have a finite size, albeit so minuscule. If there is no size then it really does not exist!

To get the full framework of reality we can drop general relativity like a hot potato and the indeterministic stance of quantum mechanics and adopt the microbit model which is a deterministic particle-based model (it is really a deeper and philosophically revised quantum mechanics model) in absolute space that unifies physics and leads to a unification of biology as well (see Part 1 of this book). The renowned mainstream, though of late extremely critical Freidwart Winterberg, who is one of the four respected students of Heisenbrg stated in a lecture at Imperial College , University of London that:

It is the failure to quantize Einstein's gravitational field theory formulated ina Riemannian curved space-time which has led to a profound crisis in modernphysics, no less profound than was the crisis of physics at the beginning of the 20th century, resolved by the special theory of relativity and quantum mechanics.

To overcome the present crisis several leading theoretical physicists have entered a maze of speculations from which there appears to be no es-

---

138 Lincoln, Don. (2012). "The Inner Life of Quarks", *Scientific American*, p. 39.
139 Ibid., p. 40.

cape: The conjectured existence of higher dimensional spaces, previously reserved by the spiritists as the seat for the ghosts of the dead, not supported by a single piece of physical evidence, with all physics laboratories still three-dimensional.

In my talk I will present compelling reasons why the special theory of relativity, and by implication the general theory of relativity, cannot be the ultimate truth describing the physical Universe. And the same must be said about quantum mechanics with its strange, over 10 meters experimentally verified, superluminal quantum correlations.

The Ptolemaic system was cast in the concrete of circular motions, permittingus to add an arbitrary number epicycles. In a similar way Einstein's Universeis cast in the concrete of geometry, permitting us to add an arbitrary number of (higher) dimensions.[140]

For those wishing to get into the technical mathematical aspects of the difficulties in combining non-Euclidian metrics with "virtual particles in quantum mechanics" are encouraged to review a transcript of this very important lecture. To end our discussion of quantum mechanics as a deterministic system, we shall cite Thomas Phipps, where in his second edition of *Old Physics for New* he discusses the drifting into "La-La-Land" of contemporary quantum mechanics based on the Copenhagen Interpretation, where c-number parameters that tell us the locations of particles in 3-space or phase space are lacking:

Despite all earnest talk about observers and observability, the experts' currently spavined "quantum mechanics" is crippled by a manifest lack of parameters needed to tie it meaningfully to reality.[141]

---

140   Lecture presented at Imperial College, London, September 3-6, 2004: *Physical Interpretations of Relativity Theory - IX*, "The Einstein Myth and the Crisis in Modern Physics", F. Winterberg, University of Nevada.

141   Ibid. p. 319, *Old Physics for New*, 2nd Edition.

Chapter 5

The Mass Problem

Bo Lehnert and photon mass

Let us now examine Physicist Bo Lehnert's concept that the photon possesses mass. According to Lehnert, whose latest book is entitled *Revised Quantum Electrodynamics*, the photon does have a mass, as we state as well, in the microbits model. This does not mean that the electron does not interact with the photon; it can and does but not in the manner of the standard model which is based on virtual popping up from nowhere and then slipping backinto nowhere. Though Lehnert's model is not like that of microbits, there are some strikingly similar conclusions. In a personal email to this writer, he states:

> Many thanks for your interesting and kind comments on the photon mass. I fully agree with the points which you make. Also I have not been aware of the results of your investigations on problems related to the shortcomings ofthe Standard Model..... I thank you for referring to my investigations. I alsoagree with you that, with all respect, the Higgs theory may not be the only way to the truth, and that it is a rather complex approach, based on spontaneous, nonlinear interaction in two steps. There have been some doubts expressed on this by G. Veltman and S. Hawkings among others.

He remarks in a preamble to his aforementioned new book that:

> In conventional theoretical physics and its Standard Model the guiding principle is that the equations are symmetrical. This limitation leads to a number of difficulties, because it does not permit masses for leptons and quarks, the electron tends to "explode" under the action of self-charge, a corresponding photon model has no spin, and such a model cannot accountfor the "needle radiation" proposed by Einstein and observed in the photoelectric effect and in the two-slit experiments.

Lehnert's model resolves many issues some of which, he summarizes, are:

> The point-charge-like behaviour of the electron comes out from the theory as a consequence of a nonzero net electric charge.

> A revised process of renormalization makes it possible for the electron to have finite and nonzero net charge, magnetic moment, rest mass, and angular momentum (spin) and also a finite size and internal structure.

Concerning electromagnetic wave phenomena, Lehnert states:

> The present theory leads to a model of the individual photon which has anonzero spin. Photon spin and photon rest mass are two sides of the same intrinsic property.

Concerning the nature of light

In my correspondence with Lehnert on a clarification of his position with respect to thedouble-slit experiment, he states (as directly quoted from my email communication with him) the following points:

> From my basic equations on a photon wave packet, there are obtained twosolutions in cylindrically symmetric geometry. One has comparatively extended transverse dimensions, and the other is needle-like. With the properties of these two modes in mind, an interpretation of the experiments is made somewhat in the sense of the Copenhagen school byBohr. The photon of my theory has like the neutrino a rest mass, and I therefore introduce the hypothesis that it can perform "photon oscillations" between the two obtained states, in analogy with neutrino oscillations. For both photon modes energy and spin are conserved.In this way the photon in the two-slit experiments can successively behaveboth as a wave of extended transverse dimensions and as a needle-shaped particle-like geometry when passing through the double slits. For the individual photon both particle behaviour in the form of needle-like radiation and a wave behaviour in the form of interference phenomena can be realized. This satisfies the necessary criteria for the observed behaviour in two-slit experiments, and it also contributes to the interpretation of such experiments. For the W, W and Z bosons, a Proca-type equation being analogous to that of the present theory can possibly be applied to the weak

field case. This would provide the bosons with a nonzero mass, as an alternative to the Higgs concept.[142]

In postulating finite sizes and structure for the electron and a mass for the photon, Lehnertis in total agreement with the principles and conclusions of the microbit model, in at least this respect. What appears to be happening in the world of physics is that: The quantum mechanical side has adopted the no mass of photon from Relativity –a theory which we have shown to be false because of internal contradictions. Adopting this false view of a massless photon incorporated into the Standard Model which requires a symmetry of the equations, it has led to a problem in which in order to explain the W and Z particles having a mass, the Higgs field has had to be introduced with the Higgs particle. After the Higgs particle was proposed it had to be found or the entire structure would have had to be scrapped or revised intensely. The Large Hadron Collider costing a great deal of funds was built and lots on contractors have made money on this! Desperation set in to discover the Higgs and a lot has been at stake despite high sounding phrases like: "We are seeking the truth" and "It will be good to go beyond the standard model". The discovery of the Higgs was determined in terms of energy level expected. After colliding trillions upon trillions of particles they are identifying one of these particles within that energy range as the Higgs.

Higgs: A Unicorn in Sheep Clothing

The whole venture to find the Higgs particle does not seem like mature scientific investigation in terms of logic. To coin an analogy it is as if: In a murder case, the police framed a wrong theory that did not make sense and had holes in it. The theory was concocted by the police chief. A certain person (culprit) with a certain description was being sought. All eyes were on the police's performance: They were having a tough time finding the murderer. Eventually they found someone who was almost the same in appearance and was of the same ethnic background and accent. The police chief then said:"It's as good as catching the real man; and the public won't know!" There was then a pressrelease which stated that: "The dangerous foreign criminal has been finally arrested! Let's celebrate and drink some champagne!"

---

142 See also: Lehnert, Bo (2012) *Revised Quantum Electrodynamics*, pp. 126-127.

Therefore, really it appears to be the case that the physics establishment has devised a unicorn of its own making which they, through correlation and causation fallacy, are now identifying with Higgs. Not only has a unicorn been invented but it is being erroneously being stated that the unicorn has been found (notwithstanding a Nobel prize being awarded for this unicorn). The media in general knows nothing of the deep fallacious history of relativity (despite the fact that it was they who collectively propagandized Einstein and relativity without technical reflection). When one becomes enmeshed in ultimately wrongtheories they become institutionalized. One has to learn about this from history and not repeat these mistakes which we have repeated twice over the last 100 years with respect toGR and the interpretive aspects of quantum mechanics. And all this tells us nothing about unification or gravity!

The Higgs Particle and the Emperor's New Clothes: The Photon has Mass

If one examines the microbits model: the simplest unificatory model existable, one does not need the Higgs particle. Indeed, according to the Microbit Model the Standard Model is incorrect to a large extent because of its incorporation of the Higgs. Not only that, but any extended model based on the same type of 'exchanges' cannot and will never be able to explain gravity which involves directional forces that can only be explained by two things: contact and pressure. So any model that really explains gravity through particles must have this net directional pressure feature; it must be mechanistic but not of the LeSage type or the type of explanations being sought in the 19th Century by many. This is the mechanism for gravity explained in FME V.1 and in the latest version of the microbits explanation (*Microbits: A New Unified Physics*) in terms of basic principles based on differential forces caused by a field of 'g-particles' acting on principles of microbit collisions, governed by the three s's (stickiness, squashability, and spin). You can read the details of how this transpires in: *Microbits: A New Unified Physics*, which is available online free of charge as previously mentioned.

I will not elaborate the details of the solution to gravity in this book, because I am focusing on more philosophical and methodological aspects, but suffice it to say that essentially the explanation of gravity *also* leads to an extension in the so-called Newton's laws by two more laws. Using these five laws, the whole of mechanics, from the micro to the macro, can be explained, and it truly unifies physics in a mechanistic way. This is explained in Chapter 2, in the above link to the book (available without cost).

In Quantum Mechanics the ascription of a massless photon has been inadvertently borrowed from relativity which we have shown to be logically false. Its actions are on other particles as described in FMEv.1 (see pages 45 to 49 of the online version of the book). It too is comprised of microbits of course, and the microbit grouping's action on particle composites that are larger than itself confers mass in the relational way that we have hiteherto described. The photon itself therefore does indeed have mass as it is affected by the ambient g-particles. What has been found in the LHC is not the Higgs particle that gives mass to everything but what we call 'mass' is the interaction between the stuff in the object and the ambient g-particles. Gravity does not therefore have to travel at speeds faster than light to affect objects; it surrounds them. The microbit model answers Newton's perplexing wonder about the illogicality of action at a distance. It answers why and how attraction mechanically works as opposed to only repulsion. In the microbit model, all particles have mass because the g-particle (I am not calling them gravitons as these already carry a baggage) pervades space as an extension field that evolves/settles after the Big Bang. Concerning mass and the equation E=mc2, it will indeed come more into the general public's purview that Einstein was not the first to formulate this and never had a proof for it and the proof of its validity will come only with a most generalized proof for special case of objects that relate to the speed of light in vacuum that does not resort to calculations through Einsteinian relativity. With microbits this equation is perfectly natural as microbit concepts draw no distinction in essence between matter and energy. The reason for this of course is that everything is comprised of microbits and "mass" and "energy" are simply human classifications due to the type of measurement of the state in which microbits happen to be, both in terms of motion and groupings. This does not mean that such demarcations are not useful; they are, but the mechanics of what is going on behind the terms "mass" and "energy" are required for clear thinking and advancement. Furthermore, a new energy equation will have to eventually be formulated that will incorporate new terms that will have to include the concept of microbits and particles that exceed the speed of light in vacuum and no causality will be affected. Normal causality will be shown to hold. The ultimate law of conservation will be applied, which is that microbits never vanish but are only re-grouped.

Chapter 6

Towards Quantum Realism:
John Bell, for whom the bell tolls or the Inconvenient Rise of Quantum Determinism

From the Quranic perspective and indeed from basic logic, the Universe does not generate itself, is not self-aware or evolving towards consciousness etc. Furthermore, the Quranic view is based on mind independent reality. The particles exist as a reality in space at a specific location and with a specific motion and there is no such thing as the collapse of the wave function. In addition, nothing created can travel instantaneously as a spooky action at a distance. The Universe of particles in absolute space is based on cause and effect—based on the design and pathways of the microbits and all the emergent laws that arise from them due to cause and effect. The microbits, in fact, form a system that is neither analogue nor digital, neither emergent nor non-emergent, but the microbits have properties of all these in a unique mix, all of their own. For example, gravity, according to the microbits' model, is based on particles that emerged from the Big Bang and the gravitational force, and acceleration due to gravity are a result of the jittery motion of these particles imparting net directional forces. 'Newton's Laws' etc. are indeed a result of intervening particles that he surmised. The microbits are very orderly and based on rules and this allows us to formulate laws based on ensemble particle behaviour at the submicro level Therefore, for example, as stated in FME v. 1, the experiments testing the EPR thought experiment through Alain Aspect and subsequent tests that purport to violate Bell's inequality are being misinterpreted through measurement. There is no instant coordination to produce strong correlation. As discussed by Professor Bryan Sanctuary143 and through papers written by Joy Christian at Oxford University Bell's model was too simplistic and did not account for all statistical possibilities of rotations or spinning orientations of particles in space. In other words, by basing statistical limits, a very restricted model of electron and photons was shown to violate Bell's inequalities, but since the inequality is itself incorrect,

---

143   Professor of Chemistry at McGill University.

it means that locality holds sway and Bell's violation can be explained through regular statistics and that quantum mechanics, as a result, does not violate the equality. No instantaneous correlation between the recordings of the two particles that arise from a common source.

The very basic reason why the inequalities are incorrect is that contrary to the prevailing obscurantist and pseudo-sophisticated views, the electron has an actual spin in 3–D space in principle just like macroscopic objects. It does spin about an axis, and indeed, has a 3-D structure. It spins on various tiltable axes depending on the nature of the other particles surrounding it. When a probe lines up on one of its indistinguishable axes it disturbs the ontologically existent and unobserved spin. The fact is that Bell's Inequality is to be expected to be violated, as the electron is not a point particle with only a binary set of spins as has erroneously been considered. In the Stern-Gerlach experiment, when one measures the spin in the z direction the particle is so affected that it orients in that direction and its spin in the other directions become non-existent. Of course if these electrons come from a common source there is bound to be strong correlation but that correlation is statistically determined by an ensemble of particles and that correlation is also affected and is sensitive to perturbation depending on the environmental set-up as the two electrons part company. However, an electron spins in an unknowable direction (with current technology) when it is not being measured. It does have a spatial configuration and specific motion. The data set is larger and the probabilities are therefore to be expected as $2\sqrt{2}$ instead of 2 in the more complex situation of particle's real spin in 3-D space. Bell's Inequality was hence based on very naive concepts which the physics community bought into and, as usual, because it is a complex subject the media bought into it too; it got taught at universities and the non-specialist public just accepted it as they rely on the scientific authorities. New age mysticism also jumped the band-wagon and started to support this idea.

As a result, when one examines all the evidence, there is no action at a distance or spooky action at a distance. The probability for correlation as found in the supposed violation of Bell's Inequality arises due to simple statistics taking this larger data set of hidden variables. In fact, this whole episode is the fallacy of correlation-causation. It is highly ironic that over the last 50 years, Bohr's interpretation and its variants have not recognized this basic fact of motion, perhaps because of the combined reasons of having a kind of a mystical outlook to nature and also because of confusion arising from a logical positivistic perspective of believing the existence of something only if measured as being scientific, which mutated into the ontological non-existence of something unless it is measured. This is the beginning of the collapse of 'entanglement' and a reversion to a unitary view of physics where there is no separation between 'classical' and 'quantum', as such. All our textbooks will have to be re-written on this subject that touches upon interpretation. This will also have an effect on the technology of information processing systems (such as quantum computing) —to bring it back to reality from the pie-in-the-sky. This whole incorrect outlook towards nature is what I call naïve abstractionism and, as we saw earlier, is at the root of and plagues special and general relativity. If only Einstein had used pure logic against his own conclusions, as he did against quantum mechanics (as per the EPR argument which he participated in) he would have really achieved something of real significance rather than illusory significance, which is now poised like a deck of cards at the edge of a precipice, ready to collapse into oblivion. This, correct view, in fact, corresponds with the microbit concepts of actual concrete reality of particles in space at the smallest levels. It should be a big lesson and make physicists realize that mathematics is only a measuring and statistical tool to measure the Mind Independent Reality out there. When we make mathematical models or yardsticks, if we do not model physical reality well enough, we will end up with inaccurate, incorrect or totally false conclusions. The time is now over for Quantum Mechanics, based on the ontologically indeterminate view, and this is eventually going to lead to Quantum Determinism, which is really just part of the overall Deterministic view of nature that was created by the Determiner. University of Liverpool physicist, Werner A. Hofer rightly and unequivocally states:

> The experimental results obtained in Yves Couder's group and theoretical results by Gerdard Grossing indicate that the wave-like distribution of trajectories of electrons in interference experiments are most likely due to the quantized interactions leading to a discrete set of transferred momenta.144

---

144 Hofer, Werner A. (2012). "Quantum mechanics: A new chapter?", http://arxiv.org/pdf/1209.1029v1.pdf, p. 1.

The emerging picture, from the preceding sections, is one of a scientific revolution with a depth and scale not seen since the quantum revolution itself, about a century ago. ...[145]

What is removed, is the additional weight quantum mechanics carried with it in the form of contradictions, paradoxes, impossibilities, and plain weirdness. There is no quantum weirdness left, once the extension of electrons, the role of wavefunctions, the specifics of rotations in three dimensional space, and the consequences of discrete interaction energies and momenta are thoroughly understood. This will almost certainly not be welcomed by some colleagues: after all, this quantum weirdness made for hugely exciting research programs and research papers for the last two generations. It remains to be seen, which of the more outlandish predictions,possible only within the ill-defined conceptual framework of conventional quantum mechanics, will in the end survive.[146]

Couder's experiment, that was first performed in 2006, (see Youtube: http://www.youtube.com/watch?v=W9yWv5dqSKk) shows that a spherical drop of silicon floats atop a liquid where waves are created and that a symbiotic relationship develops between thedrop (analogous to a particle) and the waves in the fluid that guide the drops and many of the properties of the quantum world of the submicroscopic are the same as in this analogous macroscopic realm. As mentioned in a previous section, in 2001, we (Muslim and I) had the same explanation (in principle) as Couder's unusual explanation for the double-slit experiment.Although Couder is examining this analogously we should remember that this analogue can turn out to be true of the actual principles involved at the quantum level. This is because the patterns in nature are the same at all levels. This is pointing to the veracity of the microbit model wherein the 'waves' are actually smaller sized particles that affect the trajectories of the electron. The explanation of the photon through the double-slits using the microbits' model has also been explained and is the core explanation (refer to FME, online version pp. 76-83). This is really showing that de Broglie's deterministic interpretation of particles was closer to the truth and that the Solvay conference appears to have been inordinately hijacked!

---

145   Ibid., p. 7.

146   Ibid., p. 7.

In FME v.1, the reason for the 'dual nature of light' is explained in detail and also see the latest book on microbits. Couder's experiment, conducted in 2006, which was five years after the publication of FME points to the microbitic explanation of the double-slit experiment being true, in that it shows that analogous motions occur in the macro-level in quantum mechanics if there is a physical hidden structure. In the microbits' model of the double-slit experiment, we had postulated a physical foundation for the paths which electrons traverse as well as the physical mechanism by which the photon itself would behave as a particle and wave, in a logical way. The macro-level is thus shedding light on the quantum: the patterns in nature are the same at all levels. This should be a wake-up call to those who are dissatisfied with the state of quantum mechanics. It is a wake-up call to a fully deterministic explanation of reality at *all* levels.

Chapter 7

Theophysics: Putting God and Physics back into Physics

God is the centrality of the Quran. Unless we understand the relation of God to physics, we cannot understand either properly. The Quran will help us in this endeavour. But why would we bring the Quran into the picture, in conjunction with physics? Is it not the scripture of some retrogressive foreigners riding camels, wearing rags on their heads? This caricature is not far from the minds of many people in the media distorted 'reality', the fantasy land where manipulated images and juxtapositions of words and pictures bypass the critical thinking of many individuals, reinforced not in the least by current geopolitical crises! The question that would reverberate in many a mind reflecting on scientific issues of a fundamental nature is: "What the heck has the Quran to do with science, let alone with the frontiers of physics?" Well, to answer this, let us analyse the issue step by step: Muslims believe that the Quran is a direct revelation of the maker of the cosmos, the designer of the physics in which we are engulfed. In the last century, many of the verses in the Quran pertaining to discoveries have been verified. These things could not have been known by Prophet Muhammad and include the Big Bang, the expanding Universe and galactical formation. This of course lends credence to the claim that the Quran is indeed a revelation because there is no other place from which Prophet Muhammad could have gotten this information, unless one were to believe in far-fetched theories that have no credibility whatsoever and tend to 'pass the buck' and are indeed very laughable. Some of these explanations are embarrassing to say the least, as for example: *aliens?*: but where is the evidence for aliens descending 1,400 years ago? *Some secret knowledgeable person existed who used to give the Prophet information?*: but where did that person get the knowledge from? *The Greeks had that knowledge?*; someone should take Greek history 101 to know that this was not possible, and so on and so forth.

In addition to the amazing scientific correlation that the Quran thrusts upon those who are thinking and not lazy to investigate or prejudicial and have made their minds up because they had a bad experience with 'religion' (i.e.

priests etc.), or were unduly repulsed by the behaviour of governments and individuals in countries with majority Muslim populations that are behaving in diametric opposition to the Quran, the Quranic position also assists in coming up with an understanding of how we are to analyse nature properly. These ways are more subtle and methodological and in this chapter they shall be discussed at some length. We use our reason to investigate nature and arrive at the truth. The methodology is the same with respect to determining the veracity of the Quran: We use reason and investigate the Quran and find that it matches our conclusions from nature. We also see certain principles in the Quran which we can compare with nature to advance our knowledge. The entire investigation must be based on non-contradiction: intra-Quranic; intra-Universe; inter-Quranic and Universe.

The Quran lets us know what is possible and what is not possible in the Universe. Personally, this writer is only concerned about the truth and would willingly embark on jettisoning the Quran through a parabolic trajectory into a garbage can, if it were inconsistent. However, when time after time it proves to be true, it would be rather imprudent and impudent to engage in such unwarranted aerodynamic recycling activities. So now let us examine these concepts very carefully before we plunge deep into physical concepts.

Logic/Methodology

First and foremost, the Quran emphasizes that non-contradiction in the methodology ought be used to discover the truth. The Quranic verse states:

> Do they not ponder on the Quran: If it were from other than God surely
> you would find many inconsistencies in it.[147]

Therefore, there must be no internal or external contradictions in an explanation of the workings of nature. Once we have such contradictions we know that the theory is false. And this is precisely why Special Relativity fails—it fails the test of internal consistency. As such it cannot be true from this alone, in addition to the concepts of space and time themselves. One way to see this internal contradiction is Herbert Dingle's now famous example, which was used in FME

---

147 Quran 4:82

v.1, (and also in the updated book) and which no one has been able to depose simply because it is impossible to prove the logicality of illogicality.[148]

The Reality of Existence

The global structure of existence has a bearing on how we view how we came into being and has everything to do with the big question of existence; indeed, it is the foundation, and the key to answering many other 'sub-questions'.

The Quran also stipulates that this reality exists and is real and is therefore not an illusion. even though it is sustained and maintained by God, or the Mind of God, it exists as a reality and we experience that created reality149. For example, a verse in the Quran states that:

> He [God] it is who created the cosmic systems and the Earth in the Truth.[150]

The Quran states that this Universe was created in the truth or in the Reality. As such, its existence is not illusory. In volume 2, of the Microbits series, and in Part 2 of this book, M. Muslim and this writer showed how this Universe is the imagination of God and in this sense is His sustained creation. Therefore, God is the absolute reality and all of nature is dependent on God's thoughts for existence and hence sustenance. But this does not mean that the Universe is unreal or we generate reality when we think.[151] (By 'His' it is not meant that 'God' is an anthropomorphic male type of being.'It' could be used but 'Him' has been used instead as it carries the idea of a Conscious Being better, associated with power). This is why the modern interpretation of quantum mechanics, as espoused by the school of Niels Bohr, is gravely at odds with the Quran and therefore reality/logic. We shall be taking this up in great detail later on, to see where and how this fatal error is being made.

Idea of Unification

We need to get back basics: absolute space, which is what the Quran points towards. Indeed, rather than multiple dimensions, in the Quran it speaks of the

---

148 Ibid., *From Microbits to Everything (Volume 1)*, pp. 144-147. On the internet version pp. 137-141.

149 Ibid., *From Microbits to Everything (Volume 2)*, pp. 105-122.

150 Quran 6:73.

151 Banaei, Mehran and Haque, Nadeem. (1995). *From Facts to Values: Certainty, Order, Balance and their Universal Implications*, p. 108.

Universe as existing in space. Space itself is never objectified. If it were, then the Big Bang verse in the Quran would never have been revealed the way it has been. After all, God knows how 'He' originated the Universe and the Big Bang and Quranic verse would have explicitly stated the creation of space with matter/energy.

The Quran speaks of the order of the processes in the Universe and the interconnections between things. Even in Quranic language, the Quran never splits things into spiritual and physical etc. There is God and His creation and both of these comprise two levels of existence. We exist as conscious entities and experience reality out there in space. Since there is one mind directing the Universe there ought to be unity. The general sense of unity within the diverse elements of the Universe is replete in the Quran. The Quran also states in clear Arabic, about 1,400 years ago that the Universe originated from the initially derogatory Hoylian term: the "Big Bang":

> Do those who cover the truth not see that the rest of the Universe (the heavens, or literally all those which are above) were one piece. And We [God] suddenly split/ripped them apart, and made every living thing from water. Will they (even then) not believe?[152]

And it is expanding:

> I (God, or "We" literally) have created this Universe with a force; indeed, I am (We are) definitely expanding it.[153]

Therefore, even physically, the Quran states that the Universe was once united in an 'observable' (i.e. realizable) manner. The integration and flawlessness of the universal laws, and hence its inherent unity, is depicted in the following verse:

> [It is God] who has created seven levels of cosmic clusters in integral conformity with each other. You can see no flaws in the beneficent one's creation; look again: can you see any cracks in the system? Were you to look repeatedly, your eyes would become strained and vision weakened [in an effort to find the flaws].[154]

---

152 Quran 21:30.
153 Quran 51:47.
154 Quran 67:3.

Notion of Space and Time in the Quran

In the Quran, four things are spoken of:

1. The heavens: the visible/realizable Universe we see up there by eye or instrumentation i.e. planets, stars and galaxies and other gaseous/dust matter.[155]

2. The Earth.[156]

3. What is between them, (space and also unknown things (matter/energy), which once known get shifted into #1).[157]

4. What is under the Earth.[158]

Number four above is not relevant for our discussions and will be left out of the analysis. There is a belief which is unfounded and erroneous, as we shall discuss in some detail below, that the creation of the Universe of matter and energy from the Big Bang was also the event of the creation of space. Space and time being fused together due to the incorrect impetus given by Einstein earlier, plus the misuse of Gaussian non-Euclidean mathematics made physicists select one of the several options to describe the Universe, leaving aside the model which postulates the pre-existence of absolute space yet the 'explosion' of the Big Bang within that pre-existing objectless region in space. That space itself could not have arisen with time is in fact recently highlighted in an article in the Scientific American, not to debunk Einsteinian physics, which the author appears to be following assiduously, but to avoid the problem that occurs when we include space as part of the expansion. This has been discussed already on page..... The Quranic view is that space—absolute space—pre-existed matter/energy, in which the Big Bang occurred. The reason is as follows: The Big Bang verse states:

> Do those who cover the truth not see that the rest of the Universe (the heavens, or literally all "those which are above") and the Earth were one piece. And we split suddenly them/ripped them apart, and made every living thing from water. Will they not believe?[159]

---

155   Quran 2:117.

156   Quran 2:22.

157   Quran 20:6

158   Quran 20:6

159   Quran 21:30.

As argued in From Microbits to Everything, Volume 2, this passage refers to the aforestated points #1 and #2 only, with #3 excluded. Since this verse only includes #1 and #2 and not #3, #3 cannot be the space compressed into the Big Bang; in other words space was not contracted into the Big Bang and was always ever-pre-existing. The Quranic verse does not state that those things which are above, that is, the 'heavens', the Earth and "space" were compressed to one point. In this context seven heavens, (see Part 3 of this book) means the clustered system of the Universe which includes the cluster of stellar systems (level 2) which are the galaxies, (level 1 being stellar systems), the cluster of galaxies (level 3), the cluster of cluster of galaxies or superclusters (level 4), the cluster of superclusters (level 5) and the cluster of cluster of superclusters – i.e. the whole Universe (level 6) and finally the entire Universe which is a cluster of cluster of cluster of superclusters (level 7). These are the seven heavens (saba samawati23 in Arabic literally means the "seven which are above") that the Quran is referring to in verse 67:3 (and in numerous other verses in the Quran) when this verse is applied to the space outside the Earth.

From these basic principles, one can actually derive the microbits' view, in the sense that it must be based on the unification of matter and energy and hence must be particle based; it must have originated from the Big Bang and it must be a concrete reality out there. In addition, in the Quran, a crucial ingredient is added: that of 'the balance' which in Arabic is al-mizan. The only logical interpolation one can make is that after the Big Bang split, there was only one type of particle, and out of this, all other particles emanated. In this sense we are not looking for one grand equation but one particle that unites everything. At certain points in the development of this Universe the four laws develop: electromagnetism; the strong force, the weak force and gravitation; the law behind the evolution of the four laws is the nature, motion and interaction of microbits in absolute space. Due to the interrelationship between all the particles, and the fact that from this model they are just groupings of the microbits and are the interplay of the one type of particle that forms everything in absolute space, the mathematics that will describe this view in the future is the mathematics of the motion of the microbits from the Big Bang, derived from simple rules concerning the microbits themselves, which are outlined in FME v.1 and in the latest installment, the book: *Microbits: A New Unified Physics.*

Two Basic factors which govern the Universe according to the Quran

The Universe governed and founded upon microbits, exhibits two Laws that are in the Quran:

1. **The law of static and dynamic balance. (*Al-mizan*: mentioned several times in the Quran but see especially verse: 55:7).**
   (There is a third type of balance that is responsible for evolution which is a subset of the dynamic balance which has been discussed in Part 1 of this book, and will not be taken up here, but readers are encouraged to read this part too).

2. **Complementarity or parity. (*zawjayn*: mentioned many times in the Quran as for example:51:49).**
   Parity, in which, for example, we have a particle and its anti-particle, has its basis in motions that are opposite (in actual spin for example) as we stated in FME v.1, and not subatomic placards stating "positive" and "negative".

The law of the balance is a clue that we are dealing with action and reaction, a tug of war between the microbit comprised particles that essentially gives us all the forces and the stability or lack thereof, including the novel idea of how an attractive force (i.e. the solution to gravity) operates without action at a distance. These particles are always moving and impart pushing and pulling. Net pushing causes repulsion and net pulling causes attraction. The pulling aspect works because of the rule of the Three S's. Without the mechanical pulling component comprised of two of the three S's: Squashability and Stickiness of the microbits, there would be no gravity in the Universe and indeed no Universe. Note that anyone purporting the existence of particles, if they are to be complete in their description, must ascribe some type of properties to them! When particles were first being considered by Rutherford etc. they were looked upon as 'hard' spherical objects.

Without an understanding of the foundation of the Universe, we cannot get ahead and will come to dead ends and false leads. But once the foundation is understood, it serves as an understanding for all phenomena over time. Although some recent attempts at understanding gravity that are based on mechanistic models have been proposed, they suffer from the fatal flaw that they exclude the reality of the fact that all objects down to some cut-off point have a gravitational field around them and that the inverse square law relation holds. Therefore, a mechanical model that makes contact and explains such a field is the only promising candidate to explain what gravity really is, that is, what that 'field' really is.

A slight but crucial revision to the solution for gravity is being made in the book Microbits: A New Physics that explains gravity fully. It will be available in 2025.

Note that an interesting verse in the Quran (chapter 13, verse 2) exists concerning the existence and invisibility of forces that play the major role in holding the Universe together and hence a tug of war. The Quran states that invisible columns support the structure of the Universe; as anyone studying rudimentary/elementary statics would know, this involves solely action and reaction forces that produce equilibrium. In addition, from a process perspective there is parity because there is only repulsion and attraction. The 'parity structures/entities/elements' are part and parcel of the mizan. The Quran therefore introduces physicality in three-space as the answer to the workings of the Universe, not abstract mathematical equations or abstract spaces etc. The mathematics must represent and mirror that reality, otherwise it is mere fantasy. This Universe is an engineered concrete reality and not some illusion or mathematical abstraction.

The Non-Existence of Dark Matter and Dark Energy: Modern Day Epicycles

In FME v.1, the issue of the accelerating Universe which requires a repulsive expansional force was not covered. It was discovered in 1998 that the Universe is expanding and since then this has been confirmed through further observational data. A cosmological constant had to be included in Einstein's equations of general relativity to account for this. Therefore, it is surmised that there is a repulsive pressure created by the cosmological constant through Dark Energy. Yet no one has been able to find this Dark Energy, but a few researchers have generated computer models to account for the motions by putting in these hypothesized particles in the models and then even producing pictures and computer simulations showing a distribution of these particles!

According to the microbits view: Outside this Universe there is only objectless space and no such thing as friction or other things (particles) to impede the expansion of the Universe; the only thing that could slow the Universe down is the self-gravity of its components but we are in phase where the gravitational attraction between galaxies is now overcome by the constant force that appeared at the Big Bang and remained constant creating a situation of acceleration. In this view then there is no Dark Energy as such. As far as Dark Matter goes, it is simply a mis-realization of how gravity works which is made of the evolving distribution and equilibrated settlement of g-particles (gravity particles that are too small to perceive and are of course each themselves spherical groupings of microbits) and the emergent interaction of g-particles emanating from each star creating that emergent field. It is because of the distribution of g-particles as an emergent field that creates the higher velocity in the outlier stars of the galaxies, not a halo of dark matter. Likewise, the end of the Universe will also be heralded by a command and the 'flat' Universe will collapse upon itself, back to a 'point'. Just as the beginning and its expansion rate was fixed (albeit influenced by the internal inter-gravitational 'stickiness' of the galaxies) so too is its end. With respect to Dark Energy which refers to the acceleration of the Universe, rather than its slowing down, it has become a problem finding Dark Energy; this is a rather embarrassing situation in physics now and at the forefront of theoretical resolution. In Part 2 we proved the existence of a single God and that the Universe had to have had a beginning. Likewise, the command from the Entity produced the origin. So too its end, for there is nothing in the Universe that will contract it and as it expands it will keep on expanding. Its expansion can only happen by a creative will that is not part of the Universe (i.e. the type of non-anthropomorphic God we discussed in Part 2 of this book). We therefore get this idea that this is not a God of the gaps, but certainly a God of beginnings and ends. The Quran in the same chapter speaks of the Big Bang and the Big Crunch that were subject to the commands or wills to expand and contract. After investigating the Quran and the logic of existence and creation it appears that the two terminals of the Universe: its beginning and end are set by the Creator. It is where physics has to head on meet so-called theology (though I make no distinctions between these subjects): Theophysics There are no particles that expand the Universe. The expansion is purely a command of the Creator that starts the Universe rolling. At the same time it is not the God- of-the gaps because there was no (this) Universe in the first place before the Big Bang so that there could be any gaps in causal explanations of processes within the it. The force is a constant force or command for the Universe to continually keep expanding. The expansion of the Universe is not connected to something going on inside the Universe but came from and is sustained by, the outside operating within the Universe, just as the lump of the Universe as a unity appeared from the command of God from God's mind as an imaginational product from its non-existence and the non-existence of any other Universe that could give rise to it. There was nothing in space that evolved the singularity—it was simply a direct command to BE and then a command split the lump which coincided with the command 'expand continuously'.

Since the Universe is comprised of unitary particles that split from one quasi-singularity due to an external force, that is, a force that was Conscious, then an internal force becomes redundant. The causative factor for the initial splitting did not involve any internal force but all the now splitting components are flying apart because of that initial conscious force to split imparted. If that causative force was external we do not need and there cannot be an internal causative force. One can use Ockham's Razor on this matter. Though Bo Lehnert dismisses Dark Energy for a number of reasons as the cause of this acceleration of the Universe with which this writer concurs, he, however, proposes that there is internal photon pressure due to zero-point energy, that is, due to a gas cloud of zero point energy photons leading to a radially outward directed pressure force160. It plays the role of 'dark energy'. However, I believe it is (or may be) even simpler than that, as outlined above. From this the atheists and astrophysics are being forced into see God as the only explanation of the reason for the accelerative expansion of the Universe as this entity would be seen to be the cause of the existence of the singularity, its explosion and its continued expansion and acceleration—all three aspects being external to the Universe through divine fiat and subject to a single command "Be", to put it in human linguistic terms. Thereafter, we have the microbits evolving through laws creating biological structures, entropy etc., wherein no God-of-the-gaps is present.

These ideas are further strengthened by the Quran itself in which it is stated:

> We have constructed this Universe **with a force** and We are indeed **expanding** it.[161] Here is the transliteration of the original Arabic:

> Wa As-Samā'a Banaynāhā **Bi'ayydin** Wa 'Innā Lamūsi'ūna.[162]

---

160 Lehnert, Bo. 2012. "Zero point energy as origin of dark matter and dark energy", *American Institute of Physics Conference Proceedings*, Volume 1445, pp. 102-114.
161 Quran 51:47
162 Quran 51:47

Note that the Quran is not stating that God is expanding the Universe with an inbuilt force in the Universe but that the Universe was initiated with that force which continues to expand it, where the word musiuna has only one meaning: expanding (it is a plural present participle of the Arabic verb ausa which means to make wider). What is meant here is that God does not say in the Quran that: "I have created a force in the Universe which has expanded it or which is continuing to expand it, or by which I am expanding it." But "I created the Universe with (the Arabic word "Bi") a force...". It is very subtle but there is a difference between "with" and "in". This is such a subtle point that it is being missed, assuming anyone asked the question in the first place! There is a big difference between with and in. But in normal human discourse depending on the context with can mean in. So let us look into this further in the English language and it is generalizable to Arabic. If someone says that they cooked this curry with green chillies what they mean here is that with = in. By this they mean: The chillies are in the curry. (This discussion is making me hungry!). As another example, if they were baking a cake and they were to put an ingredient in it which was the cause of the expansion of the dough they could still say: "I am expanding the cake with ingredient X". Therefore, in this case, "with" also means that they put something "in" the cake. However, in the context of the expansion of the Universe with and in distinctions become very significant. And since the Quran is very precise and without ambiguity—indeed, it is stated in the Quran itself that it is mubeen (pristinely clear); "with" cannot mean two things here—it either means there is something in the Universe that is expanding it—in terms of some particles, or that there is an external factor, in the sense of not being part of the Universe. We must take the apparent meaning here: 'with' means that which is external. In order to avoid ambiguity if God really meant that there is a part of the Universe that is making it expand, it would have been stated categorically: it would have been stated in Arabic as: "We have created this Universe with a force inside it", or "We have created a force in the Universe that is expanding it". Since such a categorical statement has not been used, it can only mean that some external force not part of the Universe but certainly having causation to it, and that it is God's command at its very inception, to 'split apart' as stated in verse 21:30. If the force was imparted at the inception of the Universe and is external to the Universe, it would remain so as a sustained force. This force would not disappear and then be left to some particles in the Universe to continue its expansion. If this line of argumentation is true, as a consequence, the current accelerated expansion of the Universe is due to the initial Force which remains constant minus the decreasing stiffness or resistance to expansion (akin to friction as an analogue) which decreases over time as the galaxies spread out. This leads to either a runaway accelerating Universe, whose acceleration varies over time, or a constant acceleration, if the resistance does not vary (as currently measured using Cepheid variables). From the latest data it has been gathered that the initial expansion was accelerating, then there was a period of deceleration and now we are in the period of acceleration. Why so? According to the Quranic analysis and microbit concepts, initially there was no gravity, as gravity is emergent and arises only when particles reach a certain size; there is a cut-off point. Therefore, the particles were not resisting expansion by self-attraction. In the second phase as the early galaxies started to form (i.e. when gravitation had emerged) the closer galaxies offered more resistance to the constant expansion force (the sustained command for expansion given by the Creator at the initiation of the Universe). Finally comes our era or phase, when the galaxies are far enough and do not offer such resistance to expansion and we see acceleration. We may have to revise the rate of acceleration in the phases etc. with new data, but the basic principles that are being discussed which concern an external force to the Universe, will remain.

As an epilogue to this discussion the precision of the Quran must be highlighted: Those who know the Quran and examples of its precision with words will know that this precision must also have been used in selecting the words describing the expansion, that is used in the Quran's expanding Universe verse (51:47), and this refers to the initial external force that is the pure will of God and is not some form of particle pressure in the Universe. Indeed, we know from all other examples that the Quran is precise to the utmost and there is no reason why it should be imprecise here, let alone the fact that the author of the verse and the expansion of the Universe are the same and the mapping should be perfect and descriptive to the utmost of what happened/is happening in physical space. This verse ties- in with the Big Bang verse of "the Universe and earth were one piece which We ripped apart..." and also "We will show them our signs in the horizons...until they know that this is the truth". I do not know what could be farther than the origin of the Universe, in this case in time.

Lastly, in the Quran, in the same chapter as the Big Bang verse, it is also stated that the Universe will collapse onto itself just as it was in the beginning. Just as God issued a command to start the Universe with a force, the direction of the force will reverse due to His command and not because there is some inherent pressure within the Universe to do so. To draw an analogy the Universe is like someone starting up an evolutionary factory (where everything evolves and is determined by laws set by the factory maker) with a switch turned on and then turned off when the job is done. The beginning and end are entirely due to divine fiat that have nothing to do with anything inherent in the system, but that which operates through a command concerning a will or power to expand the Universe that is not through particle pressure but a pure command. In relation to a discussion of the originative force that created and propels the Universe into expansion it may be fitting to end with the following quote of Dean Turner, one of the Editors of "The Einstein Myth and the Ives Paper":

> ...modern science and philosophy will never be able to make real sense out of anything so long as God is left out [of the picture].[163]

In the end, one can see that all this running away from God as Creator of the Universe has badly backfired and we are literally having to face God. It is as if God were standing at the start line of a race track and someone started to run away from Him, not realizing that after a full lap he/she would meet God head on still standing there at the starting line!

Based on microbits, there is another subtle reason why it has to be an external command. Since there is nothing other than the microbit which was congealed together as one piece (as the Quran also states) there are no other particles to make the Universe expand. And if there were no other particles then they could not have popped into the Universe later on. Added to that, the coalescence of microbits could not be causing the outward pressure (rather they are congealing, so to speak, rather than creating that outward pressure).

To add a jarring but cautionary note to this discussion that brings in God to the picture: Phipps has remarked (in a personal communication with this writer on this topic) that: "I do not personally approve of using religion of any kind as a basis for science...my impression is that in the West, little progress was made in science until the subject freed itself from religious domination. I fear that merely substituting another religion [such as Islam] will require the lesson to be learned over again. To put it another way, I view the main trouble with

---

163 Turner, Dean and Hazelett, Richard, (Editors), (1979). *The Einstein Myth and the Ives Papers: A Counter Revolution in Physics*, p. 33.

Einstein's relativity to be that it has become a religion and has thus immunized itself from critical thinking [emphasis is mine]."

If Islam is merely followed as a dogmatic and mystical belief system (which, if one hazards a guess, comprises tragically at least 90% of those who profess Islam) then Phipps's comments are most valid. However, if Islam is followed properly, that is, if the Quran is properly understood in its proper context and implemented, as in the past, where it was followed more than in the present, by which it brought about the revolution of inductive science, and other complementary forms of rationality, that is, our modern experimental method, through Ibn al-Haytham, Al-Beruni, and many others, then it is a boon rather than a curse. The Catholic Church has been instrumental in shaping modern reactions to 'religion' in the West, when the Church suppressed rationality and science, creating the lingering schizoid situation where the almost inextricable science-religion divide in the psyche of most of mankind still reigns supreme and is difficult to expunge using reason.

Since absolute flat space retains its rightful position, with the Microbits' view, we can consider how that singular entity we call God is connected to absolute space as the ground for all that exists; it indeed will tell us more about the nature of the Creator and His relation to human consciousness, purpose etc., let alone 'His' existence through discarding the basis for the obfuscating escapist arguments that tend to generate multiverses, imaginary time, curved spaces and other such fictions. One of the consequences of the model is that time is just a measure of motion, so really one can talk about what happened 'before time'. That is because time is nothing but a measure of motion of particles and as we discussed in From Microbits to Everything: Universe of the Imaginator: The Philosophical Implications, Volume 2:

> Consequently, according to this view, the Big Bang was created within the absolute space of God, who is not only transcendent of particles but has created those particles within 'His' space and sustains them. In From Microbits to Everything, Volume 2, we also showed exactly how and where the Quran speaks of this.[164]

---

164 Haque, Nadeem and Muslim, M. (2007). From Microbits to Everything: Universe of the Imaginator: Volume 2, Optagon Publications Ltd., Toronto, p. 114.

Secondly, with this notion of space being the indivisible and an infinite place where this singular consciousness is synonymous with the Sensorium of God as explained Newton, one is able to realize how the creation of particles forming themselves over time, result in complex nervous systems in such a way that they access this consciousness and become conscious, personalizing and privatizing that consciousness, leading to the unique self of each individual sentient creature.[165] This, of course, is diametrically opposite to saying that we are part of God, for we are only imagined products of God's thoughts and cannot therefore be part of the essence of God and at the same level of God. Thereby, we cannot merge into God etc. and other such illogicalities that mysticism throws upon us.[166] At the same time, however, this view explains the specificity of the whereness of God without the localization of God in space. Yet God is relational to this Universe as the Ground of all being and the Universe being within His space as an imaginational product. And the huge bonus is that this realization of the 'whereness of God' leads to the complete foundational solution to the problem of consciousness (discussed in Part 2)– details to be determined as our knowledge advances. God is not part of this Universe in any way, shape or form, but all particles that are comprised of microbits, all matter and energy are products of His Mind and hence His imagination. This is who and what God truly is and this is the ultimate just estimate of God, any other view being below this concept/fact.

There has been a lot of talk recently about the creation of the Universe from nothing, but the above physics based on microbits not only unifies physics and biology but so too does it unify 'science' and 'religion'. This is because the concept of what 'space' and particles are, is clarified and a clear distinction is made between the two. As a corollary, 'time' is understood. As far as space goes: once upon a time people used to have a rational concept of One God as being nothing like the human being but nonetheless perceived God as existing in the upper heavens with the angels. When this kind of childish view was shattered with our understanding that God is not somehow localized in some upper place in the heavens, we were left with a 'placeless' God. This placelessness and non-specificity has been exploited by atheists who say not only that God does not exist but also as to where is God? Now those who consider themselves as rationalist

---

165 Ibid., p. 52, p. 105-122, p. 195.

166 Ibid., p. 102., pp. 105-106.

theists cannot or do not want to answer the 'whereness' of God. This is because they are averse to mysticism and pantheism. However, their correct conclusion on this point has led them to become overcautious and not realize that they are missing the boat on a complete answer to the question of 'God'. Obviously, 'God' is not a spatially limited object of some type in space because "He" is unlike matter or energy. Since there cannot be an outside to God or side by side etc. it would be more rational to conclude that God is some other dimension that is synonymous with His mind and that we are in His mind. That would be more rational than saying that the inside/outside question is not valid, particularly when no reason, or good reason is given for asserting this. Although some may say He is another dimension outside our space and time dimensions, there is no evidence of any other dimension and even if it is postulated that God is some other infinite entity, that the inside/outside question is not valid, particularly when no reason, or good reason is given for asserting this. Although some may say He is another dimension outside our space and time dimensions, no evidence exists of this 'dimension', for it is just lame speculation.

The simplest answer, using Occam's razor, and which accounts for consciousness being readily accessible and integral to us, is that consciousness is the property of space itself and that the transcendent one whom we call God, the one and incomparable, is this transcendo-immanent space, this God being one and incomparable, and coinciding with Surah Ikhlas (chapter 112) in the Quran and the attributes of God, including that God has a Self and is conscious and that we are a product of His infinite mind and hence that Mind's creative abilities. This view of God is the basic one that Newton and others had which is perfectly logical and by the process of elimination by contradiction, anyone can realize this reality. It seems astonishing and too simple that this is the case but it is and we proved this in Part 2 of this book.

The critics of this position on God believe (erroneously) that if it is being held that space is God, albeit objectless space, then because it is assumed by them at the outset that space is a creation, it means that God is being misidentified with His creation and therefore anyone holding this supposed blasphemous view, saying that objectless space is God, is tantamount to worshipping His creation because 'space' is a creation. They first assume that space was created by God and then state that there is no proof that it was objectless uncreated space. In other words they assume that which is a question to be investigated as a purported created thing and are not thinking about what 'nothing' really means; 'space' is not nothing but it is not particles. Secondly, Surah Ikhlas states that there is nothing comparable to God, but then these critics think that a storage space, or a container space is like objectless space and therefore this ascription of consciousness to objectless space as the Reality or God, violates Surah Ikhlas because it is stated that there is nothing like God. However, the fact is that the last verse in Surah Ikhlas is not saying that God is Inconceivable, but that God is Incomparable. This is what the language of the Quran in that verse is clearly stating. However, this poses a problem for some critics because then it means that intellectually, God is Conceivable, as for example being the ground of all being, the plane of all existence described logically as objectless space (though we cannot experience objectless space). The question repeatedly posited to these critics as to whether we are inside or outside God, dogmatically, is evaded. However, only two options, confront us: inside or outside? What is the third? To see this, one can pose the question in another way: "Are we inside or outside the Mind of God?" To evade the sheer conclusiveness of the answer to this basic question, some critics of this view have had to resort to saying that we cannot attribute a Mind for God! Obviously, God's mind is not like ours, but it is a mind, nonetheless! This is where rationality in the 'rational theists' thought breaks down. Therefore, overall they are not being totally rational. Their rationality has a limit. Whereas the rationality of atheists breaks down earlier, the 'rational theists' rationality breaks down at a higher level. It is like a high jumper; the atheists' rationality breaks down at 3 ft, whereas the 'rational theists' who are not really being totally rational, have a breakdown at 6 ft, for they cannot clear the bar at this height! Their rationality breaks down because they do not want to complete the thought process. The answer is very obvious to the simple question posed about the 'whereness of God'. What we must be careful about, however, is what we mean by inside, in the "inside and outside question".

Penultimately, to counter the consciousness of God as being synonymous as infinite unitary objectless space, (what we can call the entityfication of space as a 'catch phrase') it is pointed out (again erroneously) that if one cannot explain/ describe, for example, colour to a blind man, because it is beyond his senses, then how can God be explained to us as objectless space, because God is beyond all senses! Lastly, it is stated that if this is the view of God then how come the Quran does not contain this view or why did the Prophet not speak about it (this is a fallacy known as appealing to authority)?

Let us add some further arguments to show the groundlessness of the critics argumentations and also tackle the latter two points one by one and show the additional fallacies inherent in these arguments that purport to show the invalidity of the long-overdue entityfication of space, which is actually a blatant reality. As this writer has belaboured to illustrate, the view of objectless space or this Universe being the imagination of God is wholly rational as there cannot be 'outside' or side by side with God. God is infinite. If we are the imagination of God then we are not the essence of God and all microbits are the imaginationof God too. Therefore, any object that we can think of, even if it were to have space in it, like an empty box, or 'storage space' like a USB device, cannot be likened to infinite objectless space that has no boundaries and is infinite and particle-less. In addition, this space is where the property of the singular consciousness lies, which gives rise to all consciousness, by will. It is therefore unlike anything else that exists or can exist. This is all discussed in volume 2 of the microbits' series. Furthermore, as was shown in Part 2, 'space' was not created. 'Space' expanding with 'matter' leads to a problem with respect to the conservation of energy, as discussed; moreover, the Quran does not speak of the creation of 'space', but only of matter and energy (i.e. microbits), arising from the Big Bang; this has also been discussed in FME v. 1.

The proof for God is entirely based on logic and not dependent on our seeing God. It depends on the concepts of matter/energy and non-matter/non-energy, which is space; therefore, it is fallacious to draw parallels between the proof for God and God's nature with the un-experience-able nature of colour to a blind man, for instance. What is being claimed here is that those holding to the 'objectless space' view of the Creator are claiming that they know the details of the existence of something which cannot be seen or experiencable and they are describing God, just as if a blind man could see the colour blue and describe it. However, the fact is that stating that this Universe is the created imagination of God who is not based on particles and is infinite too, means never being able to see God, and that is perfectly rational and no one who holds this view of 'objectless space' as being the locus of the infinite singular consciousness of God as being that consciousness (a personal God) is synonymous with unimaginable objectless space, is stating that we can experience God visually ever, not even in the hereafter, because, to re-iterate: God is not made of particles and 'He' is infinite. This God is the Ground of Being as objecteless space, particle- less and isotropically conscious and has to do with pure logic and the evidence of the

Universe as a finite particle based system. Indeed, there is no correspondence between the analogy of not seeing the colour blue if you are blind and 'seeing' that this is who and where God is, because the description of God is purely based on the most logical parameters and not visual seeing. This argument is a prime example of the 'fallacy of conflation' and a 'straw man fallacy'.

This view of God is actually in the Quran and has been discussed at length in From Microbit to Everything: Universe of the Imaginator: Volume 2 based on several Quranic verses cited in that book and therefore is from the source of Islam. Whether the Prophet Muhammad got into these technicalities or not is a moot point and totally irrelevant; now it is crucial to get into this discussion due to the nature of the debate on God, because of the advance of science and its misuse of space and time, to take God out of the picture, not present 1,400 years ago in terms of extremist and dominant atheism and relativism. Indeed, if the Prophet were he alive today he would find all of these developments most fascinating and engaging because he was 100% open to reasoning and not bound to some tradition and one would have been able to be engaged in a sane discussion with him on all these points.

The issue of consciousness that intersects with physics (proper ideas of space and time) is crucial from another perspective: To draw upon an analogy, if someone said that the earth was not flat, in prehistoric times, others would think it an absurd idea; they would say it makes no sense because if it were a ball and we were on it we'd fall off—so it can't be a spheroid! That conclusion seems like common sense because the flat-earther never took into consideration gravity properly because you cannot see gravity. Likewise in this case, consciousness as the property of space is not being factored into the issue of God, and as a result of this major disastrous oversight by humanity, the notion of absolute objectless space, the plane or ground of all being as a singular personal entity, the eternal Imaginator, who gives rise to everything by His will is not seen as therefore being the actual solution to the mind-body problem. At the same time the solution/realization of the total separateness and otherness of God is not realized as the answer. In fact, the nature of the consciousness of God is seen as something not thinkable about—a falsely created taboo subject which stifles and limits our knowledge and the desire for the truth which is beckoning us to search further. Most of the Muslim world has been indoctrinated over the centuries not to think of such an issue.

Postulating the existence of God as the basis plane for existence is the most logical conclusion one can arrive at and hence the most scientific too. Using the STOP argument (discussed in Part 2 of this book) that establishes the basis plane of all created existence, and an intelligent conscious , that is, the one that created the Universe by imagination, this plane makes the existence of the Universe contingent on the thoughts of such a formless being, infinite in extent, who made all that exists through conjuring in Its Mind identically structured unit particles (microbits) that combine in various forms to produce a maximally diverse Universe (i.e. 'physics'). This is indeed the only logical conclusion one can reach. But this of course leads to other questions, as to why the Universe was created. These have been answered in great depth and purported completeness in Volume 2 of the microbits series. Yet, the brute fact remains, not as a refutational argument, but one whose answer is itself self-evident but nonetheless perplexing and ever to remain so, even when we die and come face to face with this being that created all, which is: why does such a being exist eternally, as opposed to the non-existence of such a being; but if such a being were non-existent, nothing would be here, but that nothing would also not be nothing (and nothing would be there to perceive that nothing!); indeed, it would be something, though not conscious and if that was the case then we would not be here to ask the question! So the existence of this Universe and sentient consciousness demands the eternal existence of this ever existing consciousness, and though perplexing, this final answer was, is and ever will be the only answer, which if questioned, is answerable.

What future researchers must consider are the following factors:

1. The irrefutability of the new arguments that prove God: These arguments involve clear and logical concepts of 'space' and 'time' and not the gobbledygook of relativity and pretentious obfuscations of quantum mechanics as currently understood in the opulent halls of academia, where we are told to accept Physicist Richard Feynman's words as the ultimate invidious situation, where no one can understand quantum mechanics, but that's the way reality is!

2. The interconnection between the arguments based on space, time and motion lead to understanding the nature of God, as God is now 'placed' somewhere, but not in the usual finite sense of 'somewhere'.

3. This leads to the solution to the consciousness problem from #2.

4. The imminent collapse of both Einsteinian Relativity and the modern interpretations of quantum mechanics lead us towards a sophisticated version of determinism, based on finite-sized particles in absolute space. Since God exists and therefore created the Universe, then by force of logic the Universe must be deterministic.

Given these emerging factors, this new new physics, based on the foundation of microbits will lead us to a greater understanding of that unseen intelligence which ultimately sustainsthe Universe, not to mention the emergence of technologies such as: revolutionary propulsion systems that will lead us to the stars with great speed, to systems of transportation that levitate, to communication systems that transfer information many times faster than the speed of light in vacuum, to energy that draws continuously from 'space' etc., to drive industry and transportation without pollution, to unimaginable advances in biology, to almost human-like robots. And all this is to empower the 'masses'and eliminate financial hardships, health problems and environmental destruction, to name a few major benefits. Indeed, all these developments will make current advanced technology appear almost stone-age-like! If you think this is a rather far-fetched notion, then you are indeed like a stone-age person who, if shown a video by a time traveller from the 21st Century C.E., would not be able to believe or comprehend that one day we would have planes, internet, and rockets! A move towards this scenario can be made byconducting vital experiments that are pointing in this new direction for physics, tocorroborate certain results, rather than engaging in, or being subjected to elaborate and sinister cover-ups and suppression by the 'Establishment'. It is now up to the next generation of physicists and philosophers to take up this challenge.

Conclusion

In order for the world to change toward socio-environmental egalitarianism and to bring the unification of humankind bent on various forms of inner and outer destruction and exploitation of fellow humans, animals and nature we need to tackle and understand what consciousness really is. It is in understanding consciousness that the bridge between God and humankind is built, and all our ideas and concepts will then flow properlyfrom this, as being a complete and integrated view of life, devoid of atheism, mysticism, dogmatism and selective-reasoning. Indeed, this is the only way by which all of us individually and therefore collectively can fulfill our potential. The proper understanding of Consciousness is the bridge that will unify humankind as it will show the proper relationship between God and humanity and the unity between proper science and proper religion which are really one and the same. And once this transpires, it will assist us in solving the myriad problems that we are facing in all areas of life: personal, social, environmental and others. In reality, therefore, these two Quranic verses are linked together and foretell the future of humankind:

> They ask you about **the ruh**; say it is a command from your Sustainer/ Lord;in order to know about it you have been given little knowledge.[167]

> We will show them our **signs** in the horizons and **within themselves** [i.e. chief of which is **the ruh**] until they know that this is the truth; is it not sufficient that your Sustrainer/Lord is a witness over everything?[168]

The knowledge of the *ruh*, or the command which is our instantiation or fractionalization of consciousness will be known as a sign within ourselves. This "new" new physics will play a foundational role in this renaissance of common sense and reason with its support from the Quran, which itself seeks to liberate humankind with the understanding of the origin, proper direction and future of humankind, from the clutches of irrationality, megalomaniacal control, greed, selfishness, delusion and fear, to a wholly rational participatory engagement in the Universe that is peaceful, just, intelligent, creative and generous. With it, hopefully, will be engendered the employment and deployment of further technological advances and their non-harmful utilization, that are bound to develop in time, because this reformed view of reality clears the concepts of space and time and allows us to clearly think about what consciousness is, and, concomitantly, God and His or 'Its' real relation to us. But for this to transpire we need to extricate ourselves from entrenched illogical ideas concerning the foundation of space and time. Entrenched illogical ideas tend to be clung on to because of vested interests, be they institutional or psychological. However, such entrenched views stop the growth of the individual in examining this wonderful and amazing creation which we are given to understand, or more accurately, which is our responsibility to understand in this Quantum Traverse.

---

167 Quran 17:85
168 Quran 41:53

Endnotes

1. Some common objections and agreements with relativists/string theorists
    etc.:

One of the objections to the microbits model is that we are reverting back to the old physics. However, it must be stressed that it is not important whether something is old or not but whether it is logical (could we call this the 'age fallacy'?). It has been shown in FME v.1, and in this book that the notion of absolute space makes sense. If one has discarded an 'old' method that is shown to be consistent, whereas the new method has problems at its foundations, it is not logical to continue with the 'new method'. Something which is contradictory cannot be the foundation of physics. If one does not think that this is important then one does not think that cause and effect and non-contradiction are the foundations of truth and of physics. This writer wishes such a person 'good luck' in navigating through his or her life in a causational Universe! If non-contradiction is not important or true as the foundation of truth, then anything goes and that is what has begun to happen. But how different is that than primitive mythological notions of the Universe, despite the 'modern view' garbed in 'papers' and academia at posh Universities. This is a serious question. Where is this institutionalization fraught with vested interests, leading us? It is conceded by some conventional physicists that there is a problem with the expansion of space and energy as outlined in this book, when it is brought up. In order to circumvent this, multiple dimensions might be seen as 'solutions' by some such physicists. But multiple dimensions are not solutions but a problem, one of which is: how do we know these exist? This is a case where the cure is worse than the problem!

It is also conceded that dark energy, dark matter, infinities are problems and that perhaps the infinities' problem lies in the notion of 'point' particles. Well then, one should drop the point particle view and adopt the microbit or microbit-like view, where particles are spherical extended objects; indeed, what else could an object be! One cannot also hide behind 'fields' because it begs the question as to what they are, and how did they originate? Superstrings only compound the issue, with their multiple dimensions and are no solution; they lead to a complex dead end. If anything salvageable will come out of this misguided venture, it will be mathematical techniques and imagination/creativity. But imagination and creativity have to be grounded in reality to determine the truth, or at least approach it.

2. Professor Thomas E. Phipps Jr., born on January 26, 1925 and died on 2016 had an illustrious career in: research in theoretical, experimental and applied physics. He graduated with a Ph.D. in Nuclear Physics, from Harvard University in 1951. His interest, research and advances in fundamental physics are no doubt displayed in his Magnum Opus: the latest book, published in 2012: *Old Physics for New: a worldview alternative to Einstein's relativity theory*, 2nd Edition.More details on Phipps can be found at: http://conf17.worldnpa.org/index.php?module=pagemaster&PAGE_user_op=view_page&PAGE_id=12&MMN_position=13:13

3. Professor Bo Lehnert's, born in 1926 is currently Professor of Plasma Physics and Fusion Research at the Royal Institute of Technology, Stokholm, Sweden and is a member of The Royal Swedish Academy of Sciences, the organization that promotes scientific knowledge internationally and awards a number of important prizes, the most well-known which is the Nobel Prize. He has, like Phipps, a great interest in fundamental physics research, and remains active in presenting papers at various international conferences on the frontiers of physics. His latest book, that has been briefly discussed in this book on some key issues, is: *Revised Quantum Electrodynamics*. For a more detailed biography please see:http://www.kth.se/polopoly_fs/1.195577!/Menu/general/column- content/attachment/bo-lehnert.pdf.

As noted above, both Bo Lehnert and Thomas Phipps each had been involved in physics for over 60 years and are still active in research. This continuing research gave them a critical attitude, and wisdom that is rarely possessed by the younger generation of physicists that are being churned out at universities, and are unaware or uncritical of the numerous foundational inconsistencies that have arisen in fundamental physics and the truly logical and realistically bound theoretical advances that are being made, awaiting observation and advanced testing.

4. Stephan J. G. Gift was until recently, a Professor at the Department of Electrical and Computer Engineering Faculty of Engineering, The University of the West Indies, St. Augustine, Trinidad, West Indies. He has written numerous concise articles, debunking Einsteinian Relativity and has an upcoming new book showing the fallalies of Special Relativity..

Acknowledgement

I am deeply indebted to Professors, Lehnert, the late Phipps and Gift for their feedback that has assisted in giving this work greater clarification, depth and scope.

Bibliography

Banaei, Mehran and Haque, Nadeem. (1995). *From Facts to Values: Certainty, Order, Balance and their Universal Implications*, Optagon Publications Ltd., Toronto.

Davis, Tamara. (July, 2010). "Is the Universe Leaking Energy", *Scientific American*.

Ellis, George E. R. (August, 2011). "Does the Multiverse Really Exist?", *Scientific American*.

Gift, Stephan J.G. (2004). "The Invalidation of a Sacred Principle of Modern Physics", *Physics Essays*, Volume 17, number 3. (Available at www.scribd. com)

Gift, Stephan J.G. (2010). "Light Speed Invariance is a Remarkable Illusion", *PhysicsEssays*, Volume 23, Issue 1. (Available at www.scribd.com)

Gift, Stephan J.G. (2001)."A Negation of Einstein's General Theory of Relativity and a Returnto Newtonian Gravitation.", *Physics Essays*, Volume 14, Number 4. (Available at www.scribd.com)

Haque, N. and Banaei, M. (2011). "Bridge between Science & Religion", Scientific GOD Journal, November 2011, Vol. 2, Issue 8. (Available at www.scribd.com)

Haque, Nadeem and Muslim, M. (2007). *From Microbits to Everything: Universe of the Imaginator, Volume 2: The Philosophical Implications*, 2007, Toronto. (Available at www.scribd.com)

Hofer, Werner A. (2012). "Quantum mechanics: A new chapter?" http://arxiv. org/pdf/1209.1029v1.pdf

Iqbal, Mohammad. (1930). *The Reconstruction of Religious Thought in Islam*. Now available on many internet sites. Website: http://www.allamaiqbal. com/works/prose/english/reconstruction/

Lehnert, Bo. (2012). "Zero point energy as origin of dark energy and dark matter", Presented atthe International Topical Conference on Plasma Science,

Advanced Plasma Concepts, Faro, Portugal, on September 24-28. *American Institute of Physics Conference Proceedings*, Volume 1445, pp. 102-114.

Lehnert, Bo. (2012). *Revised Quantum Electrodynamics* (Contemporary Fundamental Physics), Nova Science Publications, New York.

Lincoln, Don. (November, 2012). "The Inner Life of Quarks", *Scientific American*.

Muslim, M. and Haque.(2001). Nadeem, *From Microbits to Everything: A New Unified View of Physics and Cosmology, Volume 1: The Cosmological Implications*, Toronto.

Phipps, Thomas E. (Jr.). (2012). *Old Physics for New, A worldview alternative to Einstein's relativity theory*, Apeiron, Montreal.

Terazawa, Hidezumi. (23 - 25 Jun 1999)., "Unified Supersymmetric Composite Model of All Fundamental Particles and Forces", *High Energy Physics in the 21-st Century* High Energy Accelerator Research Organization (KEK), KEK Preprint 99-46. This was presented at the 22nd International Workshop on Fundamental Problems of High Energy Physics and Field Theory, Protvino, Russian Federation,. http://ccdb5fs.kek.jp/cgi- bin/img/allpdf?199927046

Terazawa, Hidezumi. (1997). "INS Report: Possible Effects of Non-vanishing Particle Sizes in theEarly Universe", CERN, Institute for Nuclear Study, University of Tokyo, Tokyo, p. 1. This article was also published later on in: *Modern Physics Letters A*, Volume 12, Issue 38, pp. 2927-2931.

Turner, Dean and Hazelett, Richard. (1979). *The Einstein Myth and the Ives Papers, A Counter-Revolution in Physics*, Hope Publishing House, Pasedena, California.

Unzicker, Alexander and Jones Shiela, (2013). *Bankrupting Physics: How Today's Top Scientists are Gambling Away their Credibility*. Palgrave MacMillan.

Nana Oppong's (aka M. Muslim) and Nadeem Haque's updated book on physics (2025 Version) is available here: https://philpapers.org/versions/HAQMAN-2

Postscript:
The True Story of the Universe

The Need for a True Story

We need a new true story of the Universe that informs the foundations of society and our personal lives, not one that is based on myths, or falsehoods, but on reality. In this book, I have combined four areas of my intensive research over the decades to try to determine what is actually going on. What is existence and the existence of existence? Why are we here? Is there a God, and if so, what type of God are we talking about? Is there consciousness and if so, what is it exactly? Did we evolve biologically and if so, how? Is there life on other planets? Can physics be unified and if so, how? And so on and so forth...The Quran has paved the way for answering all these questions and more, and this book has presented the solutions or their framework. I have also given references to more detailed accounts of certain aspects to the solutions which can be found in my works and those of my close associates; these now form a network of knowledge for those who seek to understand reality, and implement the precepts learned therefrom to hopefully, solve critical issues in society. What, though, is that true story and what are its ramifications?

From Particles to Articles

We have gathered from proof in this book that there is something that lies behind everything in the Universe or possible Universes. It is a Consciousness that is formless, infinite in extent, all-encompassing, singular, everlasting, the First and the Last, the Innermost and the Outermost, the indivisible—that unto which nothing is comparable. It is the basis plane of all existence. It is nothing like Its creation, for logically, how could that be so? It is Eternal and has Imagination, and out of that imagination arose the Universe that It sustains. One of these Universes is the one we are in, that It imagined through the Big Bang and particles that split from the 'Big Bang' and co-joined to create all other particles, the willed-sustenance of solidity through these unit articles (acting without action at a distance at that final level). It was the interplay of these unit particles out of which all other 'forces' arose by combining into larger groupings of particles that we now have names for, think they are many, but arose from that unit particle's groupings (the atom's atom, as it were)—From Particles to Articles! And once these particles, through pathways, based on equilibrium formed, into more complex structures after the creation of stars, carbon, planets, water, life, rocks and eventually clay and the reorganization of carbon etc., into bio molecules, that further evolved into more complex structures, it was the birth of consciousness (with a small 'c'). These 'complex' lifeforms were able to access from that source Consciousness, just as an antenna accesses radio waves or a computer connects to Wi-Fi (crude but instructive analogies, nonetheless) but only on two conditions set by this creative and singular "Imaginator": These two conditions for the emergence of consciousness were the specific pattern of nervous system that would arise in the 'organism', and its operation through photons (and not just electrons); these two processes working seamlessly in conjunction in a specific formula, gave access to the Consciousness, and thus, such entities as Man 'owned' consciousness, as it were, through which it became reified; however, at its base, it was only a fractionalization of the consciousness from an In-(di)visible one, through the Imagination of this Indivisible one, where the Real had created the quasi-real, for that is the only way that indivisible consciousness could generate consciousness (or 'fractionalize'). And when such consciousness in Man arose through a re-organization of the unit particles about 13.8 billion years into the shape of Man, and then when he looked at the starry Universe and pondered as to the origin of it, his own creation and his consciousness, he saw no creator (or she saw no creator!), because Man could not see that which gave rise to everything, that 'thing' not being comprised of particles, and being the basis plane of the Universe. It was, therefore, invisible to all senses except through signs and pointers in nature, but visible through intellection, and also 'feel-able' through the direct causal connection between consciousness and the Consciousness. However, many homo-sapiens over the centuries started to either worship the Universe's components (mysticism in one form or another), equated this consciousness with the Universe itself, or eventually started to deny that there was ever any source that was Conscious with a big C, as a counter-reaction to irrationality and the exploitation of priestly classes in all formal major religions—a grave and tragic legacy. Given this invidiousness, sadly, as an irrational and fallacious over-reaction, the atheists threw out the baby with the bathwater. One day the baby, then grown up, will return and ask them why he was so unceremoniously also thrown out; why did they not throw out only the dirty water?! Indeed, there has been Silence for too long, and now, in the evolution of humankind, that Silence is slowly—perhaps too slowly in our conflict-ridden immature planet-—being broken; there will no doubt come a time when all of this will become very clear. At that time, calling something 'religious' or 'scientific' will become as meaningless as phlogiston, a relic of the past times of confusion, arrogance and subterfuge. This is what will transpire in the, hopefully, not too distant future. In that distant future, an understanding of the concepts that lead to both societal and ecological/environmental peace and justice will be achieved, exhibited in the causal diagram below, which, for those readers who would have read this book will be fully understandable:

EXISTENCE OF GOD: Conclusive Proofs linking space to the Person of 'God' (Parts 2 and 4)

↓

NATURE OF GOD: Realization of the relation between Consciousness and consciousness (Parts 2 and 4)

↓

AFFINITY: Realization that all entities are imagined creations accessing the same consciousness to gain individualized consciousness and the common origin of all species (SOES) based on directed/teleological creation
(Parts 1, 2 & 3)

↓

EMPATHY: Naturally developed due to closeness from Affinity

↓

COMPASSION: Naturally developed from Empathy

↓

JUSTICE: Concern develops as compassion motivates a person to establish justice

↓

PEACE: Can only arise from justice

What is the "Quantum Traverse"?

I think that by now the readers may be able to deduce what I mean by 'The Quantum Traverse', which is this book's title. This Universe is a one-off creation or quantum creation for us; it is a *testing ground* for the evolution and development of consciousness of us as 'higher' sentient entities. It is a place where particularized consciousness can exist, for only a brief period or sojourn, transitioning from our non-existence, existence to continued existence in another type of system after death. Therefore, it is like a traverse, that is, something we must pass through. It is, in other words, a one-way bridge and a means to an end, serving as a direction to get across. What will happen on the other side, once we have passed through, or crossed this system (i.e. the traverse), will depend on our intentions, actions/deeds; these are the only assets that we will carry forward with our selves. We will be judged concerning the nature and quality of our interactions with ourselves, other entities and the physical environment. Let us hope that our baggage of wholesome interactions is heavy, and that we do indeed end up in the right luggage reception area, in the arrivals zone of the next life, in the infinite journey of our lives!

BIOGRAPHY

Nadeem Haque was born in Kampala, Uganda in 1960. He moved to England in 1972 at the age of 12 with his parents and brother. In 1975, his family migrated to Toronto, Canada, where he has lived ever since, except in the early 1980s when he studied Civil Engineering at King's College London. He currently resides in Canada. He is the author of numerous books and articles that focus on what he calls 'Reality Studies', and under his belt, he has amalgamated a plethora of interrelated works that connect with Islam in the form of fiction/non-fiction books and articles/papers. His work has focused on various areas:

- animal rights and environment/ecology;
- the origin and nature of consciousness;
- the unification of physics;
- macro-evolution;
- history/history of science ('Pre-ancient', Ancient and the Middle Ages, is his focus);
- extraterrestrial life/extrasolar planets
- economics

In each of these areas he has tried to bridge the science and religion gap with new models and discoveries from the Quran, or tried to resolve sociological issues. In addition, Nadeem was the co-founder of the King's College Islamic Society at the University of London (in 1985), and is also one of the founders of the Institute of Higher Reasoning (IHR) which is an educational, research and think tank organization. He is the grandson of the late Al- Hafiz B.A. Masri, who is internationally known as the pioneer of Animals and Islam theological research and an ardent animal welfare activist. He is the prime co-author of *Ecolibrium: The Sacred Balance in Islam*, by Beacon Books, Manchester, published in 2021 and Editor of *Animals in Islam* (authored by Masri) published by Lantern Publishing and Media, New York, in 2022. Nadeem and his colleagues (ANALYS) were most instrumental in holding the lectures on Embryology and the Quran (Keith Moore, Marshall Johnson and Persaud) at the University of Toronto in the late 1980s and of their friend and colleague, the mathematician, Gary Miller (Abdul Ahad Omar). From these lectures, worldwide knowledge of rationality and the correspondence between the Quran and Science became more well-known.

Besides his academic/research work and interests, Nadeem is a registered professional engineer (asset management, civil/structural/building science and environmental) in Ontario, Canada, with a degree from King's College London in Civil Engineering, and an earlier degree in Economics from the University of Toronto.

The works of two writers have found their way into this book:

Mohammed Muslim, graduated from Osgoode Hall Law School, York University) with a Law Degree, and has worked as a lawyer, university professor and researcher. He originated and developed the idea of 'microbits' and specific proofs for the existence of God as well as the solution to the consciousness problem, together with the foundational contributions of Nadeem Haque. He co-authored two books with Nadeem Haque: *From Microbits to Everything: Volume 1: A New Unified View of Physics and Cosmology, The Cosmological Implications*; *From Microbits to Everything: Universe of the Imagination, Volume 2: The Philosophical Implications*. The physics book was expanded and updated and entititled; *Microbits: A New Unified Physics* and Muslim opted to use his name, Nana Oppong there. Part 2 of *The Quantum Traverse* includes some of his writings, relevant to the subject at hand, and Part 4 incorporates some of his foundational concepts of about microbits towards physics unification. Mohammed Muslim also co-wrote the section on Cosmobiosys, on the origin of life with Nadeem Haque.

Zeshan Shahbaz, is a writer/blogger/Islamic educationalist/podcaster, focusing on Philosophy and Politics, and is also an ardent human rights activist. He has a Bachelor's degree in Social Sciences from York University and a Diploma in Adult Education. He has contributed to the research on consciousness and extraterrestrial life that is included in this book. Shahbaz resides in Canada and his profession is an advisor in the area of benefits/insurance.

ACKNOWLEDGEMENTS

I would like to thank my colleague and long-time friend, M. Muslim, whose work appears from pages 49 to 67, concerning the proof for God, and cracking the hard problem of consciousness pages 71 to 86. This proof was initially published in: The Scientific GOD Journal,"New Proofs for the Existence of God: Part I: The Sesamatic Proof", Volume 2, No. 2, 2011. Muslim tackled the foundation of the consciousness problem and I elaborated and added to it in Microbits (Volume 2), also showing how all points were deduced and realized through empirical evidence, and then all were linked to the Quran. Based on Muslim's detailed proof I produced a 'Short Proof', on pages 92 to 93.

I would also like to thank Philosopher John Leslie for his kind encouragement and conversations. There are some overlaps between my views and those of Leslie in his book: *Infinite Minds: A Philosophical Cosmology* (Publisher: Oxford University Press (at the Clarendon Press, Oxford), Nov. 1, 2001. It would be essential reading to see the similarities and differences at the forefront of both Muslim and other rational philosophical and scientific thinking about God, in the 21st century. Finally, my rather late correspondence with British physiologist and biologist Denis Noble, who developed the first viable mathematical model of the functioning heart in 1960, needs to be included in this book, concerning biology and the question of God. To that end, he suggested the reading of his b, Chapter 9, entitled "The Relativity of Epistemology", Cambridge University Press, Dec. 2016. His book challenges current Darwinian evolutionary thought (molecular reductionism); more research would be needed to determine the connections between his work and mine, on life's origin and development in the Quran. In his correspondence with me on June 21, 2024, he stated: "It is a plea to acknowledge that, when it comes to questions of the deepest mysteries of the universe, it is better to acknowledge what we don't know, rather than adopt dogmatic positions that cannot be in the domain of science." Nothing could be more true, and both the 'Muslim' and 'non-Muslim' worlds need this outlook vitally.

Index

E

F

G

H

I

J

K

L

M

N

O

P

W

X